D1271284

THE WORLD AND LANGUAGE IN
WITTGENSTEIN'S PHILOSOPHY

The World and Language in Wittgenstein's Philosophy

Gordon Hunnings

sometime Professor of Philosophy
University of Natal, Pietermaritzburg

State University of New York Press

© Gordon Hunnings 1988

All rights reserved. No part of this publication
may be reproduced or transmitted, in any form
or by any means, without permission.

First published
in USA by
STATE UNIVERSITY OF NEW YORK PRESS
Albany

For information, address State University of New
York Press, State University Plaza, Albany, NY 12246

Printed in Hong Kong

Library of Congress Cataloging-in-Publication Data
Hunnings, Gordon, 1926–
The world and language in Wittgenstein's philosophy
Includes index.
1. Wittgenstein, Ludwig, 1889–1951—Contributions in
philosophy of language. 2. Languages—Philosophy.
3. Reality. I. Title.
P85.W5H86   1988   149'.94   87–6453
ISBN 0–88706–585–6
ISBN 0–88706–586–4 (pbk.)

To My Wife
Who Cares Little for Philosophy and Much for
a Philosopher

Contents

Contents

Preface

The object of this book is to explore the interrelated concepts of representation and grammar in the philosophy of Ludwig Wittgenstein. Throughout his life the problem of the connection between language and the world obsessed him and repeatedly in his writings he returned to the elucidation of the nature of a perspicuous representation of the world in language. This task dominates the *Tractatus* and continues as a major preoccupation in the grammatical investigations of the later philosophy. Indeed, the shifting images of reality reflected in language are themselves a mirror of the changes in Wittgenstein's philosophy.

This exploration of an aspect of Wittgenstein's thought is the result of studies on and off for more than a decade: sometimes more off than on, especially during the four years when I combined the chair of philosophy with the vice-chancellorship of the University of Malawi. Nevertheless, even the barrenness of university administration was illuminated intermittently by the brilliance and fertility of Wittgenstein's thought. In spite of an awareness of the great imbalance between labour expended and results achieved it seemed appropriate to make these studies available to a wider audience.

During the preparation of the sections dealing with the *Tractatus* I had the inestimable privilege of discussing the material they contain with Professor Richard Wollheim of University College, London. His criticism and encouragement were enormously beneficial to the development of my ideas and I record my debt to him with deep gratitude and abiding affection.

There are two slightly unusual features of this book on which comment seems worthwhile. The first concerns the seemingly excessive use of verbative quotations from Wittgenstein's writings. It is remarked elsewhere that Wittgenstein's literary style is reminiscent of a policeman's notebook and this adds a new dimension of difficulty to the understanding and interpretation of his work. This fact has contributed to the attribution to Wittgenstein of views which form a spectrum ranging from grotesque caricature at one end to subtle misunderstanding at the other. The use of verbatim quotations is designed to minimise misrepresentation of his views arising from inattention to the text although, of course, this is not a guarantee of correctness of interpretation. However, it possesses the additional advantage for those students who may be condemned to read this book of obviating the need to refer continually to the text to follow the argument.

The second unusual feature of this book concerns the absence of a bibliography with the exception of works by Wittgenstein. Earlier drafts of the book included a very large bibliography which has been omitted from the final version for two reasons. Firstly, large bibliographies increase production costs and make the book much more expensive than it need be. Secondly, the advance of educational technology is rendering extensive bibliographies appended to books an ornament of scholarship as obsolete as adorning the body with woad. Comprehensive bibliographies of the literature on Wittgenstein, in both books and computer-data banks, are now readily available.

I wish to acknowledge the generosity of the University of Natal in granting me sabbatical leave throughout 1984 and thank Dr M. A. Hoskin, Head of the Department of the History and Philosophy of Science at the University of Cambridge, for permission to spend my leave there. This period of sabbatical leave enabled me to finish the book whilst conducting research in other fields.

I also wish to acknowledge the kind permission of the editorial board of the *South African Journal of Philosophy* for permission to use material from my article entitled 'Wittgenstein on the Grammar of Mathematics', published in vol. 4, no. 4, 1985, in Chapter 6 of this book.

I wish to thank my wife for her patience and long-suffering and my former secretaries, Mrs M. Micklewood and Mrs S. Maltby, for typing earlier drafts of this book and my present secretary, Mrs van der Westhuizen, for typing the final version.

The author and the publishers wish to thank the following who have kindly given permission for the use of copyright material: Routledge & Kegan paul Plc and Humanities Press International, Inc., for the extracts from *Tractatus Logico-Philosophicus* by D. F. Pears and B. F. McGuinness; Basil Blackwell and Alice Ambrose, for the extracts from *Wittgenstein Lecture Notes 1932–1935* by Alice Ambrose and *Philosophical Grammar, Philosophical Investigations* and *Philosophical Remarks* by L. Wittgenstein.

Every effort has been made to trace all the copyright holders but if any have been inadvertently overlooked the publishers will be pleased to make the necessary arrangement at the first opportunity.

University of Natal G. HUNNINGS

PUBLISHERS' NOTE

Gordon Hunnings died in April 1986 after delivering the typescript, and we very much regret that he did not live to see his book in print. We would like to thank Sandy Matthews of the Department of Philosophy at the University of Natal, for kindly reading the proofs. We are most grateful to him for all his help.

Works by Wittgenstein

Abbreviation

Tractatus   *Tractatus Logico-Philosphicus*, eds D. F. Pears and B. F. McGuinness (Routledge & Kegan Paul, 1974).

PI   *Philosophical Investigations*, 3rd edn, trans. G. E. M. Anscombe (Blackwell, 1974).

Notebooks   *Notebooks: 1914–1916*, eds G. H. von Wright and G. E. M. Anscombe, 2nd edn (Blackwell, 1974).

BB   *The Blue & Brown Books*, 2nd edn (Blackwell, 1975).
'Some Remarks on Logical Form', *P.A.S. Supp.*, 9 (1929).
Notes on Logic (1913), ed. H. T. Costello, *J. Phil.*, 54 (1957). Repr. in *Notebooks 1914–16*.

RFM   *Remarks on the Foundations of Mathematics*, eds G. H. von Wright, R. Rhees and G. E. M. Anscombe, 3rd edn (Blackwell, 1978).

LFM   *Wittgenstein's Lectures on the Foundations of Mathematics*, ed. C. Diamond (Harvester Press, 1976).
'A Lecture on Ethics', *Phil. Rev.*, 74 (1965).

PR   *Philosophical Remarks*, ed. Rush Rhees (Blackwell, 1975).

PG   *Philosophical Grammar*, ed. Rush Rhees (Blackwell, 1974).
Lectures and Conversations on Aesthetics, Psychology & Religious Belief, ed. C. Barrett (Blackwell, 1966).

Z   *Zettel*, eds. G. E. M. Anscombe and G. H. von Wright (Blackwell, 1967).

OC   *On Certainty*, eds G. E. M. Anscombe and G. H. von Wright, trans. D. Paul and G. E. M. Anscombe (Blackwell, 1969).
Prototractatus, eds B. F. McGuiness, T. Nyberg and G. H. von Wright, trans. D. F. Pears and B. F. McGuinness (Routledge & Kegan Paul, 1971).

Letters to C. K. Ogden, ed. G. H. von Wright (Routledge & Kegan Paul/Blackwell, 1973).

Letters to Paul Engelmann with Memoir by P. Engelmann, ed. B. F. McGuinness, trans. L. Furtmüller (Blackwell, 1967).

RC   *Remarks on Colour*, ed. G. E. M. Anscombe, trans. L. L. McAlister and M. Schattle (Blackwell, 1977).

Lectures at Cambridge in the early Thirties, ed. G. E. Moore; *Mind*, I.63 (1954); II.64 (1955).

Lee   *Lectures: Cambridge 1930–1932*, ed. D. Lee (Blackwell, 1980).

Ambrose   *Lectures: Cambridge 1932–1935*, ed. A. Ambrose (Blackwell, 1979).

RPP I   *Remarks on the Philosophy of Psychology*, vol. I, eds G. E. M. Anscombe and G. H. von Wright (Blackwell, 1980).

RPP II   *Remarks on the Philosophy of Psychology*, vol. II, eds G. H. von Wright and H. Nyman; Vol. II (Blackwell, 1980).

LPP I   *Last Writings on the Philosophy of Psychology*, vol. I, eds G. H. von Wright and N. Nyman, trans. G. C. Luckhardt and M. A. E. Eue (Blackwell, 1982).

1

The Structure of the World

A recurring theme of philosophy from its earliest beginnings has been the nature of reality and the forms in which it is rendered intelligible to us. A variety of philosophical systems have been propounded alleging that the essential structure of reality or the world is reflected in mystical entities, geometrical constructs, abstract concepts, objects of immediate experience, or the theories of natural philosophy. These systems portrayed the world as essentially religious, mathematical, metaphysical, psychological or scientific and fashioned the furniture of heaven and earth on a model derived from the particular picture being portrayed. What a man thinks the world *contains* depends on what he thinks the world *is*; Weltanschauung precedes ontology.

FACTS AND STATES OF AFFAIRS

One of the fundamental ideas of Wittgenstein's *Tractatus Logico-Philosophicus* is that the structure of the world is mirrored in the logical structure of language. The world and language share a common logical form such that from an investigation of the structure of propositions it is possible to see how things must be in reality. This is the ontological content of the theory of language developed in the *Tractatus*, and much of the work is concerned with exhibiting the structure of propositions as the 'logical scaffolding' of the world. A consequence of this theory of language as essentially a picture of reality is that what earlier philosophers had written about the structure of the world was not only confused but unnecessary. It was unnecessary because what they tried to describe was already mirrored in the logical form of language: it was confused because the attempt to describe reality simply got between language and the world and attempted to say what could only be shown. As will become evident, Wittgenstein to the end of his life strenuously opposed all efforts by philosophers to inter-

1

pose philosophy as some kind of intermediary between language and reality.

The assertion that propositions and the world have a common logical form depends upon a number of subordinate theses which will be examined in more detail later but which it will be convenient to summarise here:

1. The substance of the world is comprised of objects which may be combined in an infinite number of ways.
2. Objects in combination form states of affairs which are logically simple and thus incapable of further analysis.
3. Complexes of states of affairs constitute facts which, because they are complex, may be resolved into their component states of affairs by processes of logical analysis.
4. The logical atoms of language are names which stand for, go proxy for, denote, refer to or represent objects; a name *means* an object.
5. Elementary or atomic propositions consist of names of objects in immediate combination and depict states of affairs by picturing them.
6. Elementary propositions are joined together into complex propositions by logical connectives or constants, 'and', 'not', 'or' and 'if . . . then'.
7. Logical constants do not represent or picture any objects in the world and function as logical operators in the calculus of propositions.
8. In principle, all significant language is analysable into sets of elementary propositions linked together by logical constants.

The essence of meaning of significant discourse consists in a picturing relation between propositions and possible states of affairs in the world. The sense of a proposition lies in its depicting a possible state of affairs and its truth lies in the state of affairs depicted actually obtaining. Throughout the *Tractatus*, Wittgenstein develops a highly sophisticated and complex picture-theory which is the basis of his contention that language is a mirror of reality. The ontology of the *Tractatus* is not the outcome of an empirical enquiry or any kind of experiential review of the 'given'. Preliminary questions concerning 'what things there are', which traditional philosophers regarded as an essential part of the prolegomenon to an ontology, were dismissed by Wittgenstein as illegitimate because the language used to try and formulate such questions mirrored in its logical structure the very things that were the objects of such enquiry. Not only are questions of this sort unnecessary; they are impossible. 'Propositions cannot represent logical form: it is mirrored in them. What finds its reflection in language, language cannot represent. What expresses *itself* in language, *we* cannot express by means of language. Propositions *show* the logical form of reality. They display it' (4.121). There is no language nor meta-language which can be employed to describe the logical form of reality because the essence of description is that of representation by picturing and what a picture depicts cannot be the subject of further depiction. This is not to deny the possibility of different pictures exhibiting different perspectives of the same state of affairs but the relation between picture and state of affairs is not picturable. This has two consequences; the first being the important point that claims to the effect that philosophy describes the relation between propositions and the world are to be rejected on logical grounds. Philosophy must not, indeed cannot, come between language and reality.

The second point is that if language does reach out to reality, without the possibility of the interpolation of some intermediary between them, then the logical form of propositions reveals something about the world a priori. From this it follows that the form of reality is not a construction derived from items of experience *a posteriori* but from logic. On the priority of logic with respect to experience Wittgenstein writes: 'The "experience" that we need in order to understand logic is not that something or other is the state of things, but that something *is*: that, however, is *not* an experience. Logic is *prior* to every experience – that something *is so*. It is prior to the question "How", not prior to the question "What"?' (5.552). The 'experience' that something *is*, which is presupposed by logic, is not a datum of experience nor a logical construction out of such experiences. Logic is prior to the fact of how the world *happens to be*, which is contingent, but not prior to the fact that the world *is*, which is necessary. The logical structure of any proposition purporting to describe *how* things are in the world must display *what* things there are as part of its meaning, and understanding its meaning is prior to the ascription of a truth-value. Logic precedes the 'How?' but is presupposed by the 'What?'.

Wittgenstein draws an important distinction between logic per se and its application (5.557). It is the *application* of logic that decides 'what elementary propositions there are' but 'that there must be elementary propositions' is known on 'purely logical grounds' (5.5562). That there *are* elementary propositions tells us something about the structure of the world independently of both experience and the application of logic. Clearly, the ontology of the *Tractatus* is not arrived at by any of the traditional routes; it is a requirement of a theory of the logical structure of propositions. It is through its role as a critique of language that philosophy is about the world without being one of the natural sciences.

This semantic route to ontology is in marked contrast to the ontology of traditional empiricism as represented, for example, by Russell, and indicates a fundamental difference between Russell and Wittgenstein at a period of Wittgenstein's development when it is commonly supposed that their views were very close if not identical. The tradition of which Russell is representative sought to answer questions about 'what things there are' by treating this as equivalent to 'what things can we know there are?'; this is the well-trodden epistemological route to ontology. Wittgenstein, on the other hand, dismissed such epistemological enquiries as an entanglement of psychological irrelevancies with the crystalline purity of logic. The importation into 'modern theory of knowledge (Russell, Moore, etc.)' of mental processes, states, beliefs and thoughts is to confuse logical considerations with 'unessential psychological investigations'. 'Psychology is no more closely related to philosophy than any other natural science. Theory of knowledge is the philosophy of psychology' (5.541, 4.1121). This view not only marks a fundamental difference between the early Wittgenstein and his mentors, Russell and Moore – it remained a dominant theme of Wittgenstein's philosophy throughout his life. What we might call the mentalist approach to knowledge in particular and language in general is something which Wittgenstein throughout his writings returns to again and again with a variety of subtle examples and counter-examples designed to call this approach in question. The notion that knowledge is knowledge of one's mental states, processes and etc., and that descriptions are ultimately descriptions of one's private experiences, mental images and the like are consistently rejected by Wittgenstein. He does this on two grounds; first, these phenomenalist accounts interpose a mass of irrelevant psychological material between language and the world which prevents us seeing clearly that language reaches out directly to reality. Second, the identification of criteria of meaning with sets of mental experiences leads to fundamental misunderstandings of the nature and use of language.

The concept of substance which Wittgenstein works out in the *Tractatus* is not that which is the ground and origin of sense experience but a corollary of his theory of the sense of propositions. This is made clear when he writes; 'If the world had no substance, then whether a proposition had sense would depend on whether another proposition was true. In that case we could not sketch out any picture of the world (true or false)' (2.0211–2.0212). It is substance, or more specifically, the objects named in elementary propositions that connect the bedrock of language with reality and provide propositions with a determinate sense. Without substance there could be no name–object relation and it is this relation that is the criterion of the truth or falsity of propositions about the world. If there were no such criterion then descriptions would comprise sets of mutually supporting propositions with no independent or objective foundation and these could not constitute a picture of how things are in the world. Ultimately, it is the correspondence of a propositional picture with reality that determines its truth and its lack of correspondence that determines its falsity. The sense of a propositional picture is the possibility that things in reality are arranged as depicted and the limits of sense in language are the limits of the possible arrangements of things. Thus, what a proposition 'represents' (2.221) or 'expresses' (3.1431) or 'shows' (4.022) or 'affirms' (4.064) 'is its agreement and disagreement with possibilities of existence and non-existence of states of affairs' (4.2). Substance and meaning are the end links of a chain. Without substance there could be no objects; without objects there could be no states of affairs; without states of affairs a proposition could have no sense, i.e. it could not 'show how things stand if it is true' (4.022); without propositions with sense, language would be devoid of meaning. If the essence of language is to picture how things stand, then for propositions to have meaning what is pictured must represent a determinate structure, and this is the role Wittgenstein assigns to substance.

The *Tractatus* opens with the dramatic remarks: 'The world is all that is the case' (1), and, 'The world is the totality of facts not things' (1.1). Wittgenstein's characterisation of the world is not to be interpreted as an epistemological thesis. His concern is with the world not as it is *known*, but as it is *determined* by the facts

(1.11). Wittgenstein makes clear elsewhere that the totality of
things would not 'determine what is the case', for 'things' or
'objects' are common to all possible worlds: 'It is obvious that an
imagined world, however different it may be from the real one,
must have *something* – a form – in common with it. Objects are just
what constitute this unalterable form' (2.022, 2.023). A totality of
things that are common to all possible worlds cannot by itself
determine how things are in reality. The real world is composed of
objects *in configurations* that determine the material properties of
the world, i.e. 'what is the case', whereas the totality of things
constitutes the substance of the world and 'can only determine a
form and not any material properties' (2.0231). It is the generation
of material properties by configurations of objects that constitute
facts and it is the totality of facts which 'determines what is the
case, and also whatever is not the case' (1.12). The crucial point is
that this determination of the world by the totality of facts is
independent of our knowing them. Wittgenstein is concerned
with what the world *is*, not with how we *know* what it is, and his
remarks are intended to reveal the structure of the world not the
structure of our knowledge. It is the world itself, not our knowledge of it, that 'divides into facts' (1.2). For Wittgenstein facts are
neither items in the stock of human knowledge nor are they true
propositions as such but the objective counterparts represented by
true propositions which hold independently of anyone knowing
them. Primarily, Wittgenstein's theory of language is a theory of
propositions rather than of names and, although names comprise
the logical atoms of elementary propositions, their epistemological
identification is a matter of no interest to him. Nor, given his basic
assumptions, is this an oversight on his part in spite of a host of
charges to the contrary by his critics. Since propositions picture
facts it follows that the world (which divides into facts) and
language (which is a truth-functional complex of propositions)
have parallel structures or, as Wittgenstein expresses it, a common
logical form. It is from this standpoint that Wittgenstein in the
Tractatus treats epistemology at best as superfluous with respect to
his aims and at worst as a confusion of psychology with logic. The
empirical content of the world is given in the propositions of
natural science whereas the tautologies of logic lack content.
'The propositions of logic describe the scaffolding of the world, or
rather, they represent it. They have no "subject-matter"' (6.124).
Their connection with the world presupposes that the world,

names and elementary propositions stand in line. Thus; 'Logic is not a body of doctrine, but a mirror-image of the world. Logic is transcendental' (6.13). In this sense too, the ontology of the *Tractatus* is transcendental.

After this preliminary sketch of the main line of thought of the *Tractatus* we must examine in more detail some of the important terms used by Wittgenstein. The two most fundamental of these are 'Sachverhalt' and 'Tatsache'. In the first English edition of the *Tractatus* C. K. Ogden translated 'Sachverhalt' as 'atomic fact'. In the more recent English edition by D. F. Pears and B. F. McGuinness it is rendered as 'state of affairs'. Both editions translate 'Tatsache' as 'a fact', and this has remained uncontroversial. But what is the relationship between Sachverhalt and Tatsache? Wittgenstein writes; 'What is the case – a fact (Tatsache) – is the existence of states of affairs (Sachverhalten)' (2). Taken by itself this seems to define unambiguously the relationship of the two terms, namely, that facts (Tatsachen) are simply *existent* states of affairs (Sachverhalten). However, this is complicated by Wittgenstein's further comment; 'The existence and non-existence of states of affairs (Sachverhalten) is reality. (We also call the existence of states of affairs a positive fact (Tatsache) and their non-existence a negative fact)' (2.06). This class of negative facts prevents the simple equation of Tatsachen with *existent* Sachverhalten, although it is clear that Wittgenstein often writes of 'facts' when strictly he means what he here calls 'positive facts' or existent states of affairs. We need to remind ourselves that facts are not verbal *descriptions* of states of affairs but are *comprised* of them. They do not *describe* reality; they are the components of it.

Ogden's translation of 'Sachverhalt' as 'atomic fact' was undoubtedly suggested by, and suggests an identity with, Russell's use of 'atomic fact' in his version of logical atomism. To what extent is there an identity between Russell and Wittgenstein here? Russell offers his own interpretation of Wittgenstein's use of 'Sachverhalt' and 'Tatsache' in his introduction to the *Tractatus*. He writes: 'What is complex in the world is a fact. Facts which are not compounded of other facts are what Mr. Wittgenstein calls *Sachverhalte*, whereas a fact which may consist of two or more facts is called a *Tatsache*; thus, for example, "Socrates is wise" is a *Sachverhalt* as well as a *Tatsache*, whereas "Socrates is wise and Plato is his pupil" is a *Tatsache* but not a *Sachverhalt*' (Russell B. 'Introduction to the Tractatus', p.X1).

In reply to Russell's question, 'what is the difference between Tatsache and Sachverhalt?', Wittgenstein stated in a letter written in 1919; 'Sachverhalt is what corresponds to an elementarsatz if it is true. Tatsache is what corresponds to the logical product of elementary props when this product is true. The reason why I introduce Tatsache before introducing Sachverhalt would want a long explanation'.[1] Unfortunately, no explanation of this interesting point, long or otherwise, was ever given. Nevertheless, this passage is of importance because of its emphasis on the correspondence between Sachverhalt and Elementarsatz, and this correspondence is crucial. Language and reality are linked through the correspondence of Elementarsatz with Sachverhalt, and it is this that enables Wittgenstein to elucidate what he believed to be the logical form of language – 'The general form of a proposition is: This is how things stand' (4.5). The logical structure of reality is mirrored in the logical structure of elementary propositions and if this image is obscured in the composite sentences of ordinary language then it is the task of logical analysis to resolve such sentences into the component elementary propositions which clearly exhibit this relationship.

The translation of 'Sachverhalt' as 'atomic fact' suggests that the distinction between Sachverhalt and Tatsache turns on the atomicity of Sachverhalte. This distinction is confirmed by Wittgenstein's letter to Russell, and on this point Russell's interpretation is correct, i.e. Sachverhalte are atomic and Tatsachen are composite or complex. On the other hand, Stenius has pointed out that if we render 'Sachverhalt' as 'atomic fact' then the formulation of the relationship between these two terms involves the awkwardness of saying 'a fact is a . . . fact'.[2] Writing later, in a passage now incorporated into the work known as *Philosophical Grammar*, Wittgenstein gave the sentence, 'Here there is a red rose', as an example of what he had called in the *Tractatus* an Elementarsatz and Russell had called an 'atomic proposition' (PG p.211). The equivalence of 'Elementarsatz' and 'atomic proposition' suggests that atomic facts were also common elements of both Wittgenstein's and Russell's accounts.

In spite of this, I shall argue later that Russellian atomic facts and Wittgensteinian Sachverhalte are different concepts except for their atomicity and that for this reason it is wise to reject the translation of 'Sachverhalt' by 'atomic fact'. A general criticism of Ogden's translation is that it suggests – unavoidably, perhaps, at the time of its publication – that the assimilation of the *Tractatus* into the framework of Russellian logical atomism is the key to its interpretation. This assimilation has inspired a number of misinterpretations of both Russell and Wittgenstein which have proved persistant. The *Tractatus* is much more than a footnote to *Principia Mathematica*. Clear warnings of misinterpretations of the *Tractatus* were sounded by Wittgenstein himself who did not like Russell's 'Introduction', and after a left-handed compliment paid to the fineness of its English style spoke of its 'superficiality and misunderstanding'.[3] (*Notebooks: 1914–1916*, p.132: cf. P. Engelmann, *Letters from Ludwig Wittgenstein*, Blackwell, 1968, p.31). If only to prevent the simple identification of the *Tractatus* with Russellian logical atomism the Pears and McGuinness translation of 'Sachverhalt' as 'state of affairs' is to be preferred.

Initially, Wittgenstein believed that Sachverhalte were logically independent: 'States of affairs are independent of one another. From the existence or non-existence of one state of affairs it is impossible to infer the existence or non-existence of another' (2.061, 2.062). This puzzling remark was repudiated later in the paper 'Some Remarks on Logical Form' published in 1929 and in other writings which have been published posthumously, but represents a position consistently adhered to in the *Tractatus*. It might seem that the logical independence of states of affairs is denied in the remarks; 'The totality of existing states of affairs also determines which states of affairs do not exist' (2.05). But here it is not the existence of any particular state of affairs but the *totality* of states of affairs. This makes Wittgenstein's argument consistent but does not make it less puzzling.

Wittgenstein's example of an elementary proposition quoted earlier, 'Here there is a red rose', represents a state of affairs which, if true, permits us to infer the falsity of 'Here there is a white rose' applied to the same rose at the same time. The falsity of 'Here there is a white rose' determines the non-existence of the state of affairs represented by this elementary proposition, which is contrary to the assertion of the logical independence of states of affairs. In this example, the existence of one state of affairs permits the inference of the non-existence of another state of affairs without reference to the totality of existing states of affairs. Since Wittgenstein himself explicitly acknowledged the view of the independence of states of affairs advanced in the *Tractatus* to be mistaken there is little point in expending effort and ingenuity in devising a defence for this doctrine. However, Wittgenstein's remarks on the nature of his mistake are interesting and worthy of comment. In Aristotelian logic the relation of the two propositions, 'Here there is a red rose', and 'Here there is a white rose' is one of contrariety and not contradiction. Two propositions are contradictories if, and only if, the truth of either implies the falsity of the other and the falsity of either implies the truth of the other. Whereas two propositions are contraries if, and only if, the truth of either implies the falsity of the other and the falsity of either leaves the truth or falsity of the other undetermined. It can easily be seen that the falsity of 'Here there is a red rose' permits no inference regarding the truth or falsity of 'Here there is a white rose' and vice versa. Thus the propositions are contraries and not contradictories. Because of the fact that two propositions that are contraries might both be false, classical logicians held that there was only one correct negation of a proposition, namely, the assertion of its contradictory. This doctrine has its counterpart in the *Tractatus* in that in the propositional calculus negation is treated as a uniform logical operator. As we shall see, it was this that Wittgenstein came to doubt and finally to reject altogether in favour of the view that negation comprised a family of instances which were not identical. 'Does the *same* negation occur in "Iron does not melt at 100°C" and "Twice two is not five"'? (PI 551). What led to this position were his reflections on the logical properties of colour-words. Wittgenstein expresses the contrariety of the two elementary propositions 'Here there is a red rose' and 'Here there is a white rose' in terms of a collision inasmuch as each proposition attempts to set its subject in the same place at the same time. This is rather like two people trying to sit in the same chair simultaneously; there simply isn't room for both. Wittgenstein, although he came to concede that two elementary propositions could *exclude* one another, still maintained that they cannot *contradict* one another. What is the difference between exclusion and contradiction here? Let p represent 'Here there is a red rose' and q 'Here there is a white rose' then p.q is some kind of contradiction and not simply a false proposition. The truth table for p.q is as follows:

$$
\begin{array}{ccc}
\text{p} & \cdot & \text{q} \\
\text{T} & \text{T} & \text{T} \\
\text{T} & \text{F} & \text{F} \\
\text{F} & \text{F} & \text{T} \\
\text{F} & \text{F} & \text{F} \\
\end{array}
$$

But, in the example we are considering, the first line of this table represents an impossible combination and should disappear. Thus, there is no logical product of p and q and 'herein lies the exclusion as opposed to a contradiction'. To express the contradiction we should have to write:

$$
\begin{array}{ccc}
p & . & q \\
T & F & T \\
T & F & F \\
F & F & T \\
F & F & F
\end{array}
$$

'but this is nonsense, as the top line, "T F T", gives the propositions a greater logical multiplicity than that of the actual possibilities'. The formation of nonsensical constructions can only be prevented by 'definite rules of syntax' and 'these will have to tell us that in the case of certain kinds of atomic propositions described in terms of definite symbolic features certain combinations of the T's and F's must be left out. Such rules, however, cannot be laid down until we have actually reached the ultimate analysis of the phenomena in question'.[4]

The price that Wittgenstein has to pay for this protection of the doctrine that elementary propositions cannot contradict one another is that they comprise kinds or types with different logical properties such that in order to represent possible states of affairs they require syntactical rules which exclude certain possibilities represented by certain truth-table combinations. The admission that elementary propositions are of different logical types and that the representations of reality depends upon rules in addition to propositional pictures is a much greater departure from the principles of the *Tractatus* than Wittgenstein realised at this stage in the development of his thought.

In addition to Sachverhalt and Tatsache, Wittgenstein uses another term, 'Sachlage', which is translated as 'situation' by Pears and McGuinness. Stenius argues against the synonymity of 'Sachverhalt' and 'Sachlage' and thinks that the difference between them is that Sachverhalt is logically simple or atomic whereas a Sachlage need not be so. He proposes therefore, that 'Sachlage' should be translated as 'state of affairs' and 'Sachverhalt' as 'atomic state of affairs'. He asserts, 'every Sachverhalt is also a Sachlage though the converse need not be true: a Sachlage need not be atomic, but if it is so it is a Sachverhalt'.[5] Black, on the other hand, regards 'Sachlage' and 'Sachverhalt' as simply interchangeable.[6] A comparison of the usage of these terms in the *Tractatus* is helpful.

Sachverhalt and *Sachlage* are said to be or to have:	*Sachverhalt*	*Sachlage*
Combinations of objects	2.01	3.21
'Things' as possible constituents	2.011	2.0122
That which objects contain the possibility of	2.012b	2.014
Logically independent	2.062	5.135
What a picture presents	2.11	2.11
Possibilities represented by pictures	2.201	2.202
Thinkable	3.001	3.02
Described in propositions	4.023c	3.11, 3.144
Represented by configurations of object names	4.0311	3.21
Represented in propositions	4.1	4.031
Internal properties manifested in propositions representing them	4.122d	4.124
What a sense of a proposition agrees with	4.2	4.031
What the truth-possibilities of elementary propositions mean	4.3	5.525

These similarities support Black's position that Sachverhalt and Sacklage are interchangeable. The interpretation propounded by Stenius is open to two objections. The first of these stems from Wittgenstein's remark: 'One elementary proposition cannot be deduced from another. There is no possible way of making an inference from the existence of one situation (Sachlage) to the existence of another, entirely different situation' (5.134, 5.135). If Stenius is correct that 'Sachlage need not be atomic' then this remark asserts the logical independence of complex as well as atomic states of affairs. This is to extend Wittgenstein's original mistake about the logical independence of elementary propositions to complex propositions as well, and this is both unjustified and absurd.

The second objection arises from the fact that Stenius is required to suppose that Wittgenstein's account of the relation of Sachverhalt and Tatsache in his letter to Russell was mistaken and that it is Sachlage which is the non-atomic counterpart of Sach-verhalt. As Professor Anscombe quite properly observes: 'I find suggestions that Wittgenstein gave an incorrect account of the *Tractatus* in 1919 quite unacceptable'.[7]

OBJECTS AND NAMES

Amongst the comparatively few philosophers who had an unmis-takeable influence on Wittgenstein was Gottlob Frege and nowhere is this more clearly the case than with objects and names so far as the development of Wittgenstein's thinking in the *Trac-tatus* is concerned.

Frege maintained a distinction between the logically complex and the logically simple that became the foundation of both Russell's and Wittgenstein's versions of logical atomism. As in physical science complex molecules can be analysed into simple chemical elements so in language complex propositions may be analysed into logically simple names, which cannot be further analysed or defined except ostensively. Thus, according to Russell, a complex proposition such as, 'this desk is rectangular, wooden, four-legged, brown and solid' may be analysed into a conjunction of logically simple or atomic or elementary propositions of which one might be, 'this colour patch is brown'.

Frege also maintained a distinction between 'concept' and 'object' which he insisted was a rigid one such that one of three principles which he laid down as fundamental for his enquiry into the foundations of arithmetic was 'never to lose sight of the distinction between concept and object'.[8] A concept is essentially predicative, that is, it is the reference of a grammatical predicate. In the sentence, 'this book is red', the predicate world is 'red', which is a concept word. That is to say, that which the concept word refers to or denotes is 'redness'. The expression 'the concept *redness*, however, names an object, not a concept.

The reference of a proper name, on the other hand, is an object and, according to Frege's distinction, the name of an object can never (by itself) be used as a grammatical predicate.[9] Why can we not say, 'this person is Alexander the Great'? In this example the object name or proper name – Alexander the Great – appears to function as a grammatical predicate in violation of the rigid distinction Frege maintains. He counters this by differentiating two different uses of the word 'is'. In most cases 'is' serves as a copula or verbal sign of predication as, for example, in 'x is green'. This asserts that something falls under a concept, that is, the object denoted by 'x' falls under the concept 'green', or the reference of 'x' is an object included under the extension of 'green'. However, in other cases like, 'this person is Alexander the Great', 'is' functions in the same sense as the equals sign in arithmetic and means 'the same as', 'no other than', or 'identical with'. The logical difference between the two uses of 'is' may be expressed thus: an equation is a reversible relation but an object's falling under a concept is an irreversible relation.

So much for names of objects that seem to function predicatively. What of concept words about which something is predicated|such|as, 'the concept F is a concept imperfectly understood'? Here it looks as if 'F' functions as a proper name, i.e. an object name, in violation of Frege's dictum that concept and object must always be distinguished. His reply to this is that, whilst 'F' can never designate an object, 'the concept F' may do so. Thus, whilst 'F' can never be a proper name, 'the concept F' may be. In maintaining the distinction between concept and object Frege is forced to concede that a concept word, though it can never be a proper name, may be part of a proper name, and, a proper name designating an object, though it can never be a concept word, may be part of a concept or predicate expression. This in turn forces him to postulate a hierarchy of functions of first, second and higher level concepts. An object falls *under* a first-level concept which in turn falls *within* a second-level concept and so on.

Frege also distinguished between proper names and names or signs of functions such that proper names always designate objects and include all those things that are not functions, i.e. cats, mermaids, truth-values and numbers are all objects in this sense. This is the route by which Frege arrived at his celebrated conclusion that numbers were objects. A number is the name of the class of classes having so many members; for example, 'three' is the name of the class of all triads. He also believed that sentences (equations) of arithmetic express thoughts, which guaranteed their applicability, and because arithmetical signs have reference, the application of arithmetic to the world gives us knowledge. Arithmetic is not a game lacking content made by making marks on paper but is a body of truths about objects in just the same way as are the other sciences.

Frege analysed 'There are just as many A's as B's' in a way that established a one–one correlation between them and offered this as a criterion of numerical identity, that is, for it being the case that the number of A's is the same number as the number of B's. Geach comments; 'Given this sharp criterion for identifying numbers Frege thought that only prejudice stood in the way of our regarding numbers as objects. I am strongly inclined to think he is right'.[10] In spite of these inclinations, Geach reports a lingering uneasiness and recounts a conversation between Wittgenstein and Frege in which Frege was asked whether he ever saw any difficulty in the view that numbers are objects. He replied; 'Sometimes I seem to see a difficulty – but then I don't see it'.[11] Philosophy still had some way to go before Wittgenstein could say of this and kindred semantic problems; 'say what you like'.

In one of Frege's most celebrated and seminal papers he argues that a sign (name, combination of words, letter) has both a reference (Bedeutung) – that to which the sign refers – and also a sense (Sinn). Thus, a = b may not be the same case as a = a since 'a' and 'b' may have the same reference but different senses inasmuch as 'a' and 'b' represent different modes of presentation. Similarly, statements about 'the morning star' and 'the evening star' both refer to the same object, namely, the planet Venus, but clearly have different senses since the former expression means the brilliant object visible in the morning sky and the latter expression means the brilliant object visible in the evening sky. The difference in the senses of 'the morning star' and 'the evening star' has always been understood, but the discovery that their references were the same was a notable advance in astronomy:

> The regular connexion between a sign, its sense, and its reference is of such a kind that to the sign there corresponds a definite sense and to that in turn a definite reference, while to a given reference (an object) there does not belong only a single sign. The same sense has different expressions in different languages or even in the same language . . . this is not to say that to the sense there also corresponds a reference . . . The expression 'the least rapidly convergent series' has a sense but demonstrably has no reference, since for every given convergent series, another convergent, but less rapidly convergent, series can be found. In grasping a sense one is not certainly assured of a reference.[12]

In the third edition of this book Black changes his translation of 'Bedeutung' from 'reference' to 'meaning' and there is no doubt that this is a more literal rendering of the word 'Bedeutung'. However, the significance of Frege's distinction between 'Sinn' and 'Bedeutung' is better represented by 'sense' and 'reference' rather than 'sense' and 'meaning' which are almost synonymous in English.

An important consequence of this distinction is to make the sense or meaning of a statement independent of its reference, including those cases where there is no reference. Statements about Odysseus, for example, have sense but no reference and the distinction explains how we can talk meaningfully about, but without reference to, non-existent objects. In short, statements without reference are not therefore senseless. In spite of the perplexing variety of Fregean objects, his theory is an advance on Meinong who postulated non-existent objects as the referents of statements about Odysseus, unicorns, mermaids, round squares and the like.

Frege also held that all true statements have the same reference, namely to the logical object 'the True' and all false statements likewise refer to 'the False'. To make a judgment about a statement represented an advance from understanding its sense, that is, a thought, to ascribing a truth-value, which is to determine its reference to 'the True' or 'the False'.

Frege's distinction between sense and reference and his discussion of the problem and its related issues profoundly influenced the philosophical development of both Russell and Wittgenstein. Function, sign, concept, object, sense, reference – all these are themes that underlie the philosophy of Russell and Wittgenstein and which charted new regions of philosophical logic. Many of Frege's conclusions and all his distinctions have proved to be controversial but for those ignorant of Frege's work the *Tractatus* is rendered needlessly obscure.

To return to a consideration of objects and names, what is clear from Frege's own account is that for him objects are not only, nor even primarily, empirical entities but a much wider category including anything which is the reference of a grammatical subject or is designated by a proper name. The concept 'horse' is not an object because concept and object are mutually exclusive, but 'the concept *horse*' is an object, because in designating the reference of a grammatical subject it functions as a proper name. Both 'name'

and 'object' are used by Frege in senses that show them to be
technical terms belonging to logic rather than ordinary language.
His hesitations, however transient, about asserting that such
things as numbers are objects arose when the logical and ordinary
applications of 'object' seemed to collide. The suppression of these
hesitations reveals a preference for the logical rather than the
experiential which, after all, is an occupational disease of
philosophers.

In the pre-*Tractatus* period of Wittgenstein's thought his
remarks about the status of the logical constants 'and', 'or', 'if . . .
then' and 'not' most clearly reflect Frege's influence. The *Notebooks*
show that during the period 1914–1916 when he made these notes
he was inclined to accept that there were such things as logical
objects. We find, for example, such entries as; 'Before any proposition can make sense (sinn) at all, the logical constants must have
reference (Bedeutung)'.[13] According to Frege, sense and reference
are conceived as logical properties of proper names, predicative
concepts, declarative sentences and logical constants as function-
names. Wittgenstein, on the other hand, makes the sense of the
proposition dependent upon the reference of the logical constants
and asserts that the sense or meaning of a proper name just is its
reference. This again differs from Frege for whom proper names
could have sense without reference. What is clear is that if Wittgenstein thinks that logical constants have reference then there
must be correspondent logical objects which they designate, represent or refer to. His position is not unequivocal, however, and
his uncertainty is reflected in his remarks on the possibility of
propositions which at that time appeared to rest 'on the principle
of signs as going proxy for objects'. In this connection he declares
that 'my fundamental thought is that the logical constants are not
proxies'.[14] (Op. cit. p.37j). This means that the logical constants
are a different kind of sign from proper names in that the former,
unlike the latter, do not go proxy for, refer to, designate, stand for
or represent any sort of object. In the *Tractatus* he comes down on
the side of this interpretation of the logical constants and aban-
dons the notion of logical objects as their referents when he writes;
'My fundamental idea is that the "logical constants" are not
representatives' (4.0312). He also repudiates Frege's assertion that
'the True' and 'the False' are objects to which declarative sentences
refer: 'It is clear that a complex of the signs 'F' and 'T' has no object
(or complex of objects) corresponding to it? . . . There are no

"logical objects"' (*Prototractatus*, 4.0102–4.01303, 4.433). This indicates that, in spite of the obvious influence of Frege on Wittgenstein, the assimilation of the objects of the *Tractatus* with Frege's logical objects is mistaken.

What, then, did Wittgenstein consider objects to be when he wrote the *Tractatus*? There are other entries in the *Notebooks* which throw light on this and suggest a parallel between objects and the material points of physics. In considering the analysis of ordinary sentences into logically simple propositions which contain names representing objects he remarks; 'The division of the body into *material points*, as we have it in physics, is nothing more than analysis into *simple components*'.[15] The analysis of sentences and the analysis of things are parallel processes resulting in the one case in logically simple names and in the other in unanalysable objects. A distinctive feature of the *Tractatus* is the development of a concept of correspondence between names and objects through a theory of pictorial representation.

Elsewhere in the *Notebooks* he writes; 'It always looks as if there were complex objects functioning as simples, and then also *really* simple ones, like the material points of physics, etc'.[16] Even the *Tractatus*, where empirical parallels of this kind are eliminated, he remarks; 'The laws of physics, with all their logical apparatus, still speak, however indirectly, about objects in the world' (6.3431).

These quotations indicate that in so far as Wittgenstein thought of objects as empirical entities there is some analogy with the fundamental physical particles. However, this analogy is of use only within limits outside of which it goes lame on us. There are two principal respects in which the analogy is sound. The first is that the processes of transforming sentences into elementary propositions containing logically simple names and that of transforming complex things into their simplest forms may both be called processes of analysis. Of course, even this parallel is severely restricted in that the analytic processes of physical science cannot really be compared with logical analysis for which no *process* has ever been postulated. The second respect in which the analogy holds is that there is some parallel between the physicists' conception of the combination of particles as the determinant of the properties of material things and Wittgenstein's notion of states of affairs as produced by the configuration of objects. J. Griffin has made the important point that Wittgensteinian objects are not to be identified with Aristotle's concept of first substance in that objects are propertyless – 'not in the sense that they are what *bear* the properties, but in the sense that they are what make the properties'.[17] For Wittgenstein, objects are 'the unalterable form' or 'substance' of the world and all material change is a function of variations in object-configurations (2.021, 2.023, 2.026–2.0272). 'In a state of affairs objects fit into one another like the links of a chain' (2.03). The possibilities of cross-linkages are the possibilities of different states of affairs. Since the *Tractatus* was written, modern physics has called in question the utility of the concept of objects as an unalterable form persisting throughout change. Since there is no question of an identity relation between Wittgensteinian objects and the atomic particles of physics, this consideration does not constitute a refutation of Wittgenstein's thesis and we need to bear in mind the shifting sense of the word 'object' here. Nevertheless, this important change in the physical analogue does affect the credibility and acceptability of the whole analogy and robs it of its apparent self-evidence and necessity. That there *must* be objects – in any sense of objects – is an assertion that has lost both its force and its fascination. The hardness of the logical *'must'* once again dissolves when exposed to conceptual change.

Be this as it may, the parallel with the analysis of complex into simple units and the idea of a correspondence between different object relations and different situations marks the limit of the helpfulness of the analogy between Wittgensteinian objects and the material points of physics. It would be highly misleading to assert their equivalence. For Wittgenstein, objects represent the *logical* form of the substance of the world and their identification was an empirical matter which was no concern of logicians. This indifference to the problem of identification of objects in the world is not because they are not empirical entities per se but because such an investigation does not fall within the province of logic. Although there are indications in the *Notebooks* of Wittgenstein's interest in physics and in spite of Griffin's timely reminder that the two predecessors of Wittgenstein most relevant to the thinking of the *Tractatus* are a mathematician and a physicist; Frege and Hertz,[18] there are other entries in the *Notebooks* which emphasise the purely logical considerations that seemed to necessitate simple objects. For example, there is the seemingly *a priori* concept: '*This*-Identical with the concept of the *object*. Relations and properties, etc., are *objects* too'.[19]

Wittgenstein later abandoned the idea that properties and relations were objects in favour of the view that they were object-configurations, just as, later still, he was to reject Russell's notion of 'this' as the only genuine logically proper name. At the time represented by the *Notebooks*, however, he thought that it is 'perfectly possible that patches in our visual field are simple objects, in that we do not perceive any single point of a patch separately'.[20] This flirtation with the idea that a simple object is a datum of experience designated by 'this' – which thus refers to whatever engages the attention at the time of speaking – was a transient affair. The view that pervades the *Tractatus* is that objects are components of the world irrespective of their empirical determination rather than components of our perception of the world. Purely perceptual considerations are not only a psychological intrusion into the field of logic but interposes irrelevant material between the relationship of language and reality which prevents us seeing clearly both the nature and the intimacy of this relationship.

That there must be objects is a requirement of the view that the form of the world is mirrored in a definite logical structure. Language and reality have a common logical form and this is quite independent of the problems of the empirical identification of the elements of either, i.e. objects and names:

> It keeps on forcing itself upon us that there is some simple indivisible, an element of being, in brief, a thing. It does not go against our feeling, that we cannot analyse propositions so far as to mention the elements by name; no, we feel that the world must consist of elements. And it appears as if that were identical with the proposition that the world must be what it is, it must be definite. Or, in other words, what vacillates is our determinations, not the world. It looks as if to deny things were as much as to say that the world can, as it were, be indefinite in some such sense as that in which our knowledge is uncertain and indefinite. The world has a fixed structure.[21]

This structure is reflected in the logical form of the proposition and 'the demand for simple things *is* the demand for definiteness of sense'.[22] The view of language as essentially sets of truth-functions of elementary propositions enabled Wittgenstein to say that 'if there is a final sense and a proposition expressing it completely, then there are also names for simple objects'.[23] The truth-value of a proposition is determined by the relation between its simple names being matched, or not, by a corresponding relation between objects in the state of affairs depicted by the proposition. The name–object relation is what ultimately guarantees the sense of language so that sentences have sense because names refer to objects. This notion of sense *through* reference though not unequivocal, as we shall see, is one strand of Wittgenstein's response to Frege's discussion of the sense and reference distinction. It was considerations such as these that led Wittgenstein to write:

> It seems that the idea of the *SIMPLE* is already to be found contained in that of the complex and in the idea of analysis, and in such a way that we come to this idea quite apart from any examples of simple objects or of propositions which mention them, and we realise the existence of the simple object – *a priori* – as a logical necessity.[24]

Primarily, then, the idea of the simple object is a requirement for the definiteness of sense in propositions and not something merely borrowed from physics. Indeed, infinite divisibility, the rejection of which is the starting point of physical atomism, Wittgenstein did not feel was necessarily ruled out by anything in the world.[25] The sense of compulsion which led him to assert the logical necessity of simple objects did not arise from the traditional arguments of physicists for an atomistic view of the world but from the need to give language definiteness of sense. The name–object relation is the raw elemental connection between language and reality; it is the point at which language hooks on to the world.

We must now turn to an important issue in the interpretation of the *Tractatus* over which there has been controversy. Is it the case, in fact, that objects in the *Tractatus* retain the ontological role to which some of the entries in the *Notebooks* appear to consign them? In short, does the *Tractatus* continue to treat objects as *things* or *elements* of the world? This appears to be the most natural interpretation of their role in Wittgenstein's scheme and this view seems to be reinforced by the explicit rejection of Frege's idea of logical objects. In the light of some of the accounts that have been given of objects in which they are interpreted non-ontologically, it is not easy to see why Wittgenstein wished to assert that the logical constants, truth-values and numbers were not objects. The ontological interpretation of objects, on the other hand, is free from this difficulty and his reason for excluding the logical constants, truth-values and numbers from the class of objects is because he finds it incredible that such things should be included amongst elements of the world. They are not items of furniture of either heaven or earth but merely part of the decor.

However, one difficulty with the ontological interpretation is this; why does Wittgenstein write of objects that they signify 'a formal concept' – like the words 'complex', 'fact', 'function' and 'number', so that 'one cannot say for example, "There are objects", as one might say, "There are books"' (4.1272)?

It will be remembered that a corollary of Frege's rigid distinction between 'concept' and 'object' was that a concept–expression could not on its own be the *subject* of a significant proposition, it must always be a *predicate*. In order to predicate something of a concept, as in the example, 'the concept "horse" is a concept easily attained', Frege was involved in the awkwardness of saying that whereas 'horse' did not denote an object, 'the concept "horse"' did denote an object. Putting this another way, the reference of a grammatical predicate (i.e. a concept) could never become the reference of a grammatical subject (i.e. an object) although a predicate–expression could be incorporated within a subject–expression and vice-versa. In effect this means that if something is a concept we can only significantly predicate something of it by a curious and artificial kind of circumlocution. Presumably, this would include saying of a concept that it has instances.

Wittgenstein has his own version of this doctrine:

When something falls under a formal concept as one of its objects, this cannot be expressed by means of a proposition. Instead it is shown in the very sign for this object. (A name shows that it signifies an object, a sign for a number that it signifies a number etc.). Formal concepts cannot, in fact, be represented by means of a function, as concepts proper can (4.126).

If something falls under a formal concept it is the nature of the propositional sign that shows this: 'Thus the variable name "x" is the proper sign for the pseudo-concept *object*' (4.1272). The difference between concepts proper and formal concepts is illustrated by the difference between functions and variable names and this is exhibited in the nature of the signs employed. This doctrine is coupled with another to the effect that what signs *show* cannot be *said*, with the result that what the *Tractatus* tries to say about objects, for example, strictly speaking cannot be said at all. That objects constitute a formal concept does not rob them of their ontological status and means only that they cannot be represented by functions but only by names. The representational form of the variable name–sign cannot be expressed in genuine propositions, it simply shows. It is not that there are no objects in reality but that the assertion that there are is both improper and superfluous according to the theory of propositional signs developed in the *Tractatus*.

Other relevant remarks in the *Notebooks* include; 'What the pseudo-proposition "There are n things" tries to express shows in language by the presence of n proper names with different references'.[26] The compulsion to speak of objects does not arise from physics, or acquaintance with examples, or any other empirical consideration, but from the logical structure of propositions. 'For we don't have any examples before our minds when we use Fx and all the other variable form–signs. . . . We portray the thing, the relation, the property, by means of variables and so show that we do not derive these ideas from particular cases that occur to us, but possess them somehow a priori'.[27]

Wittgenstein himself comes to our aid in elucidating the nature of the objects of the *Tractatus* in his later writings. In the *Philosophical Investigations*, for example, he writes; 'What lies behind the idea that names really signify simples?', and quotes a passage from Plato's Theaetetus about primary elements 'out of which we and everything else are composed; for everything that exists in its own right can only be *named*'. He adds; 'Both Russell's "individuals" and my "objects" (Tractatus Logico-Philosophicus) were such primary elements' (PI 46). This seems to me to be decisive. The 'objects' of the *Tractatus* are lineal descendents of their illustrious ontological forebears, Plato's primary elements. To treat objects as anything less than the unalterable form or substance of the world is to miss the relation between language and reality which the *Tractatus* sets out to exhibit. However, in spite of the fact that they are both primary elements there are important differences between Russell's individuals and Wittgenstein's objects that must be borne in mind. Russell's individuals are sense data which we know by acquaintance, i.e. experientially, whereas Wittgenstein's objects are not sensory but belong to reality independently of our experience and which we know only as the referents of names, i.e. logically. Language and reality are linked together by a correspondence between objects and names and a common logical structure. The simple signs of completely analysed propositions are names which represent, stand for, refer to or mean objects (3.201, 3.202, 3.203, 3.22). A configuration of objects comprising a state of affairs corresponds to the arrangement of names in a true proposition representing that state of affairs (3.21, 4.0311). The elementary proposition consists of a concatenation, or nexus, of names in immediate combination (4.22, 4.221).

This account of the elementary proposition presents us with problems. Does a concatenation of names in immediate combination mean that only names are employed in an elementary proposition and that quantifiers and function signs have all been analysed out? If so, then Wittgenstein's notation for writing elementary propositions as functions of names with the form 'fx' can only mean that 'f' is a name. This particular point will be discussed in more detail in the next section dealing with properties and relations. Wittgenstein himself elsewhere in the *Tractatus* recognises that a set of names cannot express a sense (3.142). 'Names are like points; propositions like arrows – they have sense' (3.144). Such considerations suggest that in the *Tractatus* he was uncertain whether the elementary proposition consisted only of names in immediate combination whose arrangement portrayed the sense of the proposition, or whether names occurred along with other non-representational logical signs which, together with names, expressed the sense. This interpretation raises doubts as to the appropriateness of the expression 'names in immediate combination', but is in line with Wittgenstein's later description of the elementary proposition as 'a logical network sprinkled with names'.[28]

If, as appears to be the case, a set of names expresses a sense only within the framework of a logical network then having a sense is a property of propositions. Does a name on its own have sense? The business of names is to refer and if we may speak of names as having sense at all it is through their references. The sense or meaning of a name is its reference and Wittgenstein is explicit that 'only propositions have sense; only in the nexus of a proposition does a name have meaning (Bedeutung)' (3.3). It is clear that Wittgenstein rejects the idea of a bare name in isolation from a proposition being endowed with sense by an ostensive definition. The function and status of ostensive definitions in relation to the activity of naming objects is something which is discussed in detail in his later writings. It must be remembered that logically simple or primitive names are not to be confused with ordinary proper names inasmuch as an ordinary proper name, but not a logically simple name, may be replaced by a description. The ordinary proper name 'Ludwig Wittgenstein' is associated with certain unique properties which may be incorporated into a description so that we can identify the bearer of the name and use the description in place of the proper name.

Wittgenstein now appears to be involved in an impasse. On the one hand, it is the name–object relation that guarantees that propositions have sense and that language is anchored to reality. This is the theory that propositions have sense through the reference of logically simple names to objects. The up-shot of this theory is that 'instead of "This proposition has such and such a sense", we can simply say, "This proposition represents such and such a situation"' (4.031). The essence of propositional representation is that 'one name stands for one thing, another for another thing, and they are combined with one another. In this way the whole group – like a tableau vivant – presents a state of affairs' (4.0311). From this it might be concluded that the sense of propositions pre-supposes their analysis into elementary propositions and, more importantly, that the name–object relation is established independently and prior to the determination of the sense of propositions containing them. On the other hand, from other remarks made by Wittgenstein, it is clear that the sense of propositions does not wait upon their analysis into simple components and neither a set of simple names, nor a simple name alone separated from the logical nexus of a proposition, has either sense or reference. If the sense of propositions is determined independently of processes of analysis into simple names, as must be the case if we do not know how to proceed as far as revealing elementary propositions in actual cases, then analysis is superfluous; sense is not achieved through the reference of logically simple names to objects in the world and thus, the name–object relation is not the guarantor of sense. How, then, can we come to understand the meanings of primitive signs? Wittgenstein's answer is that they can be explained by means of elucidation, i.e. their use in propositions that contain them (3.263). Since they are logically simple they cannot be defined – not even ostensively – nor can they be described; they can only be used in propositions. The later realisation that the method of the elucidation of meaning by considerations of use could be applied to many other kinds of words than simple names sounded the deathknell of logical analysis and all its works.

Without doubt there are confusions in the *Tractatus* which Wittgenstein came to recognise as such and, once again, there is little point now in a vast expenditure of effort and ingenuity in trying to resolve them. However, the point is that the analogy of the proposition as a picture of reality is not entirely invalidated if we dispense with analysis and logically simple names and objects. The predominent theme of the *Tractatus* vis a vis this analogy is that any significant proposition – including complex ones – is a picture of the situation it represents. It is not the case that only elementary propositions are pictures. Even if in the end this is too large a claim as an elucidation of the significance of *all* propositions the analogy per se is not absurd.

Let me hazard an illustration, albeit an imperfect one, of some of the main features of the picture analogy. Consider the following to be propositional signs:

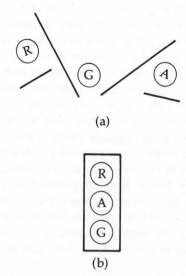

(a)

(b)

Figure 1

This group of signs as set out here, (a), does not comprise a proposition with sense. If, however, we now give these same signs the logical articulation illustrated in the second drawing, (b), then the new arrangement does constitute a proposition with sense.
The following points elucidate the proposition:

1. What the proposition portrays, depicts, expresses, pictures or represents is the arrangement of coloured discs comprising traffic signals.
2. The signs 'G', 'A', 'R' are names.
3. The signs ' – ', ' – ', ' | ', ' | ' and 'O' are the logical scaffolding of the proposition, which is, thus, a logical network sprinkled with names.
4. The sense of the proposition is *this is how things stand as regards traffic signals*.
5. Picture and reality have a common pictorial form. I.e. the arrangement of elements of the picture correspond to the arrangement of objects in the world.
6. This drawing and the statement, 'the arrangement of coloured discs in traffic signals is a vertical sequence (upwards) of green, amber and red' are *both* pictures of the same state of affairs and are logically equivalent. I.e. propositional pictures are not necessarily facsimiles.
7. The drawing and the equivalent verbal proposition in (6) have a common logical form, which they share with the state of affairs portrayed, but the propositions employ different methods of projection.
8. Since the relationship of names corresponds with the relationship of objects in reality, the proposition has the truth-value true.

I have no doubt that the early Wittgenstein would have been appalled by this gross intrusion of empirical considerations into purely logical concerns but I suspect that the later Wittgenstein might have been amused by it. This illustration is far from being an exact analogy but may serve to throw light on the interpretation of some aspects of Wittgenstein's ideas on names and objects.

PROPERTIES AND RELATIONS

Does Wittgenstein include properties and relations among objects? This is a difficult question and commentators on the *Tractatus* are divided into three groups, namely, those who think that

1. objects are bare particulars only;
2. objects include properties and relations as well as particulars;
3. it is impossible to be certain and speculation is futile.

It is clear from the *Notebooks* that at that early stage in his development Wittgenstein thought that 'relations and properties, etc. are objects too'.[29] Not only is this remark without counterpart in the *Tractatus* but there are several passages which suggest that he had swung away from the view that properties and relations were objects, to the view that they were configurations of objects. It seems as if when he discarded Frege's logical objects he also discarded the idea that properties and relations were objects. The notion of an object in the *Tractatus* is both narrower and sharper than in the exploratory remarks found in the *Notebooks*. The view that objects embraced primary elements or entities, properties and relations belongs to that stage in Wittgenstein's thought when he seriously entertained the possibility of Fregean logical objects which displayed comparable categorial diversity.

In the passage from the Theaetetus about primary elements which Wittgenstein quotes in *Philosophical Investigations* and which he identifies with the objects of the *Tractatus*, it is clear that they are bare particulars which cannot be described but only named (PI I 46). This would seem to exclude properties and relations which are not bare particulars capable only of being named. Certainly, it is difficult to conceive of relations as objects. To interpret a R b, where R is the relation 'next to', as an assertion about three objects is unnecessary if not absurd. Relations between objects are displayed by the relations between names in elementary propositions. 'The essence of a propositional sign is very clearly seen if we imagine one composed of spatial objects (such as tables, chairs and books) instead of written signs. Then the spatial arrangement of these things will express the sense of the proposition' (3.1431). This does not mean that only spatial relations of objects can be depicted by spatial combinations of names. Any relation of objects, including non-spatial ones, can be represented by a spatial combination of names, for the picturing relation need not be identical with the relation pictured. Wittgenstein thought that relational words could be analysed out of propositions containing them and displayed in an elementary proposition by relations between arrangements of names. Where a non-spatial relation is depicted we need a suitable representational convention for depicting it by a spatial arrangement of names. Thus, the analysis of the complex proposition a R b would eliminate 'R' which would be displayed by a suitable arrangement of names in an elementary proposition. For example, if 'r' is the non-spatial relation 'father of', then an appropriate spatial relation

of names would be $\begin{matrix} a \\ | \\ b \end{matrix}$, which is the representational form governing the arrangement of names in genealogical tables.

A similar treatment of properties is rather more difficult. Consider first what it might mean to say that properties are not objects but configurations of objects. How can the property 'red' be produced by a configuration of objects? Once again the analogy of objects with atoms may come to our aid. One cannot say of an atom that it is red or any other colour. Since any atom is smaller than the shortest wavelength of visible light the property of being coloured is not applicable to atoms. The property red only becomes applicable when atoms enter into a configuration such that reflection, refraction and scattering of visible light occurs and we can say of the atoms in configuration, 'this is red'. At least of this material property it makes sense to speak of it as being 'produced by' the configuration of objects (2.0231). There is reason to believe that in the *Tractatus* Wittgenstein held that *all* material properties were analogously produced.

Here the difficulties begin. Wittgenstein writes elementary propositions as functions of names having the form 'fx', '$\phi(x,y)$' etc. (4.24). We have already seen that Wittgenstein regarded 'this is red' to be an elementary proposition, i.e. using the notation of the predicate calculus, 'fa'. But if elementary propositions consist of names in immediate combination (4.22, 4.221) then either 'f' is a name or 'fa' is not elementary. If, contra Wittgenstein, 'fx' is *not* the form of the elementary proposition and further analysis is required to reach a concatenation of names, how do we proceed beyond the 'fx' stage? On the other hand, if 'f' is a name like 'a' then not only is the vital distinction between formal concept and function obliterated but properties are also objects.

One possible line of escape from these difficulties might be to emphasise once again the idea of the elementary proposition as a logical network sprinkled with names. What 'fa' shows is 'that the object a occurs in its sense' (4.1211), and this sense may be expressed in a form in which the function sign 'f' is replaced by different signs in the logical network. To hazard a further illustration, consider the proposition $\phi(a,b)$. It makes sense to regard the functional part of the proposition – its ϕ-ness – as expressed in an appropriate arrangement of the names a, b in a logical network in which the sign 'ϕ' does not occur. If ϕ expresses the property of 'having the same father' then $\phi(a,b)$ could be represented by

a   b

using the convention governing genealogical tables. In this case it is reasonable to regard this particular form of representation as a concatenation of names in a logical network which displays the property of ϕ-ness without recourse to the sign 'ϕ'. The problem with this illustration concerns the relationship between 'ϕ' and '⌐⌐⌐'. If they are simply equivalent and interchangeable then all we have is a change in signs and, plainly, a variation in the notation gets us no further. If we regard ⌐ a b as a more fully analysed form than $\phi(a,b)$ then Wittgenstein was mistaken in characterising $\phi(x,y)$ as the general form of the elementary proposition. A major difficulty of the *Tractatus* is that we are given no idea how to analyse propositions nor what 'the real primitive signs' of fully analysed forms are. From this it follows that sense does not wait upon analysis and that for the elucidation of the sense of propositions, analyses together with its implied structural relationships is simply irrelevant.

Some other difficulties with the notion of an object in the *Tractatus* must be mentioned. If the statement 'objects are colourless' (2.0232) means that they possess no properties per se, i.e. they are bare existents, what is meant by the internal and external properties of objects? An internal property is a formal property, or that which it is 'unthinkable' (logically impossible), that an object should not possess (4.123). An example might be that a simple object has the internal or formal property of being unanalysable, although Wittgenstein remarks that 'it is impossible . . . to assert by means of propositions that such internal properties and relations exist: rather they make themselves manifest in the propositions that represent the relevant states of affairs and are concerned with the relevant objects' (4.122). Internal properties of objects are characterised by the distinctive features common to the symbols employed as names (4.126). Plainly, the distinction Wittgenstein is after between internal and external properties is that between logical and material properties.

But if it is the configuration of objects that *produce* material (external) properties, what are the external properties *of* objects? Objects may be combined like the links of a chain and the external properties of an object are determined by the arrangement of objects comprising the other links. If a R b represents an existent state of affairs then 'Rb' expresses an external property of a.

What does Wittgenstein mean when he writes, 'Space, time and colour (being coloured) are forms of objects' (2.0251)? Surely not that space, time and colour are *kinds* of objects. Here, form denotes logical category: compare, 'the possibility of its occuring in state of affairs is the form of an object' (2.0141) where 'form' has this sense. If space, time and colour are categories of objects then, unquestionably, objects are ontological entities comprising the substance of the world.

However, if this interpretation is correct, what are we to make of the comment:

An atomic fact is a combination of objects (entities, things)'. Objects etc. is here used for such things as a colour, a point in visual space . . . A word has no sense except in a proposition. 'Objects' also include relations; a proposition is not two things connected by a relation. 'Thing' and 'relation' are on the same level. The objects hang as it were in a chain.[30]

This has been taken to mean that relations (and properties) *are* objects contrary to the interpretation offered above. Unfortunately this comment is not decisive because the notion of inclusion here may be read as signifying that objects are what *display* relations (and *comprise* properties). Even in this passage Wittgenstein seems to be emphasising the *thingness* of objects.

2

The Structure of Language

LOGICAL ATOMISM

Logical atomism is a theory concerning the basic structure of natural language which figured prominently in British philosophy during the early years of this century, although its antecedents are traceable back as far as Plato. A very influential version of the theory was promulgated by Russell who explicitly acknowledged the contribution to its formulation made by Wittgenstein in their discussions together in Cambridge before the First World War.

The principal thesis of logical atomism is disarmingly simple, namely that all significant assertoric sentences of natural languages are truth-functions of elementary propositions which are composed of simple, indefinable, unanalysable logical atoms or names. The truth-functional view of language supposes that the truth or falsity of a complex sentence is a function only of the truth or falsity of the component elementary propositions into which complex sentences, in principle, may be analysed. Since the relations between propositions were conceived only in terms of their truth-values, logical atomism represented the application of an extensional logic to language. In principle, all significant assertions are capable of analysis into functions of simple names – the logical atoms from which the theory derives its name – plus certain connectives or logical constants whose status varied with different versions of the theory.

Commonly associated with logical atomism was a distinction based upon Hume's dichotomy of all significant discourse into the tautologies of logic and mathematics on the one hand and the factual or empirical statements exemplified in the natural sciences on the other. A corollary of this association was the conviction, common to logical atomists, that statements of theology, metaphysics and ethics – at least as traditionally understood – lay outside the realm of what may be significantly asserted. A distinctive feature of Wittgenstein's version of logical atomism was its provision of a very sharp criterion for excluding unusually large areas of discourse, including much of the *Tractatus* itself, as nonsense.

The credibility of logical atomism depends mainly upon the fact that the question 'what does this mean?', when asked of some linguistic complex, seems to demand analysis into less complex units which must have a terminus if meaning is to be determinate. That is to say, the establishment of the foundations of the theory is the supposition that questions about *meaning* are answered by processes of *analysis* into simple components. Once this vital point has been conceded then it might be argued that if analysis may be carried on indefinitely, i.e. language is infinitely divisible, as it were, then answers to questions about meaning have no end and language is fundamentally indeterminate. If, on the other hand, analysis is ultimately a circular process, like some dictionary definitions – a is b, b is c . . . . . m is n, n is a – language seems to be equally indefinite. Since neither of the alternatives of indeterminacy nor circularity provides a secure foundation for language, and the association of meaning and analysis was axiomatic, it appeared inescapable that there must be logically primitive terms marking the terminus of analysis as a necessary condition of determinate meaning. According to this view, the bedrock of language is the logically simple name.

There are two obvious problems raised by logical analysis which have never been satisfactorily resolved and which led ultimately to its abandonment. The first is the dearth of examples of logical atoms – with the possible exception of colour words and, according to G. E. Moore, the word 'good' – and sixty years of intensive study of logical analysis have failed to yield any really convincing examples. Wittgenstein's lofty disdain as a logician for the problems of empirical identification of logical atoms could not indefinitely disguise the fact that this is a serious lack in a theory which claimed to elucidate how language is actually used with determinate meaning.

The second defect is that given that questions about meaning are answered by analysis, how does it come about that we understand complex sentences without ever undertaking their analysis? The problem is compounded by the fact that it is not that we don't need to analyse such complexes – we don't know how to do so either. Since the technique of analysis has never been demonstrated, and we have no idea how to proceed in actual cases, we are entitled to conclude that questions about meaning are rarely, if ever, answered by analysis. However, Wittgenstein himself was aware of this problem from an early stage in the development of his thinking and manifested his disquiet then. There are several passages in the *Notebooks* which indicate his recognition of the difficulty that understanding a complex proposition does not wait upon an analysis of it. For example, a complex object like, 'this watch', can be given a name and this name 'in a proposition will correspond to all the requirements of the "names of simple objects"'.[1] A name of a complex object will have a determinate meaning in a proposition without analysing either name or complex object into their simplest components – assuming that we knew how to do so. Wittgenstein asks the pertinent question; 'In order to know the syntactical treatment of a name, must I know the composition of its reference? If so, then the whole composition is already expressed even in the unanalysed proposition'.[2] The point here, I take it, is not that the syntactical treatment of the name for 'this watch' presupposes a knowledge of springs, wheels, pivots and etc., which go into the composition of the watch, but that the complex sign displayed by its form that it was composite. Nevertheless, from the fact that we can understand the meaning and use of such a name without knowing the composition of its reference, does call in question the role assigned to analysis in the elucidation of complex names and propositions. Wittgenstein's parenthetic comment is poignant: 'One often tries to jump over too wide chasms of thought and then falls in.'

He goes on to examine the proposition 'this watch is shiny' and makes the important observation, 'if a proposition tells us something, then it must be a picture of reality just as it is, and a complete picture at that'.[3] From what he has already asserted about the picturing relation between logical names and simple objects he recognises that for a complex proposition to be intelligible in its unanalysed form as a picture of reality it must be as though in a certain sense 'all names were genuine names' and 'all objects were . . . simple objects'.[4] This might have led on to a critical reappraisal and subsequent rejection of the whole apparatus of simple objects, logical names and analysis in the elucidation of the meaning of language. It is easy to see this now, but before this change in standpoint could occur there had to be a shift of attention from the investigation of language-structure to an investigation of language-function. Nevertheless, there is a prophetic ring to the remark, 'the propositions which are the only ones that humanity uses will have a sense just as they are and do not wait upon a future analysis in order to acquire a sense'.[5] Why did this not lead to a recognition of the irrelevance of analysis and an examination of the sense of the unanalysed proposition as it was actually expressed in use? The disinclination to take this step is revealed in what Wittgenstein calls 'an extremely important question', namely, does the proposition 'the book is lying on the table' really have 'a completely clear sense'?[6] It was the demand for complete clarity of sense that was the stumbling block and at that time haunted him obsessively. Even though an unanalysed proposition must have a sense as it stood, that sense was often ambiguous and, presumably, analysis would strip away the ambiguity and reveal the completely clear sense in a pure isolated form. Wittgenstein's treatment of this particular example is a forerunner of a technique he later employed in *Philosophical Investigations* for precisely the purpose of excorcising this obsession with complete clarity of sense. What the early Wittgenstein accepted as axiomatic is that if a proposition does have a completely clear sense then it must be possible to say straight off whether the proposition is true or false whatever its application. Having accepted this, his technique of investigation of the proposition is to apply it to different cases, not only to those cases where it is plainly true or plainly false, but also intermediate cases where we are in doubt about its truth-value. What constitutes his difficulty is that range of intermediate cases in which it is not possible 'to say straight off whether the book is still be be called "lying on the table"'. He concludes, therefore, that such a proposition contains 'a lot of indefiniteness' and consequently its sense 'is more complicated than the proposition itself'.[7] The outward simplicity of grammatical form disguises the complicated logical structure of its sense and the inability to read off the truth-value of a proposition for all possible applications of it is a mark of indefiniteness which can only be attributed to the outward grammatical form. At this stage it does not appear to have occurred to Wittgenstein that indefiniteness might well be a feature of some applications of an elementary proposition such as fa. If fa means, 'a is green' there are applications of fa to cases where green shades off into blue in the spectrum of visible light such that we might be in doubt concerning the truth-value of fa. Does this mean that fa contains a lot of indefiniteness or that its sense is more complicated than the proposition itself? Assuming indefiniteness is a problem the remedy here is not analysis – which is impossible in the case of an elementary proposition – but a convention which lays down the limits within the visible spectrum for which 'a is green' is true.

Before this insight became a commonplace, Wittgenstein believed that the truth-values of propositions of the form fx are obvious because such propositions are laid right up against reality and consequently sense is both determinate and of the same complexity, or logical multiplicity, as the states of affairs portrayed. In such propositions sense is completely unambiguous because of their form, for he held that 'the only sign which guarantees its meaning is function and argument'.[8]

This is developed in greater detail in the *Tractatus* where, through a truth-functional view of propositions, a link between language and reality is forged. The truth-conditions of complex propositions are the truth-possibilities of elementary propositions which represent 'the possibilities of existence and non-existence of states of affairs' (4.3, 4.41). Putting this another way, every proposition is a result of successive applications to elementary propositions of logical operations (6, 6.001, 6.002). So strong is the fascination of this picture of language that Wittgenstein asserts; 'Indeed, the understanding of general propositions *palpably* depends on the understanding of elementary propositions' (4.411). This does not mean that before we understand the sense of a compound proposition we first analyse it and grasp the sense of its constituent elementary propositions. The understanding spoken of here has to do with an appreciation of the structure of language: 'If we know on purely logical grounds that there must be elementary propositions, then everyone who understands propositions in their unanalysed form must know it' (5.5562). Again, this is not to know what elementary propositions there are, but that there must be such things is a 'requirement that sense be determinate' (3.23). Knowing a form is not necessarily dependent upon exemplification of the form as a form, but upon grasping the sense of an arrangement of signs which displays the form. Understanding language involves understanding both its surface grammar (the sense of the unanalysed proposition) and its depth grammar (the formal structure of the sense). Thus, analysis is not a requirement for understanding sense: 'We can describe the world completely by means of fully generalised propositions, i.e. without first correlating any name with a particular object' (5.526). Nevertheless, the possibility of the name-object correlation is the ultimate guarantor of sense. Our ordinary forms of expression may obscure the sense of a sentence but Wittgenstein believed that it must be possible to isolate and represent this sense unambiguously in a propositional picture which did not disguise the form of the facts represented. If the unanalysed sentence and the elementary propositions into which the sentence, in principle, could be analysed are *both* pictures, what difference is there between them? Wittgenstein would answer that there is a difference in the methods of projection employed and complete clarity of sense expressed in the analysed forms as opposed to some indefiniteness that may pertain. to an ordinary sentence. It is axiomatic that if a thing can be said at all it can be said clearly. Nevertheless, as we shall see, the admission that ordinary sentences, just as they stand, are pictures of facts calls in question the necessity, and even the utility, of the logical apparatus of analysis, objects and elementary propositions proposed by Wittgenstein to underpin language. An early symptom of this later disquiet is found in his recognition that in spite of the indefiniteness of the general application of 'lying' in the proposition, 'this watch is lying on the table', the situation it represents 'can *somehow* be portrayed by means of this form . . . this proposition is a picture of that complex'.[9] That 'somehow' speaks volumes and its explication was the major pre-occupation of Wittgenstein's philosophy.

This problem becomes more acute in Wittgenstein's account of the picture theory of language developed in the *Tractatus*. The theory is constructed out of a picturing relation between arrangements of objects in states of affairs and representative concatenations of names in elementary propositions. Yet, even more explicitly than in the *Notebooks*, Wittgenstein concedes that even ordinary printed sentences are pictures of reality (4.011). Again as we shall see, the credibility of ordinary sentences as pictures of what they describe rests upon agreement about methods of projection, or representational conventions, and it is through the medium of these conventions rather than problematical hidden logical structures that the sense of language is expressed.

It has been commonly supposed that the differences between Russell and Wittgenstein grew up during the middle period of Wittgenstein's development and thereafter became increasingly divergent. In fact, there were significant differences between them in their respective treatments of logical atomism. Nowhere is this more apparent than in the epistemological status of the logical atom, or terminus, of analysis. For example, Russell writes:

> The reason that I call my doctrine logical atomism is because the atoms that I wish to arrive at as the sort of last residue in analysis are logical atoms and not physical atoms. Some of them will be what I call 'particulars' – such things as little patches of colour or sounds, momentary things – and some of them will be predicates or relations and so on. The point is that the atom I wish to arrive at is the atom of logical analysis not the atom of physical analysis.[10]

I have already argued against the identification of properties and relations with Wittgensteinian objects, and there is little doubt that Russellian particulars are not objects either. The examples Russell gives show that his particulars are the impressions or sense data of traditional empiricist philosophy, which constitute the basic epistemological units out of which our knowledge of the world is constructed. A consequence of this view is that atomic propositions which incorporate proper names or 'words for particulars' are really descriptions of items of immediate experience. It was through the medium of sense data that language was related to reality. On the one hand, language is a set of descriptions of sense data, immediate experiences, mental states and processes, on the other hand, the world itself is a logical construction of sense data and the like. Sense data thus play a dual role: they are what significant assertions describe and they are also the foundations of empirical knowledge. In Russell's version of logical atomism psychological states, processes and experiences are essential intermediaries between language and reality. Sense data are what give language its content and reality its structure.

Against this Wittgenstein held that epistemology was not central to philosophy at all but belonged to the philosophy of psychology. The concern with 'thought processes' and the arguments adduced by Russell and Moore that 'A believes that p' exhibits a special kind of relation between A and p are dismissed by Wittgenstein as 'unessential psychological investigations' (4.1121, 5.541). The point he wishes to emphasise is that 'A believes that p', 'A has the thought p' and 'A says p' are all of the form ' "p" says p' (5.542). That is to say, I take it, that the assertion of 'p' is contained in, and part of p, and not something external to it deriving from the psychological state of the user, A. Assertion is a logical and not a psychological phenomenon and A's psychological states when he 'believes' or 'had the thought' p are irrelevant in the elucidation of the logic of assertion. The correlation of p with a pseudo-object A simply obscures the point which only concerns 'the correlation of facts by means of the correlation of their objects'. The soul or subject is a misconception which dominates 'the superficial psychology of the present day' but is of no concern to the logician (5.5421). In contrasting Wittgenstein's version of logical atomism with Russell's it is significant that the *Tractatus* makes no mention of sense data as the terminus of analysis. The rejection of Russell's sensory particulars is implicit in the ontology of the *Tractatus* and explicit in the remarks about psychological irrelevancies in philosophy. The conviction that sense-data analysis in looking inwards at mental states, processes and items of immediate experience gave a fundamentally misdirected account of language and reality remained with Wittgenstein all his life. He subjected this kind of analysis to detailed critical scrutiny in *Philosophical Investigations* in the examination of the so-called psychological verbs and the sections concerning the possibility of a private language. All this must be dealt with later but it is appropriate to note here that Russell's basic idea that logically proper names – the elements of language – were directed *inwards* at privately experienced particulars was consistently rejected by Wittgenstein as misconceiving the direction of the aim of language. In the *Tractatus* language reaches right out to, and is a mirror image of, reality and in the *Investigations* it reflects common forms of life. In both the early and the later writings, the criteria of correctness for the applications of words are external and public. The thesis that language consisted essentially of descriptions of logically private sensations was never embraced by Wittgenstein.

IDEAL LANGUAGE AND THE THEORY OF LOGICAL TYPES

What was the principal aim of the *Tractatus*? Resolution of this point is vital for an understanding of the *Tractatus* and also to comprehend the nature and extent of the divergence of thought between Russell and Wittgenstein. Russell contributed an introduction to the *Tractatus* which secured its publication but at the expense of an interpretation of Wittgenstein that seems to be mistaken. When Wittgenstein received a copy of Russell's intro-duction he replied, 'Many thanks for your manuscript. I am not quite in agreement with a lot of it: both where you criticize me, and when you are merely trying to expound my views'.[11] Coupled with Wittgenstein's remarks already quoted about the 'superficial-ity and misunderstanding' of the introduction we have good grounds for questioning the correctness of Russell's interpretation of the aim of the *Tractatus*. Of course, Russell saw in the *Tractatus* a great deal derived from his own work and it is not surprising that he concluded that their principal objectives were the same. Accordingly he wrote:

> In order to understand Mr Wittgenstein's book, it is necessary to realise what is the problem with which he is concerned. In the part of his theory which deals with Symbolism he is concerned with the conditions which would have to be fulfilled by a logically perfect language. . . . A logically perfect language has rules of syntax which prevent nonsense, and has simple sym-bols which always have a definite and unique meaning. Mr Wittgenstein is concerned with the conditions for a logically perfect language – not that any language is logically perfect, or that we believe ourselves capable, here and now of constructing a logically perfect language, but that the whole function of language is to have meaning, and it only fulfills this function in proportion as it approaches to the ideal language which we postulate.[12]

The principal aim of Whitehead and Russell's *Principia Mathematica* was to defend the logicist thesis, namely, that the foundations of mathematics are derivable from logic without the addition of further extra-logical principles. As part of this aim, the authors contributed to the outline of a logically perfect or ideal language by the construction of a symbolism whose elements had definite and unique meanings and whose syntactical structure prevented the generation of antinomies – particularly vicious-circle parodoxes – and other absurdities which the grammar of ordinary language permitted. The hope was that the construction of a rigorously defined and rule-bound symbolism would abolish the vagueness and ambiguity of ordinary language in much the same way as the language of mathematical physics has done for such words as energy and power, weight and mass, speed and velocity, force and acceleration, space and time. The successful employment of a language calculus in natural science inevitably raised hopes of a generalised calculus of language achieving comparable clarity for all ordinary discourse.

As Russell wrote of *Principia Mathematica* many years later:

> The reason for using an artifical symbolic language was the inevitable vagueness and ambiguity of any language used for everyday purposes . . . (we ought not) to be content with ordinary language with its ambiguities and its abominable syntax. I remain convinced that obstinate addiction to ordinary language in our private thoughts is one of the main obstacles to progress in philosophy.[13]

In spite of the extensive use of the symbolism of *Principia Mathematica*, attempting to formulate 'the conditions for a logically perfect language' is not the problem with which Wittgenstein is concerned in the *Tractatus*. The principal aim of the work is not that of laying the foundations of an ideal language but that of exhibiting the logical structure which supports the ordinary language which we all use. A clue to Wittgenstein's objective with respect to language is found in the *Notebooks* in the remark, 'I only want to justify the vagueness of ordinary sentences, for it *can* be justified'.[14] This is echoed in the *Tractatus* in the much-discussed entry: 'all the propositions of our everyday language, just as they stand, are in perfect logical order' (5.5563). This thesis is not incompatible with recognising that ordinary language also contains confusions and ambiguities and that it is possible to construct grammatically impeccable nonsense. However, Wittgenstein's fundamental position is that the analysis of ordinary sentences would reveal their underlying logical order and that the characteristic of nonsense is its failure to display any such order. Ultimately, nonsense is revealed not by what it *says* so much as by what it fails to *show*. The problem of vagueness and ambiguity arises principally from the fact that 'language disguises thought: So much so, that from the outward form of the clothing, it is impossible to infer the form of the thought beneath it' (4.002). Nevertheless, the thought or sense is there, even in ambiguous sentences, and the function of the logical symbolism is to reveal this sense more clearly rather than bring about the abolition of such sentences. The utility of the symbolism of *Principia Mathematica* for Wittgenstein does not consist in its constructability with respect to an ideal language but in its analytic potential for penetrating the disguised outward forms of language. The essence of language is that it should represent reality and the symbolism of *Principia Mathematica* turns out to be a convenient notation for exhibiting the logical properties of the representational relation. Wittgenstein is enthusiastic about the superiority of the generality-sign, '(x).fx', over various possible alternatives, because it possesses the necessary mathematical multiplicity which reveals the real, rather than the apparent, logical form of propositions of the type 'all S is P' (4.0411, 4.0031). However, a less felicitous symbolism from the point of view of displaying the real logical form is not therefore useless because 'the essence of the pictorial character' of propositions is 'not impaired by apparent irregularities' in notation (4.013). As has already been emphasised, a crucial point in the interpretation of the *Tractatus* is that an ordinary sentence (all S is P) and its equivalent expressed in the predicate calculus (x) (fx⊃gx) are both pictures, if true, of what is the case. The difference between them concerns only the mode of signification, but the function of all signs, including those of natural language, is to signify. 'Logic is not a field in which *we* express what we wish with the help of signs, but rather one in which the nature of the absolutely necessary signs speaks for itself. If we know the logical syntax of any sign-language then we have already been given all the propositions of logic' (6.124). The 'peculiar crotchets and contrivances' of logical symbolism and the notation of ordinary printed sentences both mirror the world, in spite of differences in the quality of reflection (5.511). Wittgenstein's interpretation of his early views to be found in the *Investigations* are relevant here when he comments that previously he had thought that 'if anyone utters a sentence and *means* or *understands* it he is operating a calculus according to definite rules' (PI 81). A passionate belief in the fundamental logical order of natural language is a constant theme of Wittgenstein's philosophical writings in spite of the different justifications that he gave for it.

If Wittgenstein's picture-theory of language is not confined to the symbolism of the propositional and predicate calculi but embraces ordinary printed sentences as well, then in what sense are the latter pictures? This question has been unnecessarily complicated by the supposition that a propositional picture must be a kind of facsimile of the state of affairs is depicts. For a proposition to be a facsimile is a sufficient but not a necessary condition for it to be a picture of a state of affairs. Propositions of the form 'a R b' and 'a is on the left-hand side of b', if true, *both* picture what is the case. Resemblance between picture and what is pictured is only one of the many different methods of representation, or modes of projection, that may be employed. Uncertainty with respect to the method of representation employed is one of the ways that language disguises the form of the facts. However, when the representational conventions employed are understood, then ordinary sentences not only successfully picture facts but are in perfect logical order as they stand; being a facsimile of the facts depicted is not the defining criterion of that logical order.

Consider the sentence, 'the cat is on the mat'. This fact may be represented in a variety of ways including the following:

(a)    (a) is a *facsimile* of the fact

(b)   'c'   (b) is a representational
                 —   convention which
                 m   *resembles* the fact

(c)   'c/m'   (c) uses a different method
                                                       of representation to depict
                                                       the fact in which a vertical
                                                       spatial relation is rep-
                                                       resented by a horizontal
                                                       spatial relation of symbols.

(d) 'the cat is on the mat'   (d) is also a picture of the
                                                       fact where the mode of
                                                       projection is determined
                                                       by the tactic conventions
                                                       of ordinary language.

All of these examples are what Wittgenstein would call logical pictures of facts and illustrate the point that logical pictures comprise an extended family of instances compared with ordinary pictures. Indeed, the more extended the family becomes the more strained becomes the picture analogy and it was the eventual realisation that the notion of representation is much wider and more elastic than could comfortably be accommodated within a workable picture-theory of language that led to its abandonment.

A further significant difference between Russell and Wittgenstein concerned Russell's theory of logical types and particularly its implications regarding the structure of language. The theory was designed to prevent the formation of logical antinomies of a kind which Russell diagnosed as arising from the vicious-circle principle. Examples of these paradoxes range from simple conundrums to complex problems of set theory. An instance of the first kind is afforded by the man who says 'I am lying'. If he is lying then he is speaking the truth and if he is speaking the truth then he is lying. An instance of the second kind is given by considering the class of classes that are not members of themselves, as, for example, the class of men is not a man. Let k denote the class of classes which are not members of themselves; is k a member of itself? It will readily be seen that if k is a member of itself, then it belongs to the class of classes that are not members of themselves and, therefore, is not a member of k. If k is not a member of itself, then it belongs to the class of classes that are not members of themselves and, therefore, is a member of k. Russell noted that all these paradoxes had a common characteristic which he described as self reference or reflexiveness. In each example something is asserted of all cases of some kind which appears to generate a new case which both is and is not of the same kind. This is a vicious circle arising from the supposition that a class can contain members which are defined by means of the class as a whole. Such classes comprise illegitimate totalities and are ruled out by what Russell called 'the vicious-circle principle', namely, ' "Whatever involves *all* of a collection must not be one of the collection"; or, conversely: If, provided a certain collection had a total, it would have members only definable in terms of that total, then the said collection has no total'.[15]

Applying this principle to propositional functions, we see that fx denotes one value, but not a definite one, of the total collection of arguments comprising the values of fx. That is to say that fx ambiguously denotes one of the objects fa, fb, fc, etc., where fa, fb, fc etc. are the various values of fx. If a function includes a value which presupposes that function then we are involved in a vicious-circle fallacy, for the function cannot be definite until its values are definite, and its values cannot be definite until the function is definite. Thus, the function fx is impossible as an argument to f and accordingly, as Wittgenstein remarked, the form $f(fx)$ is placed on the Index. A given range of significance of a propositional function thus forms a definite logical type, i.e. the collection of arguments for which the function has values. The combination of the vicious-circle principle and the theory of types, whilst excluding functions of the kind $f((x).fx)$, permits the arrangement of propositional functions in hierarchies. What Russell calls first-order functions are those that involve no variables except individuals, i.e. objects which are neither propositions nor functions. Second-order functions, in order to avoid violation of the vicious-circle principle, are permitted to contain as variables only first-order functions and individuals. This process may be continued indefinitely such that if the highest order of variable occurring in a function is a function of the nth order then the function in which it occurs is of the $n + 1$th order.[16]

Analogous arguments to those applied to propositional functions may be adduced in support of a hierarchy of propositions with elementary propositions forming the lowest logical type. In the propositional hierarchy a proposition of the nth order is one which involves a variable of the $n-1$th order in the functional hierarchy. The propositional hierarchy is thus derivable from the functional hierarchy.[17] Russell also held that the propositional hierarchy was derivable from the *entities* referred to by the subjects and predicates of propositions.

> In an elementary proposition we can distinguish one or more *terms* from one or more *concepts*: the *terms* are whatever can be regarded as the *subject* of the proposition, while the concepts are the predicates or relations asserted of these terms. The terms of elementary propositions we will call *individuals*; these form the first or lowest type.[18]

It is possible to construct propositional hierarchies according to the entities admitted as predicates. If we take 'men' as entities of type n, then 'wisdom' is a predicate of type $n + 1$ because it can be significantly applied to (some) men. Being a 'cardinal virtue' is of type $n + 2$ because it may be predicated of 'wisdom' and being a 'characteristic of God' is of type $n + 3$ because it may be predicated of a 'cardinal virtue'. Every attribute is of a higher type than the entities of which it may be significantly predicated, but there is nothing to prove that an attribute must always be of the *next* higher type, although Russell seems to assume this.

Wittgenstein conceived a strong aversion for what he once called 'the beastly theory of types'.[19] He accepted the need for the exclusion of functions violating the vicious-circle principle in the remark; 'No proposition can make a statement about itself, because a propositional sign cannot be contained in itself (that is the whole of the "theory of types")' (3.332). Unfortunately, the brevity of Wittgenstein's dismissal of the theory of types makes it difficult to be sure of the grounds of his rejection of it. However, he makes the point that 'In order to recognise a symbol by its sign we must observe how it is used with a sense. A sign does not determine a logical form unless it is taken together with its logico-syntactical employment' (3.326, 3.327). This remark is important both as a shadow of what was to come, and also as a corrective against the tendency, prevalent in Russell's writings, to suppose that within a calculus a uniformity of sign guaranteed a uniformity of meaning. Even within the rigid framework of a calculus the significance of a sign cannot be divorced from its employment. The fact that in the notation of propositional functions we can write the sign $\phi(\phi x)$ does not determine a possible logical form which we must then exclude by means of the clumsy apparatus of the theory of types. Wittgenstein's point, I take it, is that what seems to be a possible logical sign cannot arise in the first place because 'the sign for a function already contains the prototype of its argument, and it cannot contain itself' (3.333). It is of no importance that in $\phi(\phi x)$ the letter 'ϕ' occurs twice, because 'the letter by itself signifies nothing' and the proper and admissable logical form is given by $\psi(\phi x)$. Russell's theory of logical types seeks to prevent something that strictly cannot arise, and the so-called paradoxes, which the theory is designed to remedy, result from supposing that the same signs represent the same symbols in isolation from their logico-syntactical employment. In short, the logico-syntactical employment of signs for propositional functions already rules out the possibility of functions containing themselves as arguments quite independently of any theory of logical types. Russell's hierarchical structure of types uses a sledgehammer to kill a fly that cannot get off the ground.

Much the same considerations apply to the ordinary-language paradoxes, where the already existing tacit conventions of language, and language about language, render the construction of a hierarchy of propositions unnecessary. For example, an assertion that, 'discussion of sex should be avoided', may look superficially like more discussion of sex, and thus appear to be a violation of the very canon it seeks to lay down. A deeper appreciation of the way such assertions are actually used shows that its subject is not 'sex', but, 'discussion of sex', and, therefore, it is not self-refuting. Putting this another way, to understand the sense of a symbol is to understand its range of application as part of our understanding of the symbol. The logical type of the symbol is not something additional to understanding its sense.

Wittgenstein also objected to Russell's theory of types on the ground that 'he had to mention the meaning of signs when establishing the rules for them' (3.331). This is at variance with Wittgenstein's dictum that 'the meanings of primitive signs can be explained by means of elucidations' (3.263). That is to say, it is the use or application of propositions containing such signs which shows what they stand for, and primitive signs in isolation from the logical framework of propositions are meaningless. This seems to me to be the heart of the picture-theory of language. The meaning of a logically simple name, or primitive sign, is the object for which it stands and the only possible elucidation of its meaning is in propositions that contain it and , by so doing, display this connection. Nothing can be *said* about this connection; it can only be *shown* (4.1212). The essence of language is to show *how things stand* and there is not – because, logically, there cannot be – a significant meta-language in which the picturing relation itself is the subject of representation. The interposition of such a metalanguage between a propositional picture and what it represents would threaten the direct connection between language and reality which Wittgenstein wished to emphasise.

What, then, is the logical status of those propositions in which Wittgenstein elucidates this picturing relation in the *Tractatus*? 'My propositions serve as elucidations in the following way: anyone who understands me eventually recognises them as nonsensical, when he has used them – as steps – to climb up beyond them. (He must, so to speak, throw away the ladder after he has climbed up it)' (6.54). Hence, the famous epigram which concludes the *Tractatus*; 'What we cannot speak about we must pass over in silence' (7).

The question remains, however, if it is improper to mention the meanings of signs when establishing the rules for them then how are such rules established? Wittgenstein is insistent that rules, for example, governing equality between signs, such as 'a = b', are 'mere representational devices. They state nothing about the meaning of the signs "a" and "b"' (4.242). 'The rules of logical syntax must go without saying, one we know how each individual sign signifies' (3.334). But isn't this to know the meanings of signs before knowing the rules governing their application? The answer to this is that we must know *how*, but not necessarily *what*, individual signs signify. To know how a sign signifies is to know its logical structure, i.e. its place in the network of a proposition; it is not to know its meaning. This is how it is possible to know that there are names in elementary propositions, and the rules that govern them, without knowing what objects any particular names stand for or mean. 'In logical syntax the meaning of a sign should never play a role. It must be possible to establish logical syntax without mentioning the *meaning* of a sign' (3.33). Russell's development of the theory of types reverses this priority and derives the logical scaffolding of propositions from the meanings of the signs they contain. To Wittgenstein this seemed to be a threat to the crystalline purity of logic, which must be prior to how things stand in the world as a matter of empirical fact.

Ultimately, for Wittgenstein, the theory of types is both superfluous and impossible in its attempt to say what clearly shows and can only be shown. In trying to represent the representational relation between language and reality Russell generates a new variety of the vicious-circle principle. One of the aims of the *Tractatus* was to reject the theory of types and replace it with a picture-theory of language which simply showed what the theory of types, illicitly, tried to say. It is not too much to say that the logical structure of the *Tractatus* stands or falls on the success or failure of Wittgenstein's attempt to replace Russell's theory of *saying* through logical types by a theory of *showing* in propositional pictures. It was a shrewd counter-attack on Russell's part to point, in the Introduction, to the success with which Wittgenstein himself and managed to say the unsayable.

THE PROPOSITION AND LOGICAL SPACE

Wittgenstein had a fondness for geometrical analogies and, as we shall see, his development of the representational relation between language and reality in terms of geometrical methods of projection was an important stage in the process of conceptual growth that led to the eventual abandonment of the picture-theory of meaning. Another analogy of a geometrical kind on which the *Tractatus* trades is that of logical space, which, like its analogue Newtonian space, is primarily that of the ultimate ontological container; i.e. that which contains all things and in which all change occurs. He develops a Kantian argument when he writes; 'Each thing is, as it were, in a space of possible states of affairs. This space I can imagine empty, but I cannot imagine the thing without the space' (2.013). Presumably, the concept of logical space is introduced to render intelligible the idea of object-configurations producing states of affairs and being represented by appropriate spatial arrangements of propositional signs. Plainly, a spatial arrangement of things, projected as a spatial arrangement of signs, is a form of spatial analogy of the relation between language and reality. That this relation is construed in spatial rather than, say, mental terms tells us something important about Wittgenstein's concept of the nature of the relationship, and the directness of the link, between language and the world.

The analogy between physical and logical space occurs in a number of passages in the *Tractatus* and the features of the analogy are most conveniently displayed in a tabular form.

Physical Space	*Logical Space*
Things in space constitute the world	Facts in logical space constitute the world (1.13)
Empty space	Possibilities of states of affairs (2.013)
Spatial objects in space	Objects in all possible combinations (2.0121)
Infinity of space	Possibility of all situations (2.0131, 2.014)
Spatial point	Argument-place (2.0131)
Space as (Kantian) form of objects	Colour-space as form of visual objects (2.0131, 2.0251)
Objects in space may be described	Situations in logical space may be pictured (2.11)
In geometry	and logic alike

Physical Space	Logical Space
A place is a possibility: something can exist in it (3.411)	
Spatial arrangement of things	Expresses the sense of a proposition (3.1431)
A system of co-ordinates determines physical space	The logical scaffolding of propositions determines logical space (3.42)
Geometrical co-ordinates determine a place in space	The propositional sign with logical co-ordinates determines a place in logical space (3.4, 3.41)
Geometrical co-ordinates cannot represent that which contradicts the laws of space	Language cannot represent that which contradicts logic (3.032)

The heart of the analogy is expressed in the remarks: 'A proposition determines a place in logical space. The existence of this logical place is guaranteed by the mere existence of the constituents – by the existence of the proposition with a sense. The propositional sign with logical co-ordinates – that is the logical place' (3.4, 3.41). The way in which a proposition does this is by picturing 'a situation in logical space, the existence and non-existence of states of affairs' (2.11). What a picture represents is 'a possible situation in logical space' (2.202). The analogy affords another illustration of Wittgenstein's view of the elementary proposition as a logical network sprinkled with names. The analogue of the logical network is the apparatus of co-ordinate geometry, which is a system of signs in which we can represent any spatial situation. By suitable representation in both the propositional and the co-ordinate notations it is possible to depict the existence (or non-existance) of combinations of objects and their spatial relationships.

Difficulties arise in understanding 'the propositional sign with logical co-ordinates – that is the logical place' (3.41). Precisely what are logical co-ordinates and how are they signified in the propositional symbolism? If we apply the spatial analogy consistently, then, as geometrical co-ordinates only specify spatial points without reference to objects so logical co-ordinates do not represent objects – i.e. they are not names – and therefore belong to the logical network which determine possible object places in logical space. The specification of an object-place does not by itself tell us whether or not an object occurs there. If this is the case, and in the absence of further information, it is tempting to equate logical co-ordinates with logical constants. This would imply that the logical co-ordinates of 'p' and '−p' are different and therefore a proposition and its negation do not determine the *same* logical place but different logical places. This interpretation finds confirmation in the remark; 'The negating proposition determines a logical place *different* from that of the negated proposition' (4.0641). This comment is consistent with Wittgenstein's position as recorded in the *Notebooks* where he writes; ' "not p" and "p" contradict one another, both cannot be true; but I can surely express both, *both pictures exist*. They are to be found side by side. Or rather ' "p" and "−p" are like a picture and the infinite plane outside this picture. (Logical place)'.[20] A proposition 'p' depicts how things stand; its negation '−p' depicts that things do *not* so stand – the things in question being the same for both 'p' and '−p'. The difference between the positive and negative senses of propositions may be illustrated by a spatial diagram. For a given universe or logical space, p and −p picture, respectively, the situation represented by the shaded portions in the diagrams.

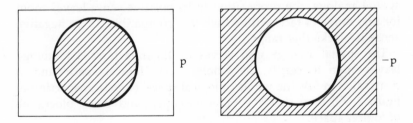

Figure 2

Each determines a different logical place but each shows clearly what things are being asserted or denied as being the case. We can interpret '−p' as meaning 'something other than "p" is the case'. The illustration also serves to show that 'nothing in reality corresponds to the sign "−" ' (4.0621). In short, the propositions 'p' and '−p' have opposite senses but picture the same reality. In terms of the spatial analogy this may easily be seen by transposing 'p' and '−p' on the two diagrams.

Wittgenstein again invokes the spatial analogy as illustrative of truth-conditions.

> The truth-conditions of a proposition determine the range that it leaves open to the facts. (A proposition, a picture, or a model is, in the negative sense, like a solid body that restricts the freedom of movement of others, and, in the positive sense, like a space bounded by solid substance in which there is room for a body.) (4.463).

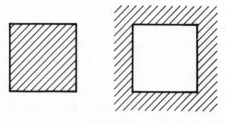

Figure 3

The corresponding entry in the *Notebooks* is accompanied by Figure 2 together with the Cartesian comment, 'This image is *very* clear and must lead to the solution'.[21] According to this use of the spatial analogy, the proposition in its positive sense leaves room for that range of facts with which it is compatible; in its negative sense it blocks that range.

The spatial analogy also serves to illustrate how 'a tautology leaves open to reality the whole . . . of logical space' and 'a contradiction fills the whole of logical space' (4.463). Inspection of figure 2 will show that 'p v −p' leaves open, and 'p.−p' blocks, all of logical space.

Black interprets the spatial analogy rather differently from the above account and suggests that the 'word "co-ordinate" can be viewed as a synonym of Zuordnung ("correlation" or "co-ordination") in 2.1514, 2.1515'. According to this interpretation, 'the co-ordinates of the propositional sign are then the links between the elements of the signs and the objects for which they stand'. In the light of this he proposes that 3.41 should be read; 'The propositional sign, together with the meanings assigned to its constituents − that is what we mean by "a logical place"'.[22]

This view is a consequence of Black's earlier suggestion that 'Objects are like the co-ordinates of empty positions in physical space, atomic facts are like the material points that sometimes occupy such positions'.[23]

This interpretation creates unnecessary confusion within the spatial analogy. A Sachverhalt (or 'atomic fact' in Black's rendering) *is* a combination of objects (2.01, 2.03–2.032) and if atomic facts are like assemblies of 'material points' then we cannot consistently liken objects to 'the co-ordinates of *empty* positions'. The key to the analogy is that a spatial point is not an object; it is an argument-place (2.0131). Although in most propositions it is the case that a designated spatial point is occupied by an object, or an argument-place is filled by a name, we must allow for false propositions that place objects where in fact they do not occur and those contradictory propositions, already noticed, that try to place incompatible sets of objects in the same place at the same time. A spatial point is a possible object–place and an argument–place is a possible name–place.

A spatial analogy of this kind comprises a plausible framework within which to develop the idea of language as a complex set of propositional pictures of reality. It tends to go lame on us, however, if we consider situations of a non-spatial kind – just as co-ordinate geometry would do in comparable non-spatial contexts. Wittgenstein sees that there must be some way in which non-spatial situations may be depicted spatially by an arrangement of propositional signs, but what he does not yet appreciate is that no extension of the spatial analogy to include a system of logical co-ordinates can lead to a solution of this difficulty. What is required here is the recognition of the role of convention in connecting language and reality, the exploration of which renders the ingenuity of the spatial analogy unnecessary. The admission that 'The tacit conventions on which the understanding of everyday language depends are enormously complicated' (4.002) is a step in the direction of acknowledging that our comprehension of these conventions is not really enhanced by looking for an underlying uniform logical structure. Nor, for that matter, do we advance much further if we take the convention of spatial representation as the paradigm of the multiplicity of all our linguistic conventions.

What the spatial analogy does do is to illustrate the fact that the notation Wittgenstein uses to exemplify the form of elementary propositions, namely, 'fx', '$\phi(x,y)$', etc. (4.24), does scant justice to the range of symbols required for an adequate representation of states of affairs. Although there is a case to be made for equating logical constants with the logical co-ordinates of the spatial analogy, it is also clear that the range of the latter must be much more extensive than the former in order to accommodate the details of the analogy. A system of co-ordinates pre-supposes a structure of axes as fixed frames of reference within which we can operate the system and these form no part of the logical structure of propositions as exemplified in the *Tractatus*. In this respect the spatial analogy gets us no further forward than we are with the characterisation of the elementary proposition as a logical network sprinkled with names. It is not Wittgenstein's disdain for the empirical identification of simple names that occasions our problem but the lack of information about this logical network. Plainly, the Whitehead–Russell notation for propositional functions is only a preliminary sketch of this network and the credibility of the doctrine that what belongs to the method of representation cannot be said but only shown varies inversely with the relegation of more and more material to the method of representation.

3

The Picture-Theory of Meaning

PICTURE, THOUGHT AND LANGUAGE

Wittgenstein says, 'We picture facts to ourselves' (2.1) and 'a logical picture of facts is a thought' (3). Although this conceives of thought as a kind of picture of the object of thought it must not be interpreted as a psychological thesis concerning the structure of mental imagery. Wittgenstein's real concern is revealed in the remark, 'The totality of true thoughts is a picture of the world' (3.01). This concern centres on the problem of the relationship between language, thought and the world, and the fundamental idea of significant language as comprised of propositional pictures of reality required thought to be the intermediate and, more importantly, the neutral link in the chain. If it is *language* that pictures what is the case then thought plays a passive role in framing our propositional pictures of the world.

This was not Russell's position, for example, for whom thought was not so much a reflection of the world as its creator. Hence the famous epigram of the British empiricists; the world is a logical construction out of sense data. If Russell had any use at all for a picture theory it would be one where our sensory experiences were what were pictured in thought and described in language. For Russell the given is sensory experience out of which we construct both the world and language. For Wittgenstein the given is the world which we picture in both thought and language.

It is hardly surprising, therefore, that in the Monte Cassino correspondence Russell's disagreement with Wittgenstein's mental neutralism expresses itself in the form of questions about the precise constituents of a thought and its relation to pictured facts. Wittgenstein brushes aside Russell's questions in a way that suggests that his account of thought was simply an accommodation of the picture theory of language and not something worked out independently. The doctrine that states of affairs and propositions depicting them had a common logical form reduced thought to a more or less mechanical function in its intermediate role between reality and language. If a more active role than this were ascribed to it, then the doctrine of the parallel structure of the world and language would be threatened and the relationship distorted by some form of subjectivism such that the utility of a picture relationship between language and reality would be seriously undermined. This pre-condition determines Wittgenstein's reply to Russell; 'I don't know *what* the constituents of a thought are but I know *that* it must have such constituents which correspond to the world of language. Again the kind of relation of the constituents of the thought and of the pictured fact is irrelevant. It would be a matter of psychology to find out'.[1] The hardness of the logical 'must' of the first sentence of this passage is very revealing and illustrates the compulsiveness of the picture theory of language on Wittgenstein at this time. Even more interesting is the dismissal of the problem of the relation of thought and the world as irrelevant and a matter for psychology. Nowhere is Wittgenstein's tendency to use psychology as a receptical for awkward problems more pronounced than here. If the world, thought and language do stand in line, as Wittgenstein suggested, then the relation of the constituents of thought to both the world and language is of prime importance in a philosophical account of them. Wittgenstein's later dissatisfaction with his treatment of Russell's questions on this point is evidenced by his meticulous examination subsequently of mental sensations, although this was undertaken as an essential part of a grammatical not a psychological, investigation.

Reverting to the *Tractatus*, 'the perceptible sign of a proposition' is an expression of a thought (3.11, 3.12), and 'the elements of the propositional sign correspond to the objects of the thought' (3.2). Does this correspondence of propositional 'elements' and 'objects of thought' mean that in some way thought is comprised of words? Wittgenstein denies this when, in answer to Russell's question 'Does a Gedanke (thought) consist of words?', he retorts, 'No! But of psychical constituents that have the same sort of relation to reality as words. What those constituents are I don't know'.[2]

In the *Tractatus* Wittgenstein does address himself to sketching out briefly the relation between thought and language. Philosophy itself is an activity which 'aims at the logical clarification of thoughts' so that thoughts which in their pre-philosophical state are 'cloudy and indistinct' become 'clear' with 'sharp boundaries' (4.112). The 'limits to what can be thought' and, thus, 'the limits to what cannot be thought' will be determined 'by working outwards through what can be thought'. This is not done by a philosophical theory concerning the nature and limitations of thought, which would be another irrelevant excursion into the domain of psychology and also involves the logical howler of trying through thought to think both sides of its own boundaries. Even were this to be possible it would not be necessary, because thought and language – like reality and language – have parallel structures. 'Everything that can be thought at all can be thought clearly. Everything that can be put into words can be put clearly' (4.116). It is the task of philosophical elucidation of the kind found in the *Tractatus* to 'signify what cannot be said, by presenting clearly what can be said' (4.115). In short, the limits of thought are the limits of language for 'what we cannot think we cannot *say* either' (5.61). This means that what the solipsist tries to say is correct up to a point, namely, insofar as there is a relation between the constituents of thought and words. It is mistaken in not recognising that there is also a relation between the constituents of thought and reality. For even though the world I speak of is in a sense *my* world it is not the world that does not exist but rather 'the subject that thinks or entertains ideas' (5.62–5.631). Wittgenstein's achievement in the *Tractatus* was to construe the relation between the world and thought on the one hand, and thought and language on the other, in terms of a picture. Hence, 'a logical picture of facts is a thought' (3) and 'a thought is a proposition with a sense' (4). Through the picture analogy the connection between the world and thought and the connection between thought and language are coupled together into a single chain.

It is not surprising that little of this appealed to Russell. The kind of relationship between thought and language which Wittgenstein envisaged as pertaining to the propositions underlying ordinary language Russell held could only be produced by the construction of an ideal language. In so far as the relation between thought and ordinary language could be conceived of as a picture Russell believed it to be a grossly distorted one and not, as Wittgenstein believed, merely a disguised one (4.002). As for the relation between thought and the world, which Russell as the chief apostle of empiricism had laboured for years to explicate, Wittgenstein's views must have seemed to be those of a naïve realist. The possibilities of distorting and misunderstanding this relationship seemed to Russell to be virtually limitless and Wittgenstein's picture analogy must have seemed a superficial caricature of the problems.

In Wittgenstein's account of thought and language a more or less passive role is assigned to thought and, in this respect, its 'psychical constituents' are reminiscent of Humean impressions. However, this is only one aspect of his idea of thought. To anticipate what must come in more detail later, consider what he says about the structure of scientific laws. As objects of thought these laws are not propositional pictures of the world but a priori insights about the forms in which the propositions of science picture reality. They are like nets of varying fineness and shapes of mesh which we impose on the world as a kind of grid or reference frame in accordance with which our descriptions of reality are formulated (6.341, 6.342). Thought here cannot consist of psychical components picturing facts, which, in turn, are pictured in propositions, because such laws are not descriptions of the world but forms for descriptions. To revert to the analogy of logical space, these conceptual nets are like the axes of co-ordinate geometry which do not describe any figure but prescribe the form for describing all figures. The essence of Wittgenstein's remarks about scientific laws as nets is that they are analogues of conceptual forms or categories of thought.

It seems then, that the interpretation of the *Tractatus* requires both a Humean and a Kantian view of thought. On the one hand thought is a bundle of psychical constituents, like Humean impressions, and on the other hand it comprises a set of conceptual forms, like Kantian categories. Thus, thought both reflects the structure of reality and also imposes a structure upon it. It would be absurd to suggest that these two notions of thought cannot be reconciled, but they do require some discussion of their roles, how they are related, and how propositions expressing scientific laws can be significant without being pictures of how things stand. The scepticism implicit in Russell's questions concerning Wittgenstein's notion of 'a thought' appears to be thoroughly justified. In spite of Wittgenstein's inclination to dismiss 'the study of thought-processes' as 'unessential psychological investigations' (4.1121) there are serious logical omissions in his treatment of thought which it is not the concern of the psychologist to repair.

The repair of these omissions was to occupy a great deal of the later Wittgenstein's attention even when the picture theory of language had ceased to be a living option for him.

For the relationship between language and reality to be construed in terms of a picture requires that the various parts of the analogy should have the following roles:

1. The world must have a determinate structure; this is the role of substance.
2. How things stand in reality must be determinable; this is the role of facts.
3. Facts must be picturable; this is the role of thought.
4. The components of a thought must be representable in words; this is the role of propositions.

Substance, facts, thought and propositions stand in series forming the links of the chain that bind together language and reality so intimately that it is possible to speak of language as a set of propositional pictures laid up directly against reality, like a ruler used to measure the distance between marks according to a series of graduating lines (2.1511–2.15121). The credibility of this claim depends upon two things. First, the extent to which facts and thought are neutral or, at least, non-distorting elements in the series. Second, the development of the picture-analogy in a way that makes intelligible the idea of a direct connection between the elements of propositional pictures and the world. The first point is dealt with by Wittgenstein's insistence that it is the world itself that 'divides into facts' (1.2) so that one cannot drive a wedge between the world and facts, and that thoughts (passively) picture facts. It is the second point which must now claim our attention as we go deeper into the detailed structure of the picture-theory of language.

Wittgenstein writes; 'The possibility of propositions is based on the principle that objects have signs as their representatives' (4.0312). This relation of representation is construed in terms of a logical picture and his elucidation of this concept depends on two key terms; 'pictorial form' (Form der Abbildung) and 'pictorial relationship' (abbildende Bezeihung). To begin with the second term first, pictorial relationship is the correlation between the *elements* of the proposition and the *objects* comprising the state of affairs which the proposition represents (2.13, 2.131, 2.1514). It is the pictoral relationship, or correlation between propositional elements and things, that enables a proposition, as it were, to reach out and touch reality (2.1513, 2.1515). The essence of a propositional picture is that it is a logical and determinate arrangement of representative signs; that is, it is a picture *of something*. A proposition is a kind of measure of reality in which the pictoral relationship is likened to 'the end-points of the graduating lines' which 'actually touch the object that is to be measured' (2.1511–2.1515).

The pictoral form of a picture is its own internal structure, that is, the determinate relationship between the elements of a picture that makes it a picture and which represents the possibility of a comparable relationship between things. The internal structure of a picture is to be distinguished from its external relationship to the things pictured. Pictorial relationship is an external relationship which subsists between the picture and the world. Pictorial form is an internal relationship between the elements of a picture which represents the possibility of a corresponding relationship subsisting between objects. In short, pictorial relationship is an element–object relation, whereas pictorial form is an element–element relation representing a possible object–object relation (2.151). 'There must be something identical in a picture and what it depicts, to enable the one to be a picture of the other at all' (2.161). This identical or common feature is pictoral form (2.17). The sense of a propositional picture must be determinable before the ascription of a truth-value, and this sense is represented by its pictorial form. Its truth-value is determined by the correspondence of its sense with reality or the lack of such a correspondence. If sense and reality do correspond the propositional picture is true and if not it is false (2.21–2.222). Wittgenstein emphasises that the truth-value of a propositional picture cannot be determined by inspection of its internal structure, or pictorial form, alone. In other words there are no propositional pictures which are true a priori; they must be compared with reality in order to determine their truth or falsity (2.223–2.225). Thus, there are no synthetic a priori propositions.

The process of comparison with reality invokes a pictorial relationship of the propositional picture, i.e. does the arrangement of elements of the picture reach out and correspond with the arrangement of things in reality? We can see that 'a R b' and 'c R d' have the same pictorial form or sense but a comparison of each with reality may show that 'a R b' is true and 'c R d' is false. That is to say, the pictorial relationship of 'a R b' is such that the elements 'a' and 'b' are correlated with the objects a and b related R in reality, whereas 'c R d' is not correlated with objects c and d related R. In this case, 'a R b' represents an existing state of affairs and 'c R d' represents a possible but non-existent state of affairs.

The truth-conditions of propositions expressed in terms of the picture analogy are as follows:

1. A propositional picture must have sense, i.e. the arrangement of elements of the picture must be representative of a possible arrangement of things. This arrangement comprises the pictorial form of the picture.
2. A true propositional picture has sense and there is a direct correlation between the elements of the picture and the objects comprising the state of affairs depicted. This correlation of elements and objects is the pictorial relationship of the picture and the pictorial form is common to both picture and reality.
3. A false propositional picture has sense but there is no correlation between the elements of the picture and the objects in the state of affairs depicted. Hence, there is no pictorial relationship between the picture and the world and the pictorial form represents only a possible and not an actual state of affairs.

There is some ambiguity in one of Wittgenstein's remarks about pictorial form: 'The fact that the elements of a picture are related to one another in a determinate way represents that things are related to one another in the same way. Let us call this connexion of its elements the structure of the picture, and let us call the possibility of this structure the pictorial form of the picture' (2.15). In the remark that follows this he writes, 'Pictorial form is the possibility that things are related to one another in the same way as the elements of the picture' (2.151). Is pictorial form the possibility of the picture's structure or is it the possibility that things are related in the same way as the elements of the picture are related? It is difficult to see what sense could be attached to describing pictorial form as the *possibility* of a picture's structure. If a picture is a picture at all it already has a determinate structure and the possibility of a structure is only the possibility of a picture. The ambiguity is resolved if we read 2.15 thus; '. . . let us call the possibility of this structure (i.e. the possibility that things in reality are so related) the pictorial form of a picture'.

Wittgenstein also writes; 'a picture cannot, however, depict its pictorial form: it displays it' (2.172). No picture can have as the subject of its representation its own structure or pictorial form. The self-representing propositional picture joins Russell's self-referring propositions on the Index.

Wittgenstein introduces a third term, 'representational form' (Form der Darstellung) in the following remarks. 'A picture represents its subject from a position outside it. (Its standpoint is its representational form.) That is why a picture represents its subject correctly or incorrectly. A picture cannot, however, place itself outside its representational form' (2.173, 2.174). How is representational form related to pictorial form and pictorial relationship? The externality of the standpoint of representational form with respect to states and affairs as subjects rules out an equivalence of representational form and pictorial form which is common to a picture and the state of affairs depicted. The fact that the correctness or incorrectness of representational form determines the truth-value of a propositional picture suggests that representational form and pictorial relationship are the same.

To illustrate the distinction between pictorial form and pictorial relationship (or representational form) consider the simple case of two objects, o_1 and o_2, represented in a propositional picture by the elements, e_1 and e_2.

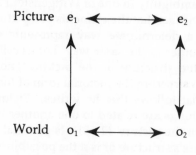

Figure 4

For this to be a true picture of the state of affairs existing as a result of the configuration of objects o_1 and o_2, the *horizontal* relationships $e_1 \longleftrightarrow e_2$ and $o_1 \longleftrightarrow o_2$ must be common. This is the relation of pictorial form.

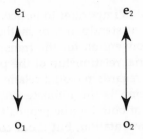

Figure 5

The *vertical* relationships in Fig. 5 are the pictorial relationship, or representational form, of the picture, and in this case the correctness of the representation determines the truth-value of the propositional picture as true. However, it must be remembered that the truth-conditions of propositional pictures also include the pictorial form in as much as the arrangement of elements may not reflect the arrangement of things. For example, using the same illustration, the *horizontal* relationship may be transposed in the propositional picture compared with what obtains in the state of affairs depicted. As may be seen (Fig. 6), the transposition of e_1 and e_2, which is a change in pictorial form, produces a change in the pictorial relationship, or representational form, such that the picture no longer connects with reality in the same way as in the former illustration. What is important to notice is that, given a different standpoint, i.e. a change in the method of representation, such as a suitable representational convention, then this picture may be regarded as true. The standpoint of the two pictures is different and if the standpoint of the first one is adopted as the criterion of correct representation then the second

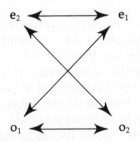

Figure 6

picture is false. What is important to notice, however, is that the adoption of a different standpoint, or method of representation, such as a suitable convention for the transposition of elements, can render the pictorial relationship of the picture correct and its truth-value true. As regards pictorial relationship, or representational form, convention is the ultimate criterion of correctness. Figures 4 and 6 cannot both be true propositional pictures for the same method of representation, but if our conventions permitted both methods of representation then both pictures would be true with respect to their different standpoints.

The realisation that the adoption of a suitable representational convention rendered any propositional picture a perspicuous one led to three consequences that ran counter to important ideas in the *Tractatus*. First, if it is the case that, given a suitable representational convention, anything can be a correct picture of anything, then the whole picture analogy is stretched to a point where it ceases to serve any useful purpose. Second, if convention is the ultimate criterion of correctness with respect to a proposition's standpoint then it is our representational conventions that should engage our attention rather than the details of problematic picture theory. Third, if convention governs pictorial relationship (the way a proposition connects with the world) then there is no reason why it should not govern pictorial form (the way elements of the proposition are arranged to represent the arrangement of things). In that case, the doctrine that pictorial form cannot be depicted, (i.e. *said*), but only displayed, (i.e. *shown*), also collapses. If convention is the key to representation then not only *can* it be said but it *must* be said for representation to be intelligible at all. Once again the omission of any detailed treatment in the *Tractatus* of the *rules* of representation is compensated for in Wittgenstein's later writings.

Having said this, I wish to emphasise, at the risk of some repetition, that Wittgenstein was not completely unaware of all this when he wrote the *Tractatus*. We do him an injustice if we do not acknowledge that he recognised that a picture's standpoint varied not only between a correct and an incorrect representation but also within the framework of correct representation. The *Tractatus* is seriously misinterpreted if we suppose that a picture has only one correct standpoint such as being a facsimile of what is represented. A printed proposition, a musical score and phonetic notation are all 'pictures, even in the ordinary sense, of what they represent' (4.011).

It is obvious that a proposition of the form 'a R b' strikes us as a picture. In this case the sign is obviously a likeness of what is signified (4.012). Nevertheless, being a likeness is an accidental feature of propositional pictures for the 'essence of this pictorial character . . . is not impaired by apparent irregularities (such as the use of # and ♭ in musical notation). For these irregularities depict what they are intended to express; only they do it in a different way' (4.013).

Certainly, what Wittgenstein regarded as the essential nature of a propositional picture is clearly displayed in hieroglyphs which depict facts by pictorial likeness, but 'alphabetic script developed out of it without losing what is essential to depiction' (4.016). A hieroglyph and its alphabetic equivalent, though their methods of representation differ, may both be correct pictures of a fact. All that is essential for depiction in

Figure 7

is preserved in 'the saint'.

ISOMORPHISM AND LOGICAL MULTIPLICITY

Variations in standpoint or pictorial relationship between different pictures of the same fact are easily accommodated in Wittgenstein's account of logical pictures but there are some difficulties associated with comparable variations in pictorial form. He asserts that for something to be a picture at all, 'there must be something identical in a picture and what it depicts', and this common feature of picture and reality he identifies as pictorial form (2.161, 2.17). If pictorial form is the arrangement of elements of the picture which displays the possibility that things are arranged in a comparable way in reality, then how can the arrangement of elements of the matchstick figure and the arrangement of elements in 'the saint' *both* be identical with the arrangement of things? In insisting on identity of form between picture and reality Wittgenstein appears to be laying down a criterion of picturing that excludes all but facsimiles. It is even less easy to detect an identity of form between a symphony and its musical score, and yet one is a picture of the other (4.011).

The relation of identity Wittgenstein wishes to establish is between the pictorial form of a propositional picture and the logical form of reality it displays. This is made clear by the following comparisons:

Pictorial form	*Logical form*
'What a picture must have in common with reality, in order to be able to depict it – correctly or incorrectly – in the way it does, is its pictorial form' (2.17).	'What any picture, of whatever form, must have in common with reality, in order to be able to depict it – correctly or incorrectly – in any way at all is logical form, i.e. the form of reality' (2.18).
'A picture cannot, however, depict its pictorial form: it displays it' (2.172).	'Propositions cannot represent logical form: it is mirrored in them. . . . Propositions *show* the logical form of reality. They display it' (4.121).

'A picture whose pictorial form is logical form is called a logical picture' (2.181).

'A picture has logico-pictorial form in common with what it depicts' (2.2).

What Wittgenstein is claiming is that a necessary condition for a proposition to be a logical picture of a fact is that the relation between the pictorial form of the proposition and the logical form of the fact must be isomorphic. Precisely, what constitutes an isomorphic relation? If we restrict isomorphism to an identity relation between pictorial form and logical form, then propositional pictures must be facsimiles subject to the following conditions:

1. Pictorial form and logical form must belong to the same categories.
2. The arrangement of elements comprising the pictorial relationship of the propositional picture must stand in one–one correlation with the arrangement of things depicted.

Isomorphism fulfilling these conditions I shall call naturalistic isomorphism and there is no doubt that some of Wittgenstein's remarks can be construed as supporting this interpretation of the relation between fact and proposition. For example, 'A picture can depict any reality whose form it has. A spatial picture can depict anything spatial, a coloured one, anything coloured, etc.' (2.171). This is the first of the two conditions for naturalistic isomorphism. 'In a proposition there must be exactly as many distinguishable parts as in the situation that it represents. The two must possess the same logical (mathematical) multiplicity' (4.04). This is the second of the two conditions for naturalistic isomorphism.

Applying these conditions strictly, however, means that a three-dimensional situation can only be represented by a three-dimensional model. A two-dimensional naturalistic picture would not satisfy the second condition of one–one correlation between elements and things because the third dimension, or Z axis, is represented by conventions of perspective. It is abundantly clear from the *Tractatus* that Wittgenstein is far from claiming that only three-dimensional models can represent situations, although such examples are the simplest kind of logical picture. Indeed, it if is true that the French practice of using dolls in the reconstruction of motor accidents in law courts first suggested to Wittgenstein the idea of language as a picture of reality, then such pictures were examples of naturalistic isomorphism.[3]

We need to remember what Wittgenstein says elsewhere when he observes, 'Every picture is *at the same time* a logical one. (On the other hand, not every picture is, for example, a spatial one.)' (2.182). This remark, and what Wittgenstein says about printed propositions, musical scores and the like being pictures, compel us to recognise naturalistic isomorphism as a sufficient but not a necessary condition of the representation of reality in propositional pictures. The class of pictures where pictorial form and logical form are identical comprise only a comparatively small subset of logical pictures. Resemblance, and still less identity, between pictorial form and the logical form are neither of them necessary conditions for propositions to picture facts. There are logical pictures where both pictorial relationship and pictorial form are related in ways that depend upon representational conventions. As Black puts it; 'there can really be no question of strict identity of logical form between proposition and fact represented but at best a parallelism of form . . . the demand for strict identity of form cannot be met'.[4]

E. Stenius in an acute discussion of isomorphism rejects the view 'that all pictures must be more or less "naturalistic"' and asserts that isomorphism presupposes only 'structural similarities'.[5] To distinguish this view from naturalistic isomorphism I shall refer to it as structural isomorphism. Stenius specifies as a condition of structural isomorphism that pictorial form and logical form have the same categorial structure. By this he means that 'it is possible to establish a one–one correspondence between the elements of each category in the two systems'.[6] The difference between naturalistic isomorphism and structural isomorphism is that the former depends upon both the conditions specified above, whilst the latter depends upon only the second condition. Stenius does consider the possibility of a picture having a 'many-one key of interpretation' but is inclined to call it a picture only in so far as it can be transformed into a structurally isomorphic representation.[7] He asserts, 'that the concept of an isomorphic picture does not correspond logically to Wittgenstein's concept of a "picture" but rather conforms to his concept of a "true picture"'.[8]

Stenius recognises, correctly, that a relation between fact and picture that consists only of structural correspondence needs a key of interpretation to render these links intelligible. Furthermore, the application of the key of interpretation, either tacitly or explicitly, is presupposed in understanding what situation a proposition pictures. Wittgenstein's doctrine that a proposition *shows* or *displays* its sense, and that what shows cannot be said, is only credible if the kind of representation in question is that of naturalistic isomorphism. Even in the case of a two-dimensional naturalistic picture that is a facsimile of what it represents although what it *shows* may be obvious this can also be *said* by making explicit the rules of perspective employed in the picture. The rules of perspective which mostly we take for granted constitute the key of interpretation which renders the picture intelligible. The point is that even the most naturalistic picture is governed by representational conventions and, in spite of some hesitations and uncertainties in the *Tractatus*, Wittgenstein recognised this. For ordinary language these conventions were 'tacit' and 'enormously complicated' (4.002). In the limited exploration of these conventions, rules, or keys of interpretation that Wittgenstein undertakes in the *Tractatus* he again invokes a geometrical analogy to help him say the unsayable, namely, methods of projection. The most familiar example of these methods is Mercator's projection according to the rules of which a spheroidal surface is projected on to a plane surface for producing maps and atlases. From the plane map (the propositional picture) on its own it would be impossible to infer anything about the shape of the original surface (the fact represented). We need to know, either that the world is a spheroid, or the laws of projection which comprise the representational convention governing the pictorial relationship of the map. The example that Wittgenstein gives is the general rule by which we project 'the symphony into the language of musical notation' and this rule is the law of projection which enables us to translate 'this language into the language of gramophone records' (4.0141). Wittgenstein adds, 'the possibility of all imagery, of all our pictorial modes of expression, is contained in the logic of depiction' (4.015). Naturalistic isomorphism is only part, and not exhaustive, of 'the possibility of all imagery'. It seems to be that the same is true of structural isomorphism.

What is not clear from the account given by Stenius of structural isomorphism is, given that to understand a propositional picture correctly we need a key of interpretation, why must the correspondence of elements between picture and fact be one–one? Why cannot the key include representational conventions with respect to the pictorial relationship other than one–one correspondence between the elements of the picture and the elements of things pictured? Presumably, Stenius has been influenced by Wittgenstein's assertion that 'in a proposition there must be exactly as many distinguishable parts as in the situation that it represents', and his comparison of this 'logical (mathematical) multiplicity' with 'Hertz's *Mechanics* on dynamical models' (4.04). There is little doubt that this is the origin of one–one correspondence between elements of picture and fact as a necessary condition of logical picturing. It is time to consider this condition in more detail.

Wittgenstein's reference to Hertz is illuminating. Black quotes the relevant passage from his work on *Mechanics* which reads as follows:

> A material system is said to be a dynamical model of a second system when the connection of the first can be expressed by such co-ordinates as to satisfy the following conditions: (1) that the number of co-ordinates of the first system is equal to the number of co-ordinates in the second. (2) That with a suitable arrangement of the co-ordinates for both systems the same equations of condition exist. (3) That by this arrangement of the co-ordinates the expressions for the magnitude of a displacement agrees in both systems.[9]

It is the first of these conditions that inclined Wittgenstein to assert that a propositional picture and the situation it represents must have exactly the same number of distinguishable parts. Presumably, in a fully analysed proposition the logical (mathematical) multiplicity would consist in a one–one correlation between the elements of the elementary proposition and elements of the state of affairs portrayed. This brings us back to the question, is a proposition a picture before it is fully analysed? In view of the fact that the understanding of sentences does not wait upon their analysis into elementary propositions we must answer, yes. This is reinforced by Wittgenstein's remarks about printed sentences being pictures and his claim that nothing essential to depiction was lost in the development of alphabetic script from hieroglyphs. If a hieroglyphic proposition and an equivalent printed sentence are both pictures as they stand then a one–one correspondence between the respective elements of picture and situation is not a necessary condition of picturing. To suppose that the one–one correspondence holds at the level of the fully analysed proposition only is irrelevant as a condition of depiction if unanalysed sentences successfully picture facts.

It should be pointed out also that Hertz's dynamical model leaves room for 'a suitable arrangement of the co-ordinates for both systems', providing for agreement between equations of condition and displacement magnitudes. The possibility of constructing a dynamical model of another system depends upon the *range* of co-ordinates of the two systems being the same and the adoption of a suitable arrangement of both sets of co-ordinates. Similarly, the construction of a logical picture of a fact requires that the *range* of co-ordinates of the two systems should be the same, which is the case, since the indefinitely large class of objects corresponds to the indefinitely large class of argument-places. Amongst the possible arrangements of both sets of co-ordinates, one–one correlation is only one of the many possibilities open to us in constructing a picture. One–one correspondence is not the only acceptable form of logical multiplicity subsisting between proposition and fact. Logical multiplicity may vary as the pictorial relationship or standpoint of the picture varies.

Consider four different ways in which a tree might be represented. In the first one, the tree is represented by a scaled-down three-dimensional coloured model faithfully reproducing the original in every detail. Since models count as logical pictures we may say in this case that the pictorial form of the model and the logical form of reality are identical. That is to say, picture and fact belong to the same categories, and the logical multiplicity of the pictorial relationship consists of a one–one correspondence between the elements of the model and the elements of the tree, i.e. the number of distinguishable parts is exactly the same. This kind of picture is an example of naturalistic isomorphism.

The second way of representing the tree consists of a picture painted by a thoroughly consistent and conscientious pre-Raphaelite. Every leaf on the tree is represented by a minute speck of green paint on the canvas and similarly with the visible boughs and trunk etc. Of this example one can say that the three-dimensional situation and the two-dimensional picture have similar categorial structures and the logical multiplicity is a one–one correspondence between the elements of the picture and situation depicted. This kind of picture would constitute an example of structural isomorphism.

The third representation of the tree is a painting by an Impressionist in which every cluster of leaves on the tree is reproduced by a blob of green paint. Here again picture and tree have similar categorial structures, but the logical multiplicity is not a one–one correspondence. A correspondence between each cluster of leaves and single blobs of paint is a many–one correspondence.

The fourth way of representing the tree is that executed by a Modernist painter in despair of ever becoming a Royal Academician. In this picture the entire tree is represented by a single splash of green paint. In this example it is still possible to speak of similar categorial structures between picture and tree, though less obviously than in the second and third cases, and the logical multiplicity is a whole-one correspondence. According to the conventions of this type of representation it could be said that the number of distinguishable parts of the tree seen as a whole and the single splash of paint is exactly the same.

Stenius's insistence on a one–one correspondence between elements as a feature of structural isomorphism and a necessary condition of picturing would require the rejection of the last two examples as true pictures. My own view is that all of these examples are acceptable as logical pictures of a fact in spite of their different standpoints. Each preserves a logical multiplicity between the distinguishable parts of the picture and the situation depicted, although what counts as a distinguishable part varies with the method of representation adopted. In the *Tractatus* Wittgenstein is not founding a logical branch of the pre-Raphaelite brotherhood. Wittgenstein's use of the concept of logical multiplicity is not confined to those cases where there is a one–one correspondence between names in an elementary proposition and atomic constituents in the state of affairs represented. In the elementary proposition where names stand for objects, from the number of names present we can draw no conclusions as to the number of objects occuring in the state of affairs represented. Wittgenstein considers the possibility that the world is infinitely complex such that 'every state of affairs is composed of infinitely many objects' (4.2211). Assuming that such states of affairs are representable, then their logical multiplicity cannot consist of a one–one correspondence between objects and names as a condition of representation because, in such a case, elementary propositions would need infinitely many names with the result that language would be fundamentally indeterminate. The possibility of determinate propositional pictures of states of affairs – especially if these may consist of infinitely many objects – rests upon the adoption of suitable methods of representation which include an appropriate logical multiplicity other than one–one correspondence between names and objects. In short, logical multiplicity is determined by the law of projection employed and belongs to the apparatus of our representational conventions.

THE PROPOSITIONS OF MATHEMATICS AND NATURAL SCIENCE

If the meaning of a proposition consists in its picturing how things stand in the world, what meaning, if any, can be attached to the propositions of mathematics and natural science? If these propositions are not pictures, how can they be saved from relegation as meaningless? A major concern of the *Tractatus* is to use the picture-theory of propositions to draw the boundaries of meaningful language in order to show what can be said and, equally importantly, what cannot be said. Indeed, the provision of a sharp criterion for the a priori exclusion of areas of language, such as theology and metaphysics, as meaningless was the principal attraction of a number of theories of meaning advanced in this century. Wittgenstein's theory was unusual in that its area of forbidden territory was more extensive than others – including as it did much of what he himself said in advancing it – but it shared a problem common to all these theories. Namely, how to prevent the formulation of the criterion of demarcation between sense and nonsense from falling on the wrong side of the distinction, and how to retain the services of certain classes of statements whose utility seemed to be indispensible. With respect to the first part of this problem Wittgenstein was unusually frank and recognised that his remarks about the picture-theory of propositions were not themselves propositions – i.e. they did not picture how things stand – but were simply elucidations to be discarded once their point was taken. The second part of the problem was not so easily, nor so paradoxically, disposed of. It is clear, for example, that mathematical propositions and statements of the laws of physics are not analysable into propositional pictures of states of affairs. It is equally clear that to reject them as nonsense because of this would be to reject areas of discourse of proven value and utility. Wittgenstein's problem was to give an account of such propositions that saved them without abolishing picturing in propositions as the criterion of meaning.

So far as the propositions of mathematics are concerned, the solution is relatively simple. Wittgenstein has already argued that the propositions of logic are tautologies 'that say nothing' (6.121) and are 'a mirror-image of the world' (6.13) only in the sense that they display 'the scaffolding of the world', i.e. they reflect form not content: 'They have no "subject-matter"'. They pre-suppose that names have meaning and elementary propositions sense; and that is their connexion with the world' (6.124). That is to say, the tautologies of logic presuppose the connection between language and reality that shows when the natural signs of language speak for themselves and this is all; 'there can never be surprises in logic' (6.1251). It is the *structure* of logic and the world that exhibits a common logical form, but the propositions of logic are without empirical content.

This makes Wittgenstein's treatment of mathematical propositions predictable. 'Mathematics is a logical method. The propositions of mathematics are equations and therefore pseudo-propositions' (6.2). They do not express thoughts and, like the tautologies of logic, the equations of mathematics show 'the logic of the world' (6.21, 6.22). They, too, reveal something about the form of the world but not its content, and mathematical propositions, far from being the paradigm of all genuine propositions, are pseudo-propositions whose use is restructed to making inferences between non-mathematical propositions (6.211). Their utility is not that they picture reality, which is why they are pseudo-propositions, but that their use permits the making of inferences between genuine propositions, which is why they are not nonsense either. This identification of the meaning of a class of propositions (albeit pseudo ones) with the *use* to which they are put might seem to be an important foreshadowing of Wittgenstein's later criterion of meaning, but at this stage he was protecting the picture-theory of meaning by adding mathematical propositions to the growing number of pseudo-propositions which strictly say nothing. Since Hume's day it had become a commonplace of empiricist tradition to divide all significant propositions into two classes. These were, the 'relations of ideas', or the tautologies of logic and mathematics, and 'matters of fact', or empirical statements, especially those belonging to the natural sciences. Wittgenstein's adoption of picturing as the criterion of propositional sense necessitated a modification of this dichotomy which resulted in the relegation of the tautologies of logic and mathematics to the status of pseudo-propositions. Wittgenstein's system in the *Tractatus* is thus a thorough-going propositional monism and the criterion of the genuine proposition is conformity to this single logical type of the propositional picture. Anything which is not of this type is either devoid of meaning altogether – nonsense – or it belongs to a special class of (useful) pseudo-propositions. The credibility of propositional monism is in inverse proportion to the size of this class of pseudo-propositions. A manifestation of the limitations of the picture-theory of language is this tendency to diminish the class of genuine propositions by increasing the class of pseudo-propositions.

Wittgenstein considers the more difficult problem presented by those propositions of natural science that are concerned with statements of physical laws, such as the law of causality. He rejects the defence of the transition from empirical generalisation to universal law that invokes some super-principle such as 'the so-called law of induction' on two grounds. First, the statement of the law of induction is 'a proposition with sense' and consequently not an a priori law (6.31). Secondly, the actual procedure of induction is a psychological one without logical justification (6.363–6.3631). He also rejects the idea that the general laws of physics may be treated as assertions of necessary connections, for Hume was right and the doctrine of necessary connections between events is sheer superstition; 'the only necessity that exists is logical necessity' (5.135, 5.1361, 6.37). What, then, of the Kantian argument that the phenomenal world is subject to a causal law as a necessary condition of experience? Wittgenstein's answer is that 'the law of causality is not a law but the form of a law', i.e. physics employs 'laws of the causal form' (6.32, 6.321). Such forms are certainly a priori but they are not necessary conditions of experience; 'all these are a priori insights about the forms in which the propositions of science can be cast' (6.34). To express the law of causality in the proposition, 'every event has a cause', does not provide an example of a synthetic a priori statement. The only genuine a priori statements are purely logical and no synthetic statement, or, in Wittgenstein's terminology, 'a proposition with sense', can possibly be a 'law of logic' (6.31, 6.3211). In this respect, Wittgenstein sides with Hume against Kant in maintaining a sharp logical distinction between a priori and synthetic statements.

What, then, is the status of propositions expressing the 'law of causality', the 'law of least action', the 'law of conservation', the 'principle of sufficient reason', and 'the laws of continuity in nature'? They are frames of reference which we apply to reality and which determine the forms of the statements of natural science. These insights or frames of reference are not explanations of reality but belong to the logical scaffolding of explanation.

Wittgenstein illustrates his meaning here with another geometrical analogy. If we imagine a white surface with irregular black dots on it, then, whatever the arrangement of these dots the picture they make can be described to any given approximation by 'covering the surface with a fine square mesh and then saying of every square whether it is black or white'. This imposes 'a unified form' on the description of the surface and, moreover, 'the form is optional' since we could use nets with different finess of mesh or having differently shaped meshes. The analogy is used to illustrate the point that Newtonian mechanics is one of the ways in which we can impose a 'unified form on the description of the world'. It does this by specifying 'that all propositions used in the description of the world must be obtained in a given way from a given set of propositions – the axioms of mechanics' (6.341). The axioms themselves 'tell us nothing about the world' but only about 'the precise *way* in which it is possible to describe it by these means' (6.342). Thus, the laws of physics 'are about the net and not about what the net describes' (6.35); they are only '*indirectly* about objects in the world' (6.3431). The propositions stating the laws of physics do not picture reality, neugher do they explain reality, nor do they describe it; they are part of the logical apparatus of our descriptions.

If the statements expressing the laws of physics are not in any sense pictures of reality, then they fall outside the propositional monism of significant language. Wittgenstein asserts that their a priori status shows them to be purely logical (6.3211) but if that were the case then they would also be tautologous and contentless, like analytic propositions (6.1, 6.11). The laws of physics are not tautologies, because from tautologies only further tautologies follow, whereas the laws of physics imply observation statements which are verifiable and, more importantly according to K. R. Popper, falsifiable (6.1222, 6.126). The truth of these observation statements leads to the provisional verification of the law from which they follow and their falsity leads to its refutation. The asymmetry of verifiability and falsifiability with respect to universal law-like statements has important consequences for scientific methodology. The point here is that laws which are in principle falsifiable cannot be tautologies which are true for all possible truth-conditions. Wittgenstein himself does not really wish to class the statements of the laws of physics with the contentless tautologies of logic because he recognises that they do have a content. Reverting to the net analogy, they are about the kinds of net we employ as forms for our descriptions of reality. More specifically, mechanics as one of our optional nets 'is an attempt to construct according to a single plan all the *true* propositions that we need for the description of the world' (6.343). To construct propositions according to a single plan is to lay down the method of representation that such propositions must employ. What Wittgenstein means by saying that our expressions of the laws of physics are only about the net is that they are explicit formulations of our methods of representation: they are the laws of projection according to which we represent reality in propositions. If it is the case that the type of net we employ is optional then the varieties of propositional forms will not be distinguishable, nor even intelligible, unless we first specify that the net we are employing has a mesh that is square or triangular or hexagonal. This constitutes the provision of a representational key without which we are unable to understand the pictorial relationship of proposition and reality. Propositions that lay down a unified form for description are not really contentless; they are about the ways in which reality may be described. As Wittgenstein himself admitted, they are both part of our logical apparatus and (indirectly) about objects in the world. Such propositions belong neither to the class of genuine propositional pictures, nor to the class of tautologies of logic and mathematics, nor to the class of pseudo-propositions which are strictly nonsense, albeit elucidatory nonsense. The emergence of this new class of hybrid propositions is the first real crack in the propositional monism of the *Tractatus*.

ETHICS AND MYSTICISM

What status does Wittgenstein accord to evaluative language of the kind used in making ethical judgements? The logical positivists, who comprised the Vienna Circle during the 1930s, were strongly influenced by parts of the *Tractatus* – particularly the treatment of the propositions of natural science as the paradigm of 'what can be said' (6.53). Their relegation of ethical propositions to the realm of emotive language brought notoriety rather than acclaim as regards the general public. According to this view, the majority of ethical statements either express one's own feelings or are designed to influence the feelings of others. The rest were at worst simply meaningless, or, at best, misconceived attempts to prescribe a moral order that traded upon the logical sleight of hand of moving from statements about how the world *is* to statements about how the world *ought* to be. Hume's genius in recognising the illicit transition from 'is' to 'ought' statements was at last widely publicised, and, in the name of outraged morality, Moritz Schlick was shot dead on the steps of his own university. His was an honourable death and philosophy received its rarest accolade – a new martyr.

To return to Wittgenstein; it would be a serious error to assimilate Wittgenstein's treatment of ethical propositions with that of the logical positivists. It is over this matter that their divergence is most marked. Wittgenstein's remarks about ethics seemed to them to reveal mystical tendencies which threatened to betray a thorough-going empiricism in the name of a new kind of transcendentalism; as though Hume would again give way to Kant. Professor Anscombe recounts a revealing conversation when she 'had occasion to remark to Wittgenstein that he was supposed to have a mystical streak: "Like a yellow streak" he replied; and that is pretty well how the Vienna Circle felt about certain things in the *Tractatus*'.[10]

Wittgenstein's remarks on ethics do not start with a disadvantageous comparison of ethical propositions with respect to the empirically verifiable propositions of science, but with an account of the accidental nature of the world. Everything that happens in the world and is the case is accidental and the concept of physical necessity is an illusion. 'The only necessity that exists is *logical* necessity' and the illusion of physical necessity arises from regarding the laws of nature both as explanations of natural phenomena and as something inviolable beyond which it is not necessary to go – like the earlier concepts of God and Fate (6.37–6.372). Consequently there is no causal nexus justifying 'an inference from the existence of one situation to the existence of another, entirely different situation' (5.135, 5.136). Induction 'has no logical justification but only a psychological one. It is clear that there are no grounds for believing that the simplest eventuality will in fact be realised. It is an hypothesis that the sun will rise tomorrow: and this means that we do not *know* whether it will rise' (6.363–6.36311).

Thus, the world is contingent and the assumption of the inviolability of the laws of nature is a modern version of an ancient but persistent superstition. This is in harmony with Wittgenstein's view of the status of the law of physics. If such laws are optional forms for the propositions we use to describe the world, then even the most impressive predictions based on them, all of which are realised, will not establish their necessity. Wittgenstein's categories of thought and experience are certainly a priori, but, unlike Kant's, they are neither necessary nor universal. The contingency of the world is mirrored in language in that elementary propositions can only show *how* things stand, not *why* or that they *must* so stand. Presumably, it was this desire to emphasise the contingency and deny the necessity of events that led Wittgenstein to assert the logical independence of states of affairs. Since the limits of representation are confined to showing how things stand, and these are the limits of meaningful language, together with the accidentality of states of affairs entails that 'all propositions are of equal value' (6.4). Putting this another way, there can be no values *in* the world because value cannot be ascribed to what is purely contingent and 'all that happens and is the case is accidental'. From this Wittgenstein concludes not that the world has no sense, but that if it were possible to speak of such a thing 'the sense of the world must lie outside the world' (6.41). But what is *higher* than the world cannot be represented in genuine propositions which can only picture what happens *in* the world so 'it is impossible for there to be propositions of ethics . . . Ethics cannot be put into words. Ethics is transcendental' (6.42– 6.421).

Wittgenstein's assertions about the world and their implications for the structure of language may be set out as follows:

Events in the world are contingent and accidental	Elementary propositions are logically independent
There is no causal nexus	Induction is without logical justification. Laws of science are *a priori* forms of propositions.
Value cannot be ascribed to what is contingent and accidental	All propositions are of equal value
The sense of the world is transcendental	Propositions cannot express what is higher. Ethics is transcendental.

The problem of life in space and time lies outside space and time	The problem of life cannot be posed within the limits of language and its solution consists in its abolition.

Wittgenstein's refusal to dismiss ethics as another brand of nonsense, albeit sublime nonsense, and his allowing even the possibility that ethics is not inferior to, but transcends, the propositions of natural science alarmed the Vienna Circle. To allow that the sense of the world may be located in transcendental values, which cannot be represented in propositional pictures, and therefore cannot be expressed at all, is to weaken seriously the thesis that language is a mirror of reality. It is to reduce this thesis to the claim that language mirrors only certain accidental features of the world whilst its sense – which it is tempting to equate with its reality – exists transcendentally although it cannot be expressed. That this sense cannot be expressed rests only upon the rigidity with which the propositional monism of the *Tractatus* is maintained. Wittgenstein's own success in transcending the limits of language in the remarks comprising the *Tractatus* opens the door to the possibility of a latter-day Kant performing another transcendental deduction in which propositions may serve as elucidations by which we might again ascend the ladder to what is higher. The further interesting possibility as to whether God can reveal himself in a contingent world is one I leave to the theologians, but, according to the canons of significant language laid down in the *Tractatus*, Wittgenstein's assertion that '*How* things are in the world is a matter of complete indifference for what is higher: God does not reveal himself in the world' (6.432) simply cannot be made.

The transcendentality of the gulf between value and fact led Wittgenstein to another important conclusion which foreshadowed his later philosophy.

The facts all contribute only to setting the problem, not to its solution. . . . When the answer cannot be put into words, neither can the question be put into words. *The riddle* does not exist. If a question can be framed at all, it is also *possible* to answer it. Scepticism is *not* irrefutable, but obviously nonsensical, when it tries to raise doubts where no questions can be asked. For doubt can exist only where a question exists, a question only where an answer exists and an answer only when something *can be said* (6.4321, 6.5–6.51).

Our predicament is not an inability to formulate the answers to philosophical problems about value, life and immortality but an inability to formulate the questions. Schlick's fear was that philosophy will never get so far as to pose a genuine problem, i.e. philosophy will somehow get lost on the way. Wittgenstein's fear was that philosophy can never get started because its very first step is to attempt to cross the threshold of what can be said. Thus, the solution of mystical problems consists in the recognition of the inability of language to express such problems at all. In short, the problems simply vanish. From this it follows that traditional philosophy in attempting to formulate and resolve these problems is rooted in a misunderstanding of the true functions of language. This leads Wittgenstein to state what he thinks to be the correct method in philosophy in a passage where he first explicitly suggests that philosophy is a form of therapy for linguistic delusions.

> The correct method in philosophy would really be the following: to say nothing except what can be said, i.e. propositions of natural science – i.e. something that has nothing to do with philosophy – and then, whenever someone else wanted to say something metaphysical, to demonstrate to him that he had failed to give a meaning to certain signs in his propositions. Although it would not be satisfying to the other person – he would not have the feeling that we were teaching him philosophy – *this* method would be the only strictly correct one (6.53).

Wittgenstein explains the origin of his own sense of the mystical as arising from 'feeling the world as a limited whole' (6.45); that beyond the world as the totality of facts there is something comprising its sense and value. One of the influences at work on Wittgenstein here is traceable back to Schopenhauer. Both in the *Notebooks* and in the later sections of the *Tractatus* there is much that is illuminated by reference to Schopenhauer, particularly the remarks about the transcendental nature of ethics, the will as the subject of ethical attributes and the distinction between the world of the happy and the unhappy man.[11]

Whatever the formative influences exerted by Schopenhauer on Wittgenstein, in the end it is the differences between them that prove to be important. The point which most sharply divides them concerns the concept of meaning. Whatever linguistic impediments Schopenhauer may have felt frustrated our expressions of mystical and ethical experiences there is little doubt that he would conceive this to be due to a personal failure to communicate adequately. That is to say, it would be possible for someone with deeper mystical insights and a more imaginative command of language to describe his mystical experiences better. For Wittgenstein on the other hand, the inability to express the mystical is neither because he denied the existence of mystical experiences, nor is it due to a personal inability to articulate such experiences, but because the logical limits of language do not permit the expression of mystical experiences in genuine propositions. It is not that what metaphysicians have struggled to express should be said more clearly and explicitly; it simply cannot be said at all because logically they cannot give meaning to the signs they wish to employ for such purposes.

Finally, the impact of early religious influences on Wittgenstein is difficult to assess, but it is possible that aspects of the Fourth Gospel and his interest in Tolstoy's religious writings affected his thinking, although his remarks are too brief to allow this to be more than a very tentative suggestion. One of the themes of the Fourth Gospel is that known as the doctrine of realised eschatology. That is to say, the end of the world does not wait upon a series of apocalyptic cataclysms culminating in a second coming of Christ but was realised in the crucifixion and death of Christ. A trace of this might lie behind Wittgenstein's remark that for the individual 'at death the world does not alter, but comes to an end' (6.431). Perhaps a little more definite is the notion of timelessness and eternal life as something presently possessed – which is a perspective of the realised eschatology of the Fourth Gospel – expressed in the remark; 'If we take eternity to mean not infinite temporal duration, but timelessness then eternal life belongs to those who live in the present' (6.4311).

Even if these slender connections with the Fourth Gospel are allowed, once again it is the differences that are important. For Wittgenstein clearly rejects the possibility of a divine revelation in a historical Jesus as a device for crossing the transcendental gulf when he asserts that 'the solution of the riddle of life in space and time lies *outside* space and time', coupled with, 'God does not reveal himself *in* the world' (6.4312, 6.432). Supposing that there was 'a word' that 'in the beginning was God', it would remain wholly transcendent and incommunicable. Nor would there be any point in speculating about its content and meaning for us for 'what we cannot speak about we must pass over in silence' (7).

4

Language and the Projection of Reality

METHODS OF PROJECTION

Wittgenstein's attitude to the *Tractatus* at the time of its publication was a strange combination of the unassailability and finality of its solution of the problems of philosophy with a conviction of the triviality of this achievement. This combination led to him abandoning further work in philosophy for about a decade and also led him to question the compulsiveness of logical necessity, i.e. the hardness of the logical *must*, when he did return to philosophy.

His renewed interest in philosophy was marked by the publication of a short article entitled 'Some Remarks on Logical Form'.[1] This paper was the only published work, besides the *Tractatus*, to appear in published form during his lifetime. It was a paper which he tended to treat with scorn and an indication of his attitude to it is given by the fact that he refused to read it at the meeting of the Aristotelian Society for which it was prepared. To some extent Wittgenstein's own feelings about the paper have influenced many of his interpreters and led to its neglect as a source of information about Wittgenstein's philosophical development. Other interpreters have incorporated some of the ideas expressed in this paper into their interpretation of the *Tractatus*, although, as I hope to show, this raises more problems than it solves.

What is the relationship between the paper on *Logical Form* and the *Tractatus*? This narrows down to two specific questions:

1. To what extent does this paper modify Wittgenstein's earlier views and what is the effect of reading back these modifications into the *Tractatus*?
2. To what extent does this paper represent a movement away

from the *Tractatus* in the direction of Wittgenstein's later philosophy?

The paper begins with a distinction between propositional form and content and the assertion that analysis will reveal propositions to be truth-functions of simple propositions. If analysis is carried far enough it will reach a terminus in atomic propositions as the ultimate, fully analysed connections of simple terms. All this is familiar ground from the *Tractatus*. However, after a criticism of ordinary language and a plea for a clear symbolism, Wittgenstein continues; 'We can only substitute a clear symbolism for the un-precise one by inspecting the phenomena which we want to describe, thus trying to understand their logical multiplicity. That is to say, we can only arrive at a correct analysis by what might be called, the logical investigation of the phenomena themselves'.[2] This necessitates an appeal to a posteriori considerations instead of simply 'conjecturing about a priori possibilities' and such a task belongs to the 'theory of knowledge'. He deals with the philosophical temptation 'to ask from an a priori standpoint: what, after all, *can* be the only form of atomic propositions?' and rejects the answers such a question inspires as 'mere playing with words'. He then roundly declares; 'an atomic form cannot be foreseen. And it would be surprising if the actual phenomena had nothing more to teach us about their structure'.[3]

Here is a definite shift away from the *Tractatus*, and its rigid adherence to the view of the a priori logical structure of language, in the direction of the realisation that 'the more narrowly we examine actual language, the sharper becomes the conflict between it and our requirement. (For the crystalline purity of logic was, of course, not a result of investigation; it was a requirement)' (PI 107). Plainly, Wittgenstein's decade away from philosophy had been well spent. The recognition that an actual inspection of phenomena described might illuminate the logical structure of the description is a more empirical approach to language than that found in the *Tractatus* where such considerations were ruled out, a priori, as irrelevant. Coupled with this is a change in attitude towards epistemology, which is no longer relegated to psychology but recognised as an indispensable tool of philosophy. 'It is the task of the theory of knowledge' both to find atomic propositions 'and to understand their construction out of the words or symbols'. This is a departure from the doctrine that the signification of the signs used in elementary propositions simply shows as part of the nature of the signs themselves. The upshot of this is that 'an atomic form cannot be foreseen'. This is a denial of one of the main stays of the propositional monism of the *Tractatus*, where Wittgenstein had argued that it was possible 'to give the most general propositional form' on the grounds that 'there cannot be a proposition whose form could not have been foreseen (i.e. constructed). The general form of a proposition is; This is how things stand' (4.5). The admission that we cannot specify a priori the forms of elementary propositions is fatal to the propositional monism of the *Tractatus* and the general theory of propositions derived therefrom. If the identification of atomic propositions and, more importantly, their forms, are determinable only as a result of empirical enquiry, then we cannot say that these forms will conform to a single logical type. Putting this another way, unless we can foresee the forms of elementary propositions, we cannot exclude the possibility of classes of propositions that, not only do not picture how things stand, but whose function cannot be explicated in terms of a picture analogy at all.

In the 1929 paper, Wittgenstein is much more inclined than he was to stress the imperfections of ordinary language. The emphasis has shifted from its perfect underlying logical order to its syntactical weaknesses. It is 'not quite adequate'; it 'leads to endless misunderstandings', it 'disguises logical structure'; it allows the formation of 'pseudo-propositions' and 'uses one term in an infinity of different meanings'. Such expressions in themselves are not inconsistent with the *Tractatus*, but what is significant is the recognition that 'conjectures about the structure of atomic propositions' based on the forms of ordinary language are 'misleading' and, particularly important, is the declaration of the task of philosophy to be to 'substitute a clear symbolism for the unprecise one'. It is worth noting as an aside here that it was known that Russell was to be present at the meeting for which this paper was prepared – even though Wittgenstein refused to read it – and that it bears the marks of the almost excessive deference which it has been remarked that he showed in the presence of Russell. The effect of this on the contents of the paper is a matter for conjecture, but there is clearly an accommodation of Russell's views and terminology at the expense of the *Tractatus*. That the aim of philosophy is the replacement of the vagueness of ordinary language by a clear symbolism tailored to the actual phenomena described is not from the *Tractatus* but rather a thesis that Russell had been advocating for years.

It has been noted already that the 1929 paper explicitly repudiates the logical independence of elementary propositions which was asserted in the *Tractatus*. From what Wittgenstein says in the 1929 paper about the mutual exclusion of propositions ascribing different colours to the same place at the same time, Stenius concludes, correctly, that this means that we can only infer the logical independence of states of affairs of *different dimensions*, contrary to the *Tractatus* which asserted the independence of all states of affairs and, thus, of all elementary propositions. Stenius, however, wishes to incorporate this modification into his interpretation of the *Tractatus* as a whole and restates Wittgenstein's earlier view thus; 'Atomic states of affairs of *different dimensions* are independent of one another. The existence or non-existence of the atomic states of affairs of one *dimension* is independent of the existence or non-existence of the atomic states of affairs of *any other* dimension'.[4] Reading back this modification into the *Tractatus* enables Stenius to repudiate what he calls 'the positivistic theory' that there 'are not any genuine entities to be spoken of besides *objects* and that all statements on predicates are in fact disguised statements on objects'. His position is that 'we must not discard the distinction between the categories, and that predicates are as genuine components of reality as are objects'.[5]

This attempt to reinterpret the *Tractatus* so as to incorporate the retraction contained in the 1929 paper creates more problems than it solves. In the first place, as Stenius recognises, a consequence of admitting the existence of elementary propositions of different dimensions is that the differences are indicated predicatively. This means that predicates remain as unanalysable constituents of elementary propositions, contrary to the ontology of the *Tractatus*, which treats objects as the primary elements whose configurations produce properties and relations. The retraction set out in the 1929 paper is not a minor modification of the ontology of the *Tractatus* but a rejection of it.

Secondly, the introduction of elementary propositions of different dimensions marks the abandonment of the position; 'There cannot be a hierarchy of the forms of elementary propositions' (5.556). If states of affairs have different dimensions then it is, in principle, possible to arrange the elementary propositions representing them in some sort of hierarchy. What Wittgenstein sets out in the 1929 paper are grounds precisely for such a hierarchical arrangement. Indeed, some such arrangement is required in order to determine whether or not the logical product of propositions leads to a collision since, according to the later view, it is only elementary propositions of different dimensions that are logically independent. The incorporation of properties and relations as unanalysable constituents of elementary propositions paves the way for a predicative hierarchy of the kind found in Russell's theory of logical types. The magnitude of this shift from the propositional monism of the *Tractatus* cannot have escaped Wittgenstein for very long. The direction of this shift is towards a grammatical investigation of the way propositions actually function as the attempt to specify this a priori becomes less and less a living option. Such a programme belonged to the future but the 1929 paper marked a stage on the way to its realisation. It represents the Parmenidean stage of Wittgenstein's thought in which the absurdities of propositional monism were becoming apparent but had not yet given way to the propositional pluralism of the *Philosophical Investigations*.

The most important part of the 1929 paper is the section on methods of projection in which Wittgenstein once again examines the way that reality is represented in language. In saying that propositions represent how things stand, which of the following senses of 'represent' are intended? 'Depict', 'denote', 'portray', 'exhibit by resemblance', 'symbolise', 'stand for', 'be image of', 'go proxy for'; be 'map', 'diagram', 'icon', 'facsimile', 'parallel', 'approximation', 'analogue' or 'family likeness' of. A number of the controversies running through the literature on the *Tractatus* illustrate the shifting senses of 'represent'. In sharpening his account of representation in the 1929 paper, Wittgenstein again invokes a geometrical analogy based on the use of various methods of projection by which we can represent plane figures of a given type by plane figures of a different type. This is achieved by using a particular law of projection which governs the form of representation of one type of geometrical figure by another. A diagram makes the analogy and its application clear.

We can imagine, Wittgenstein suggests, two parallel planes I and II such that, for example, 'every ellipse on plane I is to appear as a circle in plane II, and every rectangle as a square in II (see Fig. 8). From the figures in plane II alone 'the exact shapes of the original figures on plane I cannot be immediately inferred'.

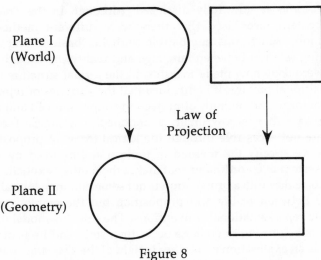

Plane I
(World)

Law of
Projection

Plane II
(Geometry)

Figure 8

For this inference to be possible we need to know the precise method of projection employed. The case of ordinary language, Wittgenstein further suggests, is quite analogous. If how things stand in the world correspond to the ellipses and rectangles on plane I then the subject–predicate and relational forms of ordinary language correspond to the circles and squares in plane II. 'These forms are the norms of our particular language into which we project in *ever so many different* ways *ever so many different* logical forms. And for this very reason we can draw no conclusions – except very vague ones – from the use of these norms as to the actual logical form of the phenomena described'.[6]

Wittgenstein goes on to make what he calls 'my first definite remark on the logical analysis of actual phenomena' and gives an example in which we imagine the visual field divided into a system of rectangular axes and numbered co-ordinates. In a description of this situation the atomic proposition employs not only a symbol representative of the colour of the field but 'the system of co-ordinates here is part of the mode of expression; it is part of the method of projection by which the reality is projected into our symbolism'. Some reference to these co-ordinates is 'an essential and, consequently, unavoidable feature of the representation'.[7] Here is a further elaboration of the idea of the elementary proposition as a logical network sprinkled with names.

The interior weakness of the account of representation given in the *Tractatus* is now fully disclosed. Although in the *Tractatus* Wittgenstein recognised that there were different methods of projection, which was compatible with his basic concept of a picturing relation between language and reality, he thought that they were somehow made manifest in the formal structure of the propositional picture. It is this idea that the varieties of representational forms, or methods of projection simply showed and could not be said that is now finally abandoned. The logical forms of facts are not accessible through the logical forms of propositions unless we specify the method of projection employed by using some system of co-ordinates that makes the method explicit. What projects reality into a proposition is not some common logical form shared between reality and proposition but the employment of suitable representational conventions. The calculus model of language is beginning to go lame on Wittgenstein and he is moving towards an exploration of another insight of the *Tractatus*, namely, the enormously complicated nature of 'the tacit conventions on which the understanding of everyday language depends' (4.002).

The concept of representation is now so elastic that it stretches far beyond the limits of anything that might be credibly called a picture. Given appropriate methods of projection a fact may be represented by such varieties of different types of sentences that the notion of a picturing relation is actually a hindrance. Wittgenstein's remark in the *Tractatus* that nothing essential for depiction is lost in the replacement of hieroglyphs by an alphabetic script puts things the wrong way round. Rather it is that nothing essential is gained by substituting hieroglyphs for sentences. I.e. a picturing relationship between language and reality is an accidental and inessential feature of our notation and not that which gives language life and meaning.

The 1929 paper reveals Wittgenstein at a crossroads. He has not yet freed himself from the constrictions of the picture-theory of meaning, even though he now realises the incorrectness of supposing that the structure of the world simply shows in the pictorial and representational forms of propositions per se. His dilemma is most obvious with respect to ordinary language. On the one hand he states:

> Where ordinary language disguises logical structure, where it allows the formation of pseudo-propositions, where it uses one term in an infinity of different meanings, we must replace it by a

symbolism which gives a clear picture of the logical structure, excludes pseudo-propositions and uses its terms unambiguously.[8]

This is the Russellian programme of philosophy in which the clarification of ideas is achieved by the replacement of the 'abominable syntax' of ordinary language by a rigorously defined logical symbolism free from ambiguity. On the other hand he also states:

> I have said elsewhere that a proposition "reaches up to reality", and by this I meant that the forms of the entities are contained in the form of the proposition which is about the entities. For the sentence, together with the mode of projection which projects reality into the sentence, determines the logical form of the entities, just as in our simile a picture on plane II, together with its mode of projection determines the shape of the figure on plane I.[9]

Modes of projection are the rules and conventions governing the various forms through which we represent reality in language. The investigation of these modes suggests a different programme of philosophy and, moreover, one which was to occupy Wittgenstein for most of the rest of his life. At some time after the preparation of the 1929 paper, and before he thought out the material now incorporated in the *Blue and Brown Books* (i.e. 1933 at the latest), Wittgenstein had resolved his dilemma and turned his back finally and forever on the Russellian programme of philosophy.

In the *Philosophical Remarks*, which were prepared in the form in which they have reached us in the summer of 1930, Wittgenstein moves further away from the *Tractatus* and, particularly with respect to the new methods of philosophy employed, towards the position represented in the *Philosophical Investigations*. The literature of Wittgenstein's middle period is extensive and illuminating and includes *Some Remarks on Logical Form, Philosophical Remarks, Philosophical Grammar, The Blue and Brown Books* and the *Remarks on the Foundations of Mathematics*, to say nothing of letters, notes by former students and memoirs. It must not be supposed, however, that there is a straightforward progression from the *Tractatus* to the *Investigations* that is traceable throughout this literature.

There is a kind of progression but it is not a simple linear one. False starts and blind alleys with respect to the stance of the *Investigations* are also present and it is no easy task to pick one's way through the criss-cross lines of thought contained in the literature of the middle period with any clear sense of direction. The work of detailed comparison between this literature and the *Investigations* has hardly begun and is likely to sustain the Wittgenstein industry for some considerable time. I count myself fortunate, and my readers more so, that the limitations of my brief do not require extensive involvement in all these complexities except those that affect the relationship between language and reality and the concepts of representation and grammar.

Returning to the *Philosophical Remarks*, Wittgenstein again uses the analogy of methods of projection to illustrate ways in which reality may be misrepresented by propositions. As in the 1929 paper, he imagines two planes in which figures on plane I are projected on to plane II by some method of projections. In this case, however, we are to adopt the rule that whatever the figures on plane I may be they are all to be projected as circles on plane II. This supposes that the methods of projection vary in order to satisfy the rule that the projected figure must always be a circle.

> In order in this case to construe the circles in II as images, I shall have to say for each circle what method of projection belongs to it. But the mere fact that a figure is represented on II as a circle will say nothing. It is like this with reality if we map it onto subject–predicate propositions. The fact that we use subject–predicate propositions is only a matter of our notation. The subject-predicate form does not in itself amount to a logical form and is the way of expressing countless fundamentally different logical forms, like the circles on the second plane. The forms of the propositions: 'The plate is round', 'The man is tall', 'The patch is red', have nothing in common (PR 93a pp.118–19).

Wittgenstein uses this argument to attack the generality of Frege's theory of concept and object which corresponds to that of predicate and subject. 'And we have just said that there is not just one logical form which is *the* subject–predicate form'.[10]

He remarks later that it is possible to use the subject–predicate form (or, for that matter, the argument-function form) as a norm of representation but in so doing concepts and objects are not the result of analysis but are, in fact, a mould into which the proposition has been squeezed. It is by this route that Frege arrived at his theory that numbers were properties of predicates (PR 115e, f pp.136–7).

In these passages Wittgenstein once again emphasises that the forms of ordinary language may be misleading as representations of reality unless we know the methods of projection employed which permit us to infer the logical forms of the facts. The *Philosophical Grammar*, written during 1932–34, exhibits a definite change in his use of the analogy of methods of projection. So far Wittgenstein has assumed that the association of projection lines from a proposition with the objects depicted is not problematical, i.e. as though the proposition and the method of projection fixed this association. He now treats a projection-method as a rule of translation which illustrates the difference between 'associate' and 'copy', that is, 'we say: "you haven't copied correctly", but not, "you haven't associated correctly"' (PG 50a p.92). The example of a table with colour words written alongside colour samples is discussed from the point of view of deciding whether or not the association of words with samples is arbitrary. Wittgenstein's conclusion is that:

> the chart doesn't guarantee that I shall pass from one part of it to another in a uniform manner. It doesn't compel me to use it always in the same way. Its there, like a field, with paths leading through it: but I can also cut across. Each time I apply the chart I make a fresh transition. The transitions aren't made as it were once for all (by) the chart (the chart merely suggests to me that I make them) (PG 52d p.94).

Here is the emergence of a new problem, namely, that propositions, even when we know the mode of projection, do not guarantee the method of their application. This is a new variable in the relationship between language and reality.

Later in the *Philosophical Grammar* Wittgenstein picks up this point again in considering a way in which the analogy of methods of projection goes lame and becomes positively misleading. 'We may say: a blueprint *serves as a picture* of the object which the workman is to make from it. And here we might call the way in which the workman turns such a drawing into an artefact "the method of projection".' This in turn suggests that 'the method of projection mediates between the drawing and the object, it reaches from the drawing to the artefact'. The picture we have in mind here is one where:

> we are comparing the method of projection with projection lines which go from one figure to another. But if the method of projection is a bridge, it is a bridge which isn't built until the application is made. This comparison conceals the fact that the picture *plus* the projection lines leaves open various methods of application; it makes it look as if what is depicted, even if it does not exist in fact, is determined by the picture and the projection lines in an ethereal manner; every bit as determined, that is to say, as if it did exist.

Here are the beginnings of Wittgenstein's exploration of ethereal connections which he was to illustrate in his later writings with a wealth of subtle examples. His point here is that the notion of the blueprint as a picture leaves open a variety of methods of application of the picture, whereas to construe ethereal projection lines as part of the picture seems to determine one particular method of application. 'And we now imagine the method as something which is attached to the blueprint whether or not it is used.' The consequence of looking at a blueprint in this way is this: 'So I am imagining that the difference between proposition and reality is ironed out by the lines of projection belonging to the picture, the thought, and that no further room is left for a method of application, but only for agreement and disagreement' (PG 4B pp.213–14).

This insight into the limitations of the simile of methods of projection is important as marking another stage in the decline of the viability of propositional pictures as the link between language and reality. Wittgenstein's earlier use of the simile leads one to suppose that, once the method of projection has been laid down along with the picture, the latter's connection with reality is both direct and assured. I.e. the projection lines reach right out of the picture and connect with things in the world. Where both ends of the connection are on view, as in the case of a picture of an existing state of affairs, the analogy is quite helpful, but there are other uses where it is not only unhelpful but positively misleading. This is particularly the case with propositions expressing intentions, or unrealised plans like blueprints, where the lines of projection that we imagine as coming from the picture seem to determine the form of reality intended. The extrapolation of the analogy to such cases makes it appear that all that is in question is the agreement or disagreement of the proposition with reality. Whereas, in fact, intentional and related propositions may be variously applied in all cases and it is not the case that there is a single and unequivocal connection with reality at all.

How then does reality enter into such propositions? This question can only be answered when we have applied the picture and drawn the projection lines from it to reality in a particular way. What this means is that questions about the meanings of propositions expressing intentions, wishes, hopes and the like, can only be answered by reference to the realisation of what was intended, wished or hoped for. The corollary of this is that the meanings of these propositions are not determined by reference back to mental process, feelings or states that may be said to accompany their expression. Of this there is much more in the later philosophy of Wittgenstein, but it is fascinating to catch glimpses of him thinking his way through his earlier analogies and beginning to identify the problems that dominate the later philosophy.

Wittgenstein comments: 'Certainly I can compare deciding on the meanings of words with deciding on a method of projection, such as that for the representation of spatial forms ("the proposition is a picture"). That is a good comparison, but it doesn't exempt us from investigating the way words signify, which has its own rules' (PG 51b p.93). What is interesting in this passage is the indication that Wittgenstein is moving away from the comparison of the meanings of words with pictures having specific methods of projection, towards a recognition of the actual complexities of the way words signify. Although references to this analogy occur in his later writings, what it was originally designed to illustrate becomes one aspect of a range of considerations which increasingly he calls the grammar of propositions. To specify the method of projection employed in connection with a proposition is to comment on the grammar of the proposition but by no means fixes it to one particular application.

Wittgenstein considers the extent to which rules of grammar and rules of representation are conventional and, therefore, in that sense, arbitrary. He examines a point to which he returns several times in the later philosophy, namely, whether reality shapes or even suggests the various rules of grammar that we use. He writes;

'Grammar is not accountable to any reality. It is grammatical rules that determine meaning (constitute it) and so they themselves are not answerable to any meaning and to that extent are arbitrary (PG 133a p.184). There are no external criteria of correctness by which we can justify such rules. However, this assertion of the conventional basis of grammar seems open to objection in the case of colour words. Surely, it might be argued, the grammar of colour words is shaped by reality because there really are four primary colours and the natural grouping of colours together is based on similarity, which does not obtain if we try to group together colours and sounds. Wittgenstein's reply is; 'whence do I derive the idea of this similarity? Just as the idea "primary colour" is nothing else but "blue or red or green or yellow" is not the idea of that similarity too given simply by the four colours? Indeed, aren't these concepts the same?' (PG 134a p.186). Whether or not similarity is independent of the concept 'primary colours' the point is that it does not determine a particular projection. A painted portrait might bear a striking similarity to one man and yet be a picture of someone else whom it resembles less. What fixes the projection in this case is not the similarity, but the name-plate placed alongside the portrait.[11]

Surprisingly, Wittgenstein makes an exception to his general argument in the case of certain rules of representation. 'I do not call rules of representation conventions if they can be justified by the fact that a representation made in accordance with them will agree with reality. For instance the rule "paint the sky brighter than anything that receives its light from it" is not a convention' (PG 134b p.186). The difficulty here is, what constitutes agreement with reality unless, contrary to what he has argued elsewhere, this is determined by similarity? If I paint a landscape picture I can follow Wittgenstein's rule by painting the sky bright orange and everything else jet black. Agreement with reality in this case depends upon a particular method of projection – one of many which I might adopt – and in this sense is conventional. More importantly, if similarity does not determine how reality enters into a picture, then even naturalistic landscapes are connected with the world by convention. As there is a gap between a picture and the methods of its application, so there is a gap between a rule and its methods of application. The recognition of this fact with respect to a rule was to become explicit in Wittgenstein's later writings. If the connection between the application of a rule and reality is conventional, then agreement with reality does not provide a justification of the rule. I suspect that the problem Wittgenstein has in mind is one which haunts him throughout the *Investigations*, namely, what makes a representation perspicous?

REALITY AND PROPOSITIONS

The previous section has shown how the immediacy of the connection between language and reality asserted in the *Tractatus* is lessened by the interpolation of methods of projection which stand between propositions and their application to the world. One can no longer, as it were, read reality straight off from propositions without regard to the rules of projection that govern the connection between them. This is not the only area of difficulty with respect to the link between language and reality with which Wittgenstein found himself faced during his middle period.

Another problem concerns the ontology of the *Tractatus* which rested on the idea of objects as primary elements. In the literature of the middle period we find Wittgenstein becoming increasingly critical of his own earlier account of objects and more inclined to use the word in its ordinary sense to denote things, rather than the ultimate constituents resulting from the analysis of things. This identification of objects in the *Tractatus* with primary elements is reinforced by Wittgenstein's later comment; 'What I once called "objects", simples, were simply what I could refer to without running the risk of their possible non-existence; i.e. that for which there is neither existence nor non-existence, and that means: what we can speak about *no matter what may be the case*' (PR 36a p.72). This passage is strongly reminiscent of the Platonic arguments for primary elements developed in the *Theaetetus*.

In some remarks on *Complex and Fact*, dated June 1931 (PR pp.301–3), Wittgenstein suggests that his account of facts as composed of objects given in the *Tractatus* rests upon a number of linguistic confusions. These include the following:

1. To represent a fact as a complex of objects is misleading in that it makes sense to say of a complex, but not of a fact, that it moves spatially.
2. To assert of a complex that it is a spatial object composed of its

parts is a grammatical comment on the words 'complex', 'part' and 'compose'.

3. To speak of a red circle as composed of redness and circularity is both misleading and a misuse of words.

4. It is an incorrect use of the word 'house' to say it is a complex of bricks and their spatial relations.

5. One can point out a fact but not point to it.

6. The description of a fact is a misnomer for the assertion of a fact.

7. The fact that a chain is composed of links does not mean the fact is composed of anything.

8. 'The part is smaller than the whole' applied to fact and constituent is absurd.

9. 'The root of this muddle is the confusing use of the world "object".'

These remarks are important for two reasons. First, they confirm the correctness of the interpretation of the *Tractatus* adopted in this book, namely, that at that time Wittgenstein thought of facts as actually *composed* of objects. Those who deny this are faced with the problem of explaining what the above rebuttal by Wittgenstein is intended to rebut. Second, these remarks illustrate the primacy of the ordinary use of words over their use in philosophy. In spite of the acknowledgement of the diversity of methods of projection and methods of application of propositions Wittgenstein never defends his earlier writings by invoking their special sense or philosophical application. Thus, 'a fact is a complex of objects' is treated as a 'bad expression' on the grounds that 'here the fact that a man is sick is compared with a combination of two things, one of them the man and the other the sickness' (PG I 20c p.58).

Another problem that threatens the link between reality and propositions propounded in the *Tractatus* concerns logical form. According to the theory of pictorial representation what makes it possible for a proposition to depict a fact is the possession of a common logical form, in some sense of 'common'. As we have seen, the supposition that 'common' means an identity relation between the logical form of facts and the logical form of propositions is a condition that cannot be met. To the extent that logical form becomes further and further removed from an identity relation, than to that extent is there the interposition of more and more material between reality and proposition. Up to a point the

Tractatus accommodates this through the admission of appropriate representational conventions governing the connection between proposition and fact. These conventions admit of a commonality of logical form without involving identity or even similarity. The realisation of the middle period that the logical form of facts and the logical form of propositions could actually collide proved fatal to Wittgenstein's earlier views on the generality of the logical form of propositions and the possibility of foreseeing the forms of elementary propositions. All this first becomes explicit in the 1929 paper on *Logical Form*.

These points are re-examined in greater detail in *Philosophical Remarks* and *Philosophical Grammar* in an extended discussion of the nature of the contradiction generated by the assertion that a given patch in the visual field has two different colours at the same time. Letting 'f(r)' mean 'there is red here now' and 'f(g)' mean 'there is green here now', Wittgenstein writes: 'If f(r) and f(g) contradict one another, it is because r and g completely occupy the f and cannot both be in it. But that doesn't show itself in our signs. But it must show itself if we look not at the sign, but at the symbol. For since this includes the form of the objects then the impossibility of f(r).f(g) must show itself there, in this form. . . . That two colours won't fit at the same time in the same place must be contained in their form and the form of space' (PR 78 a, b p.106–7). The first point to note is that a symbol is a sign with meaning, hence, looking, not at the sign, but at the symbol inevitably leads to propositions of the same propositional forms but of different logical types depending on the meanings of the signs employed. This is a complete volte-face from the *Tractatus* where he had written: 'It must be possible to establish logical syntax without mentioning the meaning of a sign.' It is this that is the basis of his magisterial rebuke of Russell and rejection of the theory of types: 'It can be seen that Russell must be wrong, because he had to mention the meaning of signs when establishing the rules for them' (3.33–3.331). This is precisely what Wittgenstein himself is now proposing, if only for the purpose of excluding syntactical constructions like 'f(r).f(g)'. The rehabilitation of a theory of logical types which follows from the possibility of arranging propositions according to the entities represented was something to which Wittgenstein. remained in steadfast opposition. As he remarked in the context of a discussion of systems of propositions; 'There's nothing to be found here which we could call a hierarchy of types' (PR 152j p.179). However, once we admit that there are propositions of different logical types the possibility of arranging these in hierarchies cannot be excluded, at least, without advancing further grounds for doing so.

The second point to note is that he discusses the problem of the simultaneous ascription of two colours to the same object in terms of the incompatibility of forms. A little later he turned his attention away from this way of looking at the problem and, instead, compared the reality of colour situations with the grammar of colour words and propositions in order to determine the extent, if any, to which reality shapes that grammar. Moreover, it should be observed that the lack of fit between the logical form of the facts of colour situations and the logical form of propositions representing them is a serious impediment to a theory that depends on a common logical form subsisting between fact and proposition. This lack of fit is due to a difference in logical multiplicity which in this example cannot be accommodated by some schema of representational conventions. The logical product $f(r).f(g)$ represents as possible a situation which in fact is impossible, thus giving the proposition a logical multiplicity in excess of what the facts allow. No juggling with a many-one or a one-many correlation between elements of fact and proposition can reconcile the collision resulting from this example in which the logical syntax permits as legitimate a representation which the facts show to be illegitimate. There is no escaping the conclusion that here fact and proposition have different logical forms and different logical multiplicities. This rules out the possibility, advocated in the *Tractatus*, of constructing the rules for a propositional syntax without reference either to the meanings of the signs utilised or the actual phenomena represented. In this case, objects as the substance of the world, no matter what may be the case, are not a sufficient foundation for the construction placed upon them in the *Tractatus* and simply fall away as both inadequate and unnecessary.

Wittgenstein recognises that 'the concept of an "elementary proposition" now loses all of its earlier significance' because the elucidation of the rules for the use of the logical constants in terms of the T–F notation 'are a *part* of the grammar of these words, but not *the whole*'. Consequently, propositions joined by 'and', such as '$f(r).f(g)$' 'are not independent of one another, they form *one* picture and can be tested for their compatibility or incompatibility' (PR 83 a–c p.111). This insight that the so-called logical

constants 'and', 'or', 'not' etc. are not constants in ordinary language was seminal and has been amplified and much discussed
in subsequent writings on philosophical logic.[12]

Wittgenstein makes a specific criticism of his old conception of
an elementary proposition on the grounds that, 'there was no
determination of the value of a co-ordinate; although my remark
that a coloured body is in a colour-space, etc., should have put me
straight on to this' (PR 83d p.111). I take this to mean that if 'f(r)'
and 'f(g)' both had the same co-ordinates and this were to be
shown in some way then it would also be shown that 'f(r).f(g)' was
impossible because ' co-ordinate of reality may only be determined *once*' (PR 83e p.111).

A recapitulation of Wittgenstein's argument here might be
helpful. The problem is that the rules of logical syntax as outlined
in the *Tractatus* permit propositional forms that depict situations
which in reality are impossible. This impossibility does not show
itself in the truth-functions, or the T–F notation, and, although
Wittgenstein is prepared to concede that these comprise only a
fragment of the grammar of the logical constants, he still insists
that 'True–false, and the truth-functions, go with the representation of reality by propositions. . . . Language *means* the totality of
propositions. . . . The truth-functions are essential to language'
(PR 85a p.113). If it is the case that truth, falsity and the truth-
functions are essential for the representation of reality by propositions then there can be no question of totally abandoning them.
But the fact remains that the apparatus of the truth-functions does
not show that 'f(r).f(g)' represents an impossible situation. Yet this
impossibility must show itself in the logical syntax quite apart
from a comparison of 'f(r).f(g)' with reality. Wittgenstein's first
attempt at solving this problem is found in the 1929 paper on
Logical Form where he suggests that the logical network sprinkled
with names which comprises the elementary proposition must
also include spatial co-ordinates which allow only one determination at a time. This suggestion is taken up and developed in the
early parts of *Philosophical Remarks* where Wittgenstein modifies
his remark in the *Tractatus* on the general form of a proposition;
'This is how things stand' (4.5). He now writes, 'If I wanted to
represent the general standpoint I would say: "You should not say
now one thing and now another about the same matter". Where
the matter in question would be the co-ordinate to which I can
given one value and no more'. This is followed by an extremely

important passage which throws light on the emphasis in the later philosophy on systems of propositions (language-games) and grammar. 'The situation is misrepresented if we say we may not ascribe to an object two incompatible attributes' (e.g. the colours red and green at the same time). 'For seen like that, it looks as if in every case we must first investigate whether two determinations are incompatible or not. The truth is, *two* determinations of the same kind (co-ordinate) are impossible' (PR 83f–84a pp.111–12). It is still not clear how this co-ordinate shows itself – what is its sign? Wittgenstein does not tell us and, indeed, moves away from the notion of co-ordinates to the more general considerations of syntax. 'Syntax prohibits a construction such as "A is green and A is red" . . . but for "A is green", the proposition "A is red" is not, so to speak, *another* proposition – and that strictly is what the syntax fixes – but another form of the same proposition. In this way syntax draws together the propositions that make *one* determination' (PR 86a p.113). What Wittgenstein is trying to formulate here is made much clearer when he makes explicit an important change in a position he took up in the *Tractatus*. There he used the analogy of a measure of length to illustrate the way in which a proposition connected with reality (2.1511–2.1515). It is the directness of this connection that is threatened in the case of the proposition 'f(r).f(g)' which, seemingly, has impeccable syntactical credentials and yet does not, and cannot, reach out to reality. In view of this, and other similar examples, he is compelled to say, not that particular propositions are laid against reality, but that systems of them do so. Waismann's notes for Christmas day 1929 of Wittgenstein's talks are worth quoting at length.

> I once wrote: 'A proposition is like a yardstick against reality. Only the outermost tips of the graduation marks touch the object to be measured'. I should now prefer to say: a *system of propositions* is laid like a yardstick against reality. What I mean by this is: when I lay a yardstick against a spatial object, I apply *all the graduation marks simultaneously*. It's not the individual graduation marks that are applied, it's the whole scale. If I know that the object reaches up to the tenth graduation mark, I also know immediately that it doesn't reach the eleventh, twelfth etc. The assertions telling me the length of an object form a system, a system of propositions. It's such a whole system which is compared with reality, not a single proposition. If, for instance,

I say such and such a point in the visual field is *blue*, I not only know that, I also know that the point isn't green, isn't red, isn't yellow etc. I have simultaneously applied the whole colour scale. This is also the reason why a point can't have different colours simultaneously; why there is a syntactical rule against fx being true for more than one value of x. For if I apply a *system* of propositions to reality, that of itself already implies – as in the spatial case – that in every case only *one* state of affairs can obtain, never several.

When I was working on my book I was still unaware of all this and thought then that every inference depended on the form of a tautology. I hadn't seen then that an inference can also be of the form: A man is 6ft tall, therefore he isn't 7ft. This is bound up with my then believing that elementary propositions had to be independent of one another: from the fact that one state of affairs obtained you couldn't infer another did not. But if my present conception of a system of propositions is right, then it's even the rule that from the fact that one state of affairs obtains we can infer that all the others described by the system of propositions do not.[13]

This is the end of the propositional monism of the *Tractatus*, namely, that all propositions are reducible by analysis to a single elementary form. Elementary propositions are not logically independent but comprise sets or systems or, in fairness to Russell, logical types. Here is the precursor of the very important notion that dominates the *Philosophical Investigations* – the language-game. The use of a given system of propositions is equivalent to playing a particular language-game. Hence also the comment, 'It is only in a language that something is a proposition. To understand a proposition is to understand a language. A proposition is a sign in a system of signs. . . . As it were *one* position of an indicator as opposed to other possible ones' (PG 84d p.131; cf. 85d p.132).

Here, too, are the beginnings of another important concept of the later philosophy. The place, function and relationship of a proposition with respect to others in the same system is its *grammar*. An examination of this concept will be undertaken in due course but it is worth observing here that what Wittgenstein has been trying to say about f(r).f(g) in terms of co-ordinates, then syntax, finally becomes coherent using the concept 'grammar'. If propositions fall into systems, or grammatical sets, then it is no longer necessary that each proposition should be laid up against reality in order to read off its agreement or disagreement.

> All that's required for our propositions (about reality) to have a sense, is that our experience *in some sense or other* either tends to agree with them or tends not to agree with them. That is, immediate experience need confirm only something about them, *some* facet of them. And in fact this image is taken straight from reality, since we say 'There's a chair here', when we only see *one* side of it (PR 225c p.282).

Provided that a system of propositions about a chair exhibit truth-functional and other relationships then the agreement, or otherwise, with reality of one proposition will determine the truth or falsity of all the others in the system. It is the internal relationships of the propositions comprising a system about a chair that entitle us to infer from the truth of the proposition 'a now occupies the chair' the falsity of 'b now occupies the chair'. Of course, it must not be supposed that for Wittgenstein the internal relationships of a system of propositions are only truth-functional ones. The purpose of his grammatical investigations is to reveal something of the enormous complexity of these relationships. What Wittgenstein is moving away from is his earlier position, 'The agreement or disagreement of its (i.e. a propositional picture's) sense with reality constitutes its truth or falsity' (2.222), towards the recognition that sense is a function of grammar. The magnitude of this shift must not be obscured by supposing that the rules of grammar are themselves shaped in some way by reality. Wittgenstein is insistent on this point:

> Can one ask: 'How must we make the grammatical rules for words if they are to give a sentence sense'? I say, for instance: There isn't a book here, but there could be one; on the other hand, it's nonsensical to say that the colours green and red could be in a single place at the same time. But if what gives a proposition sense is its agreement with grammatical rules then let's make just this rule, to permit the sentence 'red and green are both at this point at the same time'. Very well; but that doesn't fix the grammar of the expression. Further stipulations have yet to be made about how such a sentence is to be used; e.g. how it is to be verified (PG 182a p.127).

What Wittgenstein finally succeeds in making explicit here is that what rules out 'f(r).f(g)' as nonsense is not its lack of agreement with reality but its lack of a place in the grammar of our colour expressions. I.e. in the case of colour expressions what use is assigned to f(r).f(g) and how would it be verified? It looks like an expression with sense but it has no place in the grammar and this is why it is nonsense.

Here it may seem that Wittgenstein is being sheerly perverse. Why is he so reluctant to admit that grammar is shaped by reality so that the lack of a place for f(r).f(g) in the grammar of sentences about colour is ultimately because reality does not permit the simultaneous ascriptions of different colours to the same body? The syntactical mark of this incompatibility is the contrariety of 'red' and 'green' so that f(r).f(g) is nonsense because it asserts that two expressions are both true when the logical structure of contrariety forbids that they are both true. Furthermore, it is not the case that this logical structure agrees with reality and this is the bedrock on which logic, syntax and grammar rests – at least for propositions which are about reality?

This, roughly, is the position of the *Tractatus* where the sense of propositions about reality is determined by agreement or disagreement with reality. The structure of the world and the structure of language are parallel and this is mirrored in a common logical form. However, further reflection by Wittgenstein convinced him that the concepts of, 'agreement with reality', and, 'logical form', are both slippery and complex in ways indicated in the previous sections of this book. There is a biographical point to be made here. The trauma of the discovery that the logical 'must' of the *Tractatus* – this is how language and reality *must be* – simply dissolves, following a shift of standpoint, left a deep psychological scar on Wittgenstein for the rest of his life. Subsequent attempts to invoke reality as the ground of assertions that this is how things must be are treated by him with the gravest suspicion. In the *Remarks on the Foundations of Mathematics* he examines the nature of logical inference itself with a boldness that has caused consternation in some philosophical circles.

There are two changes in Wittgenstein's standpoint which are important here. The first concerns the movement away from his earlier notion, that individual propositions are laid up against reality such that we simply read off their agreement or disagreement with reality, to the later position that propositions form systems which touch reality at some but not all points. The second change is even more important and concerns the growing realisation that language is used by human beings for a large variety of purposes and the internal logic of propositional systems reflects these purposes rather than the structure of the world. Putting this another way, the rules of grammar governing propositional systems are as multifarious as are the rules of games human beings play and basically are stipulations. The justification of these stipulations does not consist in further appeals to some problematic notion of 'agreement with reality', but in their utility with respect to the objectives of the language-game. Let us revert to the example of $f(r).f(g)$. Wittgenstein wishes to rule this out as nonsense because it does not have a grammar with respect to our normal language-game of colour expressions and, therefore, the expression $f(r).f(g)$ is senseless only because we have not given it a sense. If we are inclined to say that it is nonsense because it does not agree with reality inasmuch as the world precludes the simultaneous ascriptions of two colours to the same object we might be tempted to think that the expression is senseless in some absolute sense, i.e. it could never have an application because the structure of the world forbids it. But $f(r).f(g)$ is senseless only in that it awaits the stipulation of a sense in a system of propositions that has use and therefore a grammar. Suppose we use 'and', not in the sense it has in the propositional calculus, but in ordinary language when we use it in the sense of 'and then', as, for example, in 'John took poison and died'. If we stipulate that 'and' should be used in this sequential sense then the logical product $f(r).f(g)$ has sense, a truth table (TFFF) and a coherent grammar which includes the rule $p.q \vartriangle q.p$. This latter expression is a grammatical rule which illustrates the difference in grammar between this stipulated use of 'and' compared with its use in the propositional calculus where $p.q \Phi q.p$.

Wittgenstein and his interlocutor argue as follows:

> So it depends wholly on our grammar what will be called possible and what not, i.e. what the grammar permits. But surely that is arbitrary! Certainly; but the grammatical constructions we call empirical propositions (e.g. ones which describe a visible distribution of objects in space and could be replaced by a representational drawing) have a particular application, a particular use. And a construction may have a superficial

resemblance to such an empirical proposition and play a some-
what similar role in a calculus without having an analogous
application; and if it hasn't we won't be inclined to call it a
proposition (PG 82b p.127).

It is how a proposition is used which fixes it's grammatical role
and, consequently, it's sense, rather than it's correspondence or
otherwise with reality. Even in the case of empirical propositions
which do represent reality how they do this depends on their
grammar as part of a system of propositions and not vice versa.
Sameness of propositional form is no guarantee of sameness of
function or grammar. Wittgenstein is insistent; 'What matters is
the system.' One of his illustrations of this point is an example to
which he repeatedly returns in the later philosophy. Consider the
two questions, is it conceivable that a row of trees goes on as a
series until the 100th tree?; and, is it conceivable that a row of trees
goes on as a series for ever? The similarity in form of these
questions misleads us if we suppose that this means that they
have the same grammar. Instead of looking at the form, if we ask
of each proposition what is its application, how might an answer
be found and how verified? we shall see their grammatical differences (PG 82c p.128).

On the entailment relationship between propositions with
respect to grammar Wittgenstein observes:

If $F_1(a)$ (= a has the colour F_1) entails $-F_2(a)$ then the possibility
of the second proposition must have been provided for in the
grammer of the first (otherwise how could we call F_1 and F_2
colours?). . . . Whether a proposition entails another proposition must be clear from the grammar of the proposition and from
that alone (PG pp.255–6).

In a typescript reprinted in *Philosophical Grammar* and provi-
sionally dated 1932 by the editor, Wittgenstein criticises Carnap's
attempt to construct elementary propositions on the ground that
the idea 'rests on a false notion of logical analysis'. He also declares
that the *Tractatus* was wrong because of unclarity about such
things as 'a logical product is hidden in a sentence' and the belief
that logical analysis had to reveal what was hidden like chemical
and physical analysis.

The proposition 'this place is now red' . . . can be called an elementary proposition if this means that it is neither a truth-function of other propositions nor defined as such. . . . But from 'a is now red' there follows 'a is now not green' and so elementary propositions in this sense aren't independent of each other like the elementary propositions in the calculus I once described – a calculus to which, misled as I was by a false notion of reduction, I thought that the whole use of propositions must be reducible (PG pp.210–11).

The irreducibility of all propositions to truth-functions of elementary propositions increases their diversity both in terms of content and form. The question to whose answer the *Tractatus* was largely addressed, namely, ' "How is the general concept of proposition bounded?" must be countered with another: "Well, do we have a *single* concept of proposition?" ' (PG 69b p.112). This leads on to various attempts to explain the concept 'proposition' in the course of which Wittgenstein mentions one type of explanation which he rejects and to whose further examination he returns repeatedly in the *Investigations*. In clarifying the concept 'proposition' Wittgenstein makes clear that 'I am not concerned with a feeling accompanying the word "proposition".' From the many examples he considers later it is clear that he regarded attempts to explain propositions by reference to feelings accompanying their use as a comparable intrusion of psychological irrelevancies into grammar as he had done earlier with respect to logic. He maintained this attitude even with those propositions whose function seemed to be to describe feelings, such as ascriptions of pain. His remarks on our systems of sensation-expressing propositions have proved to be interesting and controversial and must engage our attention later. Meanwhile, after excluding feelings as the criteria which determine the concept 'proposition' he observes, 'The word "proposition" does not signify a sharply bounded concept. If we want to put a concept with sharp boundaries beside our use of this word, we are free to define it, just as we are free to narrow down the meaning of the primitive measure of length "a pace" to 75cm' (PG 69d p.113; cf. 73b p.117; 76b p.120). The earlier definition, 'a proposition is whatever can be true or false' that seemed to draw the sharp boundary around 'proposition' in fact only 'fixes the concept of proposition in a particular language system as what in

that system can be an argument of a truth-function'
(PG 79a p.123).

What now of the attempts in the *Tractatus* to specify the general
form of the proposition – remembering that in German 'Satz'
means not only proposition but sentence generally – as 'This is
how things stand'? (4.5). 'In the schema "This is how things
stand" the "how things stand" is really a handle for the truth
functions. "Things stand", then, is an expression from a notation
for truth-functions. An expression which shows us what part of
grammar comes into play here' (PG 80a, p.124). This schema as the
general form of propositions is defective in that it is both too
broad and too restrictive. It is too broad in that it admits into this
general form the propositions of arithmetic such as $2 + 2 = 4$. It is
too restrictive in that it supposes that all sentences of an assertoric
or descriptive kind are to be construed on a model based on a
calculus which is only a fragment of language.

In view of the multiplication of perplexing problems concerning
the connections between reality, thought and propositions proposed in the *Tractatus* it is appropriate that Wittgenstein should
write the epitaph for the propositional picture.

> What gives us the idea that there is a kind of agreement between
> thought and reality? – Instead of 'agreement' here one might say
> with a clear conscience 'pictorial character'. But is this pictorial
> character an agreement? In the *Tractatus Logico-Philosophicus* I
> said something like: it is an agreement of form. But that is an
> error. . . . Anything can be a picture of anything if we extend the
> concept of picture sufficiently (PG p.212; 113a p.163).

The key concepts of the *Tractatus*, 'proposition', 'thought', 'picture', 'pictorial character', 'agreement', 'logical form' and 'having
in common' dissolve into extended families of instances whose
complex grammars belie the simplicity of the thesis that propositions picture the world.

THOUGHT AND REALITY

The position of the *Tractatus* is that proposition, thought and
reality stand in line. The intermediate position of thought

required that it should be both the image of reality and the prototype of the propositional picture. This largely passive role assigned to thought was hardly an adequate explanation of the construction of the law-like forms of propositions used in physics. In addition, Russell's questions about thought and its constituents in Wittgenstein's system received answers that were as unsatisfactory as they were brief and, plainly, a more detailed treatment was called for. With the abandonment of propositional picturing as the only logical type of representational relationship between language and the world the simple linear link between thought, proposition and reality is broken. Furthermore, Wittgenstein came to see that the notion of a proposition's agreement or non-agreement with reality was problematic and over-simplified the place of a proposition within a system of propositions. The rejection of the logical independence of elementary propositions together with propositional monism implies that propositions form systems of differing logical types and, for any given system, it is the system, rather than its constituent propositions, that is laid up against reality. The place of thought in all this is something which calls for explication.

Surprisingly, however, Wittgenstein does not attempt a detailed explication of thought in any positive fashion, beyond repeating Frege's idea that the thought expressed by p is simply the sense of p (PG 65b p.106). Instead he offers a searching analysis of what others, notably phenomenalists and phenomenologists, have said about the connection between thought, language and the world. The purpose of this analysis is to exhibit the extent to which philosophers have misconceived the real functions of language.

One view which Wittgenstein examines recurrently, and consistently rejects, is the concept of thought as an imperfectly understood process in the as yet incomprehensible medium of the mind. A typical example is as follows:

It is a travesty of the truth to say 'Thinking is an activity of our mind, as writing is an activity of the hand'. (Love in the heart. The head and the heart as loci of the soul). . . . It is correct to say 'Thinking is a mental process' only if we also call seeing a written sentence or hearing a spoken one a mental process. In the sense, that is, in which pain is called a mental state. In that case the expression 'mental process' is intended to distinguish 'experience' from 'physical processes'. . . . On the other hand, of course, the expression 'mental process' suggests that we are concerned with imperfectly understood processes in an inaccessible sphere (PG 64c 65b p.106: cf. PR 230f, p.287; PG 93d p.141; *Zettel* 605–7).

Although Wittgenstein dismisses as 'a travesty of the truth' the popular but naïve tendency to identify thinking with an activity of the mind, his criticisms are not principally directed against the concept of thought as an amorphous condition in a cloudy and gaseous medium. This extremely vague and generalised concept only becomes seriously misleading when it is invoked in order to offer a philosophical account of the way that language functions. Amongst his specific concerns is 'the idea that you "imagine" the meaning of a word when you hear or read it'. Basically he regards this account of the meaning of a word is mistaken even though he concedes that 'the naïve theory of forming-an-image can't be utterly wrong' (PR 12a, b p.58). Some words may be said to conjure up vivid mental images and because of this we are inclined to generalise such cases and say that the dead signs are given life by these mental images which accompany their use. This is where Wittgenstein's genius for devising counter-examples is given full scope. If I say of a green object, 'that is not red', do I have two images before my mind and is my statement the result of a (mental) act of comparison of the images plus a further (mental) act of recognition that they are not the same? With this kind of explanation of meaning all difficulties are dealt with by the expedient of multiplying the mental processes involved. Any requests for verification that these processes actually occur are turned aside on the grounds of their inaccessibility and the intangibility of the mental medium. One of Wittgenstein's self-appointed tasks was to apply Occam's razor to this proliferation of mental entities. His philosophical interests in mental events, as opposed to psychological or physiological concerns, are emphasised clearly and repeatedly in the notes of John King and Desmond Lee of Wittgenstein's lectures at Cambridge between 1930–32.[14] 'Thought is a symbolic process, and thinking is interpreting a plan.' The physiological processes involved are of no interest to a philosophical investigation. Nor does it matter where the symbolic process takes place 'whether on paper or on a blackboard. It may involve images and these we think of as being "in the mind". This simile of "inside" or "outside" the mind is pernicious'. This picture is derived from the idea of thinking as something going on in the head, harmless enough, except when we forget the picture and go on using the language derived from it in philosophical contexts. An analogous example is to picture man's spirit as his breath, as in Hebrew thought, and where we retain the language derived from it but forget the picture. 'We can only safely use such language if we consciously remember the picture when we use it'[15] Much of our language about thought and thinking derives from the ghost-pictures invoked in writings about the Hebrew spirit, the Greek soul and the Cartesian ego. The resultant conceptual confusions that pervade philosophical discussion of thought are what Wittgenstein seeks to expose. In particular his concern is to demonstrate the consequences of these confusions on philosophical accounts of the nature and function of language.

> Language is not an indirect method of communication, to be contrasted with 'direct' thought-reading. Thought-reading could only take place through the interpretation of symbols and so would be on the same level as language. It would not get rid of the symbolic process. The idea of reading a thought more directly is derived from the idea that thought is a hidden process which it is the aim of the philosopher to penetrate. But there is no more direct way of reading thought than through language. Thought is not something hidden; it lies open to us. What we find out in philosophy is trivial; it does not teach us new facts, only science does that. But the proper synopsis of these trivialities is enormously difficult, and has immense importance. Philosophy is in fact the synopsis of trivialities.[16]

Even those mystics who would strenuously oppose the idea that thought is completely accessible through language and view language as an inadequate vehicle for expressing the inexpressable can only be judged by their utterances. According to Wittgenstein, both the metaphysician in search of transcendental facts and the positivist in search of new facts are engaged in a vacuous enterprise. Philosophy is nothing but the synopsis of trivialities through grammatical investigations. 'The meaning of a word is its place in the symbolism' not the thought or process or mental state hidden behind it. It is a fallacy 'to think that there are, as it were, two series, a thought series (ideas, images) and a word series, with some relation between them'.[17] To explain the meaning of a sign is not to transcend the symbol but to describe it; 'the meaning is part of the symbol. . . . A proposition cannot be significant except in a system of propositions'.[18] Wittgenstein again explicitly denies any interest 'in thought from a psychological point of view, in its conditions, causes and effects; we are interested in thought as a symbolic process. Thought is an activity which we perform by the expression of it and lasts as long as its expression'. This point is further illustrated by the use of colour words. 'The words "red" and "green" do not require the existence of red or green things in order to have meaning. My idea or image of red is not red.'[19]

Does the assimilation of thought with its linguistic expression resolve all the philosophical problems arising from an analysis of thought? Hardly! And it is clear from Wittgenstein's examination of counter-examples to this view that he did not rest content with this simplified account of thought and language. This is made clear in the notes of Alice Ambrose and Margaret Macdonald of Wittgenstein's lectures at Cambridge during 1932–1935. Wittgenstein is recorded as saying, 'The fact that two sentences express the same thought does not mean that there is a thing which is the thought, a gaseous being corresponding to the sentences. But we must not therefore conclude that the word "thought" as contrasted with "sentence" does not mean anything. The two words have different uses'.[20]

Supposing we accept the view that the elucidation of word-meanings involve the surrounding system of propositions rather than an appeal to mental imagery, are there not a number of important cases where some such appeal is required? In another comment on the use of colour words Wittgenstein is recorded as saying, 'The word "green" . . . must be connected by an explanation to a symbol in another language, e.g. the totally different language of memory-images. But we are still using language (even if not *words*).'[21] This discloses an important strand of Wittgenstein's argument. He is far from denying the existence of mental events like memory-images, but in so far as they are invoked to explain word-meanings they belong to language. The concept of wordless language calls for further examination but the significance of this suggestion must not be underestimated. Phenomenalists, like Russell and Moore under whose tutelage Wittgenstein was brought up, made a sharp logical distinction between mental events and language. Mental events are objects of experience and it is the function of language to describe them. The phenomenalist paradigm of language-function was that of object and designation, inner and outer, thought and words. It is this model that Wittgenstein rejects and the specific form of his rejection is the abolition of this distinction between mental events and language. Memory-images and the like belong to language. The phenomenalist conception of the depth-grammar of language is translated by Wittgenstein into the topology of language. What seemed to the former to stand in a vertical relationship, as it were, is represented by him as a horizontal relationship. 'The meaning of a word is not the object corresponding to it, but the grammatical rules which apply to it'.[22] Nevertheless, the analysis of colour words provided examples which, at least during his middle period, Wittgenstein analysed in a way that went beyond grammatical rules and invoked mental events.

> It might be thought that if a mental act accompanying hearing or saying a word cannot sum up the meaning of the word in the sense in which rules define it, the mental act loses its importance. But it has importance in that sometimes, e.g. in understanding the word 'red' it is essential to have an image before one, as when one is ordered to copy the particular red of this book. Here the word 'red' is not enough. In such a case the image plus the word will function as a complete symbol, beyond which we would need nothing else. Remember, however, that in many cases a private mental act, which livens up the symbol like a soul the body, is not necessary.[23]

Here again the memory-image is not something behind the word which inspires it with meaning; it is part of the symbol. The image plus the word constitutes the complete symbol. This is not to say that the memory-image of red is what is common to all uses of the word red and Wittgenstein's examination of the 'general idea' reveals that although sometimes there is 'something before our minds' there are a series of cases 'where there is no such thing'. What is true of the word 'red' is also true of the words 'good' and 'beautiful'. In all such cases 'there is only a number of overlapping resemblances'. 'Our concepts are enormous families with various resemblances.' Wittgenstein asserts that 'one of our main philosophical troubles' is due to the tendency to look for the common element or essence underlying all instances of concept-words. In this respect he is particularly critical of the Socratic theory of knowledge contained in the *Theaetetus* because here knowledge is identified with the determination of common essences which simply are not there.[24]

Wittgenstein recurrently considers intention where it seems that the intention expressed by p must invoke a mental picture or image of p without which the intention itself could not exist, nor could we recognise the realisation of p when it occurred. Wittgenstein's reply to this is that any picture can be variously interpreted:

> hence this picture too in its turn stands isolated. When one has the picture in view by itself it is suddenly dead, and it is as if something had been taken away from it, which had given it life before. It is not a thought, not an intention; whatever accompaniments we imagine for it, articulate or inarticulate processes, or any feeling whatsoever, it remains isolated, it does not point outside itself to a reality beyond.

Wittgenstein's interlocutor objects here; 'it is not the picture that intends, but we who use it to intend'.

> But if this intending, this meaning, is something that is done with the picture, then I cannot see why that has to involve a human being. The process of digestion can also be studied as a chemical process, independently of whether it takes place in a living being. We want to say 'meaning is surely essentially a mental process, a process of consciousness and life, not of dead matter'. But what will give such a thing the specific character of what goes on? – so long as we speak of it as a process. And now it seems to us as if intending could not be any process at all, of any kind whatever. For what we are dissatisfied with here is the grammar of *process*, not the specific kind of process. It could be said: we should call any process 'dead' in this sense (PG 100a p.148).

Amongst the specific points Wittgenstein makes is that the grammar of 'physical process' includes extension in time, location in space, observation, verification, causal connection and the like. How much of this grammar carries over to the related concept 'mental process' where the unexplored process occurs unobserved in the ethereal medium of the mind? The mental process turns out to be a hypothetical construction with a fictitious function in an imaginary location. But something goes on in the head and if the experiences of imagining, thinking, expecting, intending, wishing, meaning and the like which we really do have are not processes in the mind then they must at least correspond with *brain* processes. Since brain surgery can be carried out under local anaesthesia then, with advanced knowledge, it will surely be possible for the neuro-surgeon to record and interpret nerve impulses such that he will be able to say, 'now the patient is imagining, and now understanding and now intending something'. Wittgenstein rejected this non-mentalist explanation of thought in terms of brain-processes in some interesting remarks in *Zettel* in which he dismisses as prejudice this attempt at psychophysical parallelism.

> No supposition seems to me more natural than that there is no process in the brain correlated with associating or with thinking; so that it would be impossible to read off thought-processes from brain-processes. I mean this: if I talk or write there is, I assume, a system of impulses going out from my brain and correlated with my spoken or written thoughts. But why should the *system* continue further in the direction of the centre? . . . It is thus perfectly possible that certain psychological phenomena *cannot* be investigated physiologically, because physiologically nothing corresponds to them. (Zettel pp.608–9).

Whatever the nature of the connection between thinking and brain processes may be, the fact remains that the criteria for the correct usage of 'thinking' in various systems of propositions must be located in the grammar of those systems and not in an as yet unobserved inner process. What may be found to accompany thought is not the meaning of the word 'thought' anymore than the sensation of mind-reeling that accompanies certain uses of the word 'infinite' may be said to be its meaning.

Wittgenstein makes two points with respect to intention which are crucial for an understanding of the development of his later views on the way language actually functions. The first is; 'If you exclude the element of intention from language, its whole function then collapses.' Secondly; 'What is essential to intention is the picture, the picture of what is intended' (PR 20c, 21a p.63). The first comment marks the end of the formalist view of language function in the *Tractatus*. Language is not reducible to a single type of propositional form with a fixed logical structure exhibiting a definite representational relation to reality. Propositions, even elementary ones, are as multifarious in type as the functions they are designed to serve and what gives them life is their use. If that is the case, then writ large in the grammar of our systems of propositions must be intention. 'You could say that language is like a control room operated with a particular *intention* or built for a particular purpose' (PR 31a p.69). In the light of Wittgenstein's rejection of the mind model as an explanation of the meanings of words like intention, if I intend that p, in what sense does p already exist in the intention and by what kind of act or process do I recognise the occurrence or fulfilment of p? At this comparatively early stage in the development of the later philosophy Wittgenstein concedes that the essential element in intention is some kind of picture of what is intended. But why should the picture of p be different from the proposition 'p' and why should a separate act or process be invoked to account for the recognition of the realisation of p? Our analysis has gone seriously wrong if we suppose that intention has the following components; the proposition 'p', the picture of p, the recognition of the occurrence of p as that which was intended by 'p'. It is over the analysis of intention in particular and thought in general that again the difference between Russell and Wittgenstein is crucial. Wittgenstein writes: 'For me, there are only two things involved in the fact that a thought is true, i.e. the thought and the fact; whereas for Russell there are three, i.e. thought, fact and a third event which, if it occurs, is just recognition. This third event, a sort of satisfaction of hunger . . . could, for example, be a feeling of pleasure' (PR 21b p.63).

Wittgenstein's objection to this is that if this recognition were an event independent of and external to the thought p, like a feeling of satisfaction, for example, then the event is not uniquely determined by the truth of or the realisation of p. Many other things may induce such a feeling which are logically unconnected with p. Wittgenstein remarks; 'My theory is completely expressed in the fact that the state of affairs satisfying the expectation of p is represented by the proposition p. And so, not by the description of a *totally* different event' (PR 25a p.66). A little later occurs the interesting comment:

I only use the terms the expectation, thought, wish, etc., that p will be the case, for processes having the mlutiplicity that finds expression in *p*, and thus only if they are articulated. But in that case they are what I call the interpretation of signs. I only call an *articulated* process a thought: you could therefore say 'only what has an articulated expression'. (Salivation – no matter how precisely measured – is *not* what I call expecting.) (PR 32a pp.69–70).

In what sense then does the intention expressed by p contain a picture of p and where is this picture located?

In so far as the meaning of words becomes clear in the fulfilment of an expectation, in the satisfaction of a wish, in the carrying out of an order etc., it already shows itself when we put the expectation into language. It is therefore completely determined in the grammar, in what could be foreseen and spoken of already before the occurrence of the event (PG 45d p.88).

In short, the picture of p is not a mental image or shadow of p, nor is it a feeling accompanying its use; it is nothing but the grammar of p. The central error of phenomenalism and phenomenology is to identify the symptoms of expectation, intention, wishing etc. with their meanings and consequently to embark on a hypothetical psychological analysis instead of a grammatical investigation. 'The symptoms of expectation are not the expression of expectation' (PG 91e p.138). A further consequence of this psychological analysis is that its practitioners feel compelled to invent, in addition to a series of words which already have sense, 'another series of mental elements running parallel. That simply duplicates language with something else of the same kind' (PG 104a p.152). Another consequence of this is that phenomenalists and phenomenologists represent reality in terms of hypothetical processes in a fictitious medium and so misconceive the directness of the connection between our systems of propositions and the world. According to this view the locus of language is thought in the form of sense impressions, feelings and internal reflections which give life and meaning to language. For Wittgenstein the locus of thought is language and the mysteriousness of thought arises 'because we misunderstand its grammar and feel the lack of a tangible substance to correspond to the substantive' (PG 66f pp.108–9). This is the classic case of Ryle's category mistake.

The *Philosophical Grammar* is particularly rich in comments on thought and language which are interesting in their own right and which also throw light on some of the most difficult passages to be found in the *Philosophical Investigations*. The following selection of remarks speak for themselves.

' "Thought" sometimes means a particular mental process which may accompany the utterance of a sentence and sometimes the sentence itself in the system of language' (PG 13c p.51).

An explanation of the operation of language as a psychophysical mechanism is of no interest to us. Such an explanation itself uses language to describe phenomena (association, memory etc); it is itself a linguistic act and stands outside the calculus: but we need an explanation which is *part of the calculus* (PG 33b p.70).

Plainly, Wittgenstein's detestation of Russell's hierarchies of logical types extends to Tarski's hierarchies of metalanguages.

We say that we understand (the) meaning (of a word) when we know its use, but we've also said that the word 'know' doesn't denote a state of consciousness. That is: the grammar of the word 'know' isn't the grammar of a 'state of consciousness', but something different. And there is only one way to learn it; to watch how the word is used in practice (PG 34a p.71).

We speak of understanding (a process of understanding, and also a state of understanding) and also of certain processes which are criteria for this understanding. We are inclined to call understanding a mental process or a state of mind. This characterises it as a *hypothetical* process etc., or rather as a process (or state) in the sense of a hypothesis. That is we banish the word 'understanding' to a particular region of grammar (PG 41a p.82).

We may say 'Thinking is operating with symbols'. But 'thinking' is a fluid concept, and what 'operating with symbols' is must be looked at separately in each individual case. I might also say 'Thinking is operating with language' but 'language' is a fluid concept (PG 65a p.106).

The idea that one language in contrast to others has a word order which corresponds to the order of thinking arises from the notion that thought is an essentially different process going on independently of the expression of the thoughts (PG 66a p.107).

One imagines the meaning as something which *comes before* our minds when we hear a word. What comes before our minds when we hear a word is certainly something characteristic of the meaning. But what comes before any mind is an example, an application of the word. And this coming to mind doesn't really consist in a particular image's being present whenever I utter or hear the word, but in (the) fact that when I'm asked the meaning of the word, applications of the word *occur* to me (PG 75a pp.118–19).

The sense of a proposition (or a thought) isn't anything spiritual; it's what is given as an answer to a request for an explanation of the sense. . . . The sense of a proposition is not a soul. . . . It is only in a language that something is a proposition. To understand a proposition is to understand a language (PG 84c, d p.131).

What I really want to say is this: the wish that he should come is the wish that really *he* should really *come*. If a further explanation of this assurance is wanted, I would go on to say 'and by "he" I mean that man there, and by "come" I mean doing this . . .'. But these are just grammatical explanations, explanations which *create* language. It is in *language* that it's all done (PG 9lb, c p.143).

If we imagine the expression of a wish as the wish, it is rather as if we were led by a train of thought to imagine something like a network of lines spread over the earth, and living beings who moved only along the lines. But now someone will say: even if the *expression* of the wish is the wish, still the whole of language isn't present during this expression, yet surely the wish is! So how does language help? Well, it just isn't necessary that anything should be *present* except the expression. You might as it were locate (look up) all of the connections in the grammar of language. There you can see the whole network to which the sentence belongs (PG 101b, c, 102a p.149).

We ask: 'Does the hand above a table wish (that it should be so much higher)?' Does anything, spiritual or material, that we might add, wish? Is there any such situation or process that really contains what is wished? – And what is our paradigm of such containing? Isn't it our language? Where are we to find what makes the wish *this* wish though it's only a wish? Nowhere but in the expressed wish (PG 102f p.150).

'I arrive in Vienna on the 24th of December!' They aren't mere words! Of course not; when I read them various things happen inside me in addition to the perception of the words: may be I feel joy, I have images, and so on – But I don't just mean that various more or less inessential concomitant phenomena occur in conjunction with the sentence; I mean that the sentence has a definite sense and I perceive it. But then what is this definite sense? Well, that this particular person, whom I know, arrives at such and such a place etc. Precisely: when you are giving the sense, you are moving around in the grammatical background of the sentence. You're looking at the various transformations and consequences of the sentence as laid out in advance; and so they are, in so far as they are embodied in a grammar. (You are simply looking at the sentence as a move in a given game.) (PG 104d p.153).

When I think in language, there aren't meanings going through my mind in addition to the verbal expressions; the language is itself the vehicle of thought (PG 112a p.161).

'The proposition determines in advance what will make it true'. Certainly, the proposition 'p' determines that p must be the case in order to make it true; and that means: (the proposition p) = (the proposition that the fact p makes true). And the statement that the wish for it to be the case that p is satisfied by the event p, merely enunciates a rule for signs: (the wish for it to be the case that p) = (the wish that is satisfied by the event p). Like everything metaphysical the harmony between thought and reality is to be found in the grammar of the language (PG 112d pp.161–2).

If it is grammar that provides the connections which render lines of thought an intelligible concept then it is misconceptions about grammar which give rise to the erroneous analyses of thought found in phenomenalism and phenomenology. Wittgentein makes this general criticism more specific when he points out that

> all our forms of speech are taken from ordinary, physical language and cannot be used in epistemology or phenomenology without casting a distorting light on their objects. The very expression 'I can perceive x' is itself taken from the idioms of physics, and x ought to be a physical object – e.g., a body – here. Things have already gone wrong if this expression is used in phenomenology, where x must refer to a datum. For then 'I' and 'perceive' also cannot have their previous senses (PR 57b, c p.88).

One of Wittgenstein's most celebrated examples arises from precisely this kind of error, namely, construing the grammar of expressions like 'I have toothache' as though it were the same as the grammar of expressions like 'I have money'. Of the latter expression, but not the former, it makes sense to ask questions about ownership and what the differences are between my money and other people's money. In the case of sensations like toothache the notion of ownership, which is part of the grammar of material possessions, simply has no application. It makes no sense in speaking of sense data to say either that someone else does or does not have them. Similarly, it is also 'senseless to say that *I*, as opposed to someone else, have them' (PR 61a p.90). Thus, the expression 'I feel his pain' is nonsense for precisely the reasons that 'I feel my pain' is nonsense (cf. PR 65a, 66b pp.94, 95).

A comparable error arising from an erroneous interchange of grammars occurs with the expressions "A man makes his appearance" and "an event makes its appearance". The persuasiveness of this comparison leads us to think of an event as standing at the door of reality as a man may stand at the door of a room (PG 90d p.137). It is also a misunderstanding of grammar that leads us to suppose 'that the endless series of cardinal numbers is somehow before the mind's eye whenever we use that expression significantly' (PG 106a p.155)).

Given that language is the vehicle of thought how does Wittgenstein now view the connection between thought and reality? In the *Tractatus*, where it was also the case that the thought expressed by p was roughly equivalent to the sense of p, this connection was exhibited by the agreement or non-agreement of p with reality.

Quite apart from the fact that the notion of agreement and non-agreement with reality becomes increasingly complex as the nature of representation through picturing is broadened, there is the additional complication of the relation of p with the propositions in the same system. What has changed in the middle period of Wittgenstein's development is not the essential character of thought but the shift from propositional monism to the recognition of the multiplicity of propositional forms which comprise systems of propositions. What gives p the type of structure it has is not its relationship to reality but its relationship to other propositions in the same system, i.e. its grammar. The relation of p to the system is likened by Wittgenstein to that between a particular mark on a yardstick and the system of marks that enable us to use it for purposes of measurement. It is the yardstick as *a system of measurement* that compares with reality rather than individual marks on the yardstick. For the marks or signs to link up with the world the yardstick and the object to be measured must belong to the same space. Applying this analogy Wittgenstein writes:

> What is the connection between sign and world? Could I look for something unless the space were there to look for it in? Where does the sign link up with the world? To look for something is, surely, an expression of expectation. In other words: How you search in one way or another expresses what you expect. Thus the idea would be: what expectation has in common with reality is that it refers to another point in the *same* space' (PR 32b p.70).

This spatial analogy is repeatedly invoked and particularly for various examples of expectation. For example, the expectation of p is like the hollow shape of a body in space and its occurrence is like the solid shape filling it (PR 34a p.71). Putting this another way, 'In expecting the part corresponding to searching in a space is the directing of one's attention'. The fact that with expectation we always know it to be expectation 'shows that expectation is immediately connected with reality'. Another reason for this is that in anticipating an event our expectation constructs a model of it, but this model 'must be essentially related to the world we live in', independently of its truth or falsity, as a condition of sense. Thus the presents reality which forms the ingredients as it were of our expectations is the guarantor of their direct connection with reality.

For of course you couldn't say that the future the expectation speaks of – I mean the concept of the future – was also only a surrogate for the real future. For I await in just as real a sense as I wait. . . . That is to say the yardstick of language must be applied at the point which is present and then points out beyond it – roughly speaking, in the direction of the expectation (PR 34c, 35a, b pp.71–2).

An even more interesting application of this analogy is the following:

If I want to tell someone what colour some material is to be I send him a sample, and obviously this sample belongs to language; and equally the memory or image of a colour that I conjure by a word belongs to language. The memory and the reality must be in *one* space. I could also say: the image and the reality are in *one* space (PR 38a, b p.73).

Or as he puts it a little later: 'I will count any fact whose obtaining is a presupposition of a proposition's making sense, as belonging to language' (PR 45a p.78).

How useful is this new version of the spatial analogy? Wittgenstein himself concedes that whilst is is easy to see that a yardstick and the object to be measured must be in the same space it sounds absurd to say that words must be in the same space as an object whose length is described in words or in the same space as a colour (PR 45b pp.78–9). At this point he reintroduces the idea of a system of co-ordinates to accompany the use of colour words. Even though this introduces into language an element which it doesn't normally use it does show the connection between language and reality (PR 46a p.79). Whatever the merits of a co-ordinate system as part of a calculus which we construct this does not elucidate the way we successfully use colour words in ordinary language and it is this that is Wittgenstein's major preoccupation.

In the more mature observations to be found in *Philosophical Grammar* Wittgenstein does not pursue the spatial analogy in quite the same detail but concentrates on more direct elucidations of the grammar of systems of propositions. He analyses reading in a way that breaks the dependence of the concept on an internal operation and then comments:

Every such more or less behaviourist account leaves one with the feeling that it is crude and heavy handed; but this is misleading; we are tempted to look for a 'better' account, but there isn't one. One is as good as the other and in each case what represents is the *system* in which a sign is used. ('Representation is dynamic, not static') (PG 60b p.100).

The point is that what the system represents is reality and what obscures this point is the idea that the objects of thought are in the mind or in the head or even in our thoughts (PG 96a p.143). Such a picture really does get between reality and its representation in language and diverts our attention away from the directness of the connection between systems of propositions and the world. 'It is as a calculus that thinking has an interest for us; not as an activity of the human imagination. It is the *calculus* of thought that connects with extra-mental reality' (PG 111a, b p.160).

What Wittgenstein is seeking to reveal is that in the explication of the logic of concepts there is no place for the psychological accompaniments of concept-words, i.e. mental events, states or processes; such explication is grammatical. The most strikingly original part of Wittgenstein's argument is the maintenance of this position in the analysis of such psychological verbs as thinking, wishing, intending, expecting, understanding, hoping and the like. Even with these concepts it is their grammar rather than mental experiences associated with them that gives their meanings. Those philosophers who tend to dismiss this kind of enquiry as linguistic in a pejorative sense have failed to grasp the devastating consequences of the later Wittgenstein's investigations on empiricist theories of knowledge based on sense-data analysis. Wittgenstein's impact on a great deal of 20th century epistemology can hardly be exaggerated – and this is to single out only one of his achievements.

Given that grammar is the bed-rock at which the spade of enquiry turns what becomes of reality now? To what extent, if at all, are the rules of grammar shaped by reality? To this important question we must return.

5

From Pictures to Grammar

THE BLUE AND BROWN BOOKS

Wittgenstein's preliminary studies for the *Investigations* are known as the *Blue and Brown Books* and consist of notes of lectures delivered in Cambridge between 1933 and 1935. Their interest lies in the explicit repudiation of some of the main contentions of the *Tractatus* and the exploration of a new approach to language that is refined and more carefully formulated in the *Investigations*. As aids to the interpretation of the *Investigations* they are frequently invaluable and for the historian of philosophy they throw light on the stages in the development of his thought. From an historical point of view the late 1920's and early 1930s mark a turning point in the development of modern philosophy. Not only was this the period which saw the beginnings of Wittgenstein's later philosophy but in 1932 Gilbert Ryle published an astonishingly seminal paper on what would now be called linguistic analysis.[1] This parallelism in thought between Wittgenstein and Ryle is comparable to that between Leibniz and Newton with respect to the infinitesimal calculus – though happily, the more recent case has been free from the acrimonious controversy that marred the relations between Leibniz and Newton. The new directions of Wittgenstein's thought are already apparent from those notes which survive and which are dated before the publication of Ryle's paper. There is no evidence to suggest that Ryle was aware of these new directions and, indeed, his references to Wittgenstein in the paper itself are to the *Tractatus*. To what extent, if at all, Wittgenstein might have derived some encouragement and reinforcement of his views from Ryle's paper it is not possible to say from the written evidence available.

The most cursory examination of the *Blue and Brown Books* reveals that problems of language and the representation of reality are treated from a standpoint quite different from the *Tractatus*. The opening sentence of the *Blue Book* delineates the central

126

problem with which both books are concerned, namely, 'what is the meaning of a word?'. Any feeling that we are on familiar ground here is quickly dispelled by the seemingly unphilosophical treatment which the question receives. Instead of an attempt to distil the essence of meaning from a word or to isolate the sense that distinguishes a living symbol from a dead sign we are asked to consider what counts in practice as an explanation of meaning? The question is treated analogously with the way that the question 'what is length?' is dealt with by looking at how we actually measure length. That ostensive definition unambiguously bestows meaning on a word by its indication of the object designated by the word and that this avoids the circularity of verbal definitions is a philosophical gambit which Wittgenstein declines. Ostensive definitions can be misunderstood since the act of pointing and naming does not uniquely determine which property or quality of the object indicated is being referred to. To say, 'this is x' or, 'this is called x' does not discriminate between an object's name, colour, shape, texture, hardness and etc., unless we provide additional information, and this presupposes the existence of a language in which this information can be conveyed. But ostensive definition is supposed to be the way in which the *foundations* of language are laid by correlating words and objects. Now it seems that these correlations can only be understood if we use langauge to make them precise, e.g.; 'By x I did not mean . . . but I meant the property . . .'. At this point the suspicion of circularity returns.

Similarly, the *Brown Book* begins with the suggestion attributed to Augustine, although it was already ancient in his day, that we acquire our mastery of language by first learning the names of things. Wittgenstein compares this account with the workings of a simplified model language where such name–object correlations seem credible and then considers more sophisticated forms of language where it does not.

Clearly, the task that Wittgenstein has set himself is that of placing the extensive set of problems concerned with meaning in language, together with what philosophers – including himself – have said about them, in the context of our actual employments of words in a great diversity of different situations. As a method of philosophy this is a strikingly different approach to these problems than that found in the *Tractatus* or any other work of philosophy traditionally reckoned as such. Frege and the early

Wittgenstein, for example, conceived of signs as acquiring life when they were combined in propositions with sense. Clarity of meaning was to be achieved by the isolation of this sense and its expression in an unambiguous logical symbolism that revealed the essence of meaning. To this the later Wittgenstein remarks; 'If we had to name anything which is the life of the sign, we shall have to say that it was its use' (BB p.4e). Analysis has given way to grammatical investigation.

One of the influential ideas which Wittgenstein examines from the vantage of this new perspective is that of the proposition as a picture. This investigation covers two quite different accounts of the proposition as a picture. The first of these is that made familiar in the *Tractatus* of the logical structure of the proposition as picturing the structure of reality. The second account which may be attributed to a phenomenalist thesis of epistemology, is that of the proposition as picturing mental percepts, states and processes. With regard to the first account of the proposition as a picture, namely, his own earlier view, he attributes its origin to a linguistic confusion due to a misconstruction of such substantives as 'objects of thought' and 'fact' and a failure to distinguish between different meanings of the work 'exist'. 'Talking of the fact as a "complex of objects"' springs from this confusion (cf. *Tractatus Logico-Philosophicus*)' (BB p.31d). What stems from such misconstructions is the inclination to construe the object of thought not as the fact itself but as the shadow of the fact and then to give names like 'proposition' and 'sense of the sentence' to this shadow. The proposition as a picture of reality is rendered most credible by the selection of examples in which the picture resembles the fact represented by it. However, what destroys the persuasiveness of the examples in which similarity between the elements of the proposition and the elements of reality is the form of representation adopted is the recognition of the multiplicity of our methods of projection.

If we keep in mind the possibility of a picture which, though correct, has no similarity with its objects, the interpolation of a shadow between the sentence and reality loses all point. For now the sentence itself can serve as such a shadow. The sentence is just such a picture, which hasn't the slightest similarity with what it represents (BB p.37c).

Wittgenstein has now appreciated the implications of his admission in the *Tractatus* of the variety of our methods of representation and that similarity is a sufficient but not a necessary condition of picturing. To realise that the concept of the proposition as detailed in the *Tractatus* is an irrelevant interpolation between sentences and reality is not simply a repudiation of propositions but a rehabilitation of sentences. If the picturing relation is governed by representational conventions then sentences too are pictures and there is no need of propositions to underwrite them. In that case the connection between reality and language is not through the intermediary of propositions but, as it were, directly through sentences. This must not be taken to mean that each descriptive sentence is laid up against reality but rather that sentences form systems, or language-games, which represent reality. Thus to determine the sense in which a sentence is a picture of reality requires that we know its place in the language-game, i.e. its grammar, and that we know the representational conventions that link the language-game to reality.

It has been made apparent in the last section of this book that Wittgenstein strongly resists the idea of a proposition as a picture of mental activities and much of the *Blue and Brown Books* are devoted to an examination of this idea.

> In fact one may say that what in these investigations we were concerned with was the grammar of those words which describe what are called 'mental activities': seeing, hearing, feeling, etc. And this comes to the same as saying that we are concerned with the grammar of 'phrases describing sense data' (BB p.70a).

As has been noted, he sets his face against the concept of meaning which equates it with mysterious mental processes.

> Let's not imagine the meaning as an occult connection the mind makes between a word and a thing, and that this connection *contains* the whole usage of a word as the seed might be said to contain the tree (BB pp.73–4).

I will not repeat what has been written in the last section, although the discussion needs to be resumed later in the light of the mature comments in the *Investigations* and some of the posthumously published notes written towards the end of his life. In this respect it is worth recalling that he gave up the attempt to revise the *Brown Book* as 'worthless' and instead began working on what we now know as Part I of the *Investigations* (cf. BB Preface pp.vii–viii). Although it will be convenient to refer back to the *Blue and Brown Books* for purposes of comparison with and sometimes illumination of the later work these notes remain preliminary investigations only. Their most important use is as a source of information on the new methods of philosophy that Wittgenstein was developing.

What comes out clearly in this connection is that the objective of these new methods was to provide a cure rather than a solution for philosophical problems. The seemingly jaundiced view of philosophy characteristic of the later Wittgenstein in part reflects his dissatisfaction with the work of Frege and Russell but, more particularly, is inspired by an increasing awareness of his own errors in the *Tractatus*. The therapy that he now proposes includes the following: performing philological substitutions in which certain misleading forms of expression are replaced by others having an equivalent use but in which the misleading feature is absent (BB p.32a); appealing to such considerations as how we learned the meanings of words (BB p.10b), the study of model language-games (BB pp.67c–68a), the invention of new uses for words (BB p.28c), and the carrying out of linguistic experiments (BB p.42b). These investigative techniques are to be applied to a variety of examples including the relation of language to mental activities; the possibility of private experience (BB p.16b); the grammar of 'wishing', 'thinking', 'understanding' and 'meaning' (BB pp.6e, 16a, 19c); illustrations of the actual employment of 'to know', 'to expect' and 'to long for' (BB pp.23a, 30c); and the criteria for personal identity (BB pp.61ff). The point of this kind of linguistic analysis is to illustrate that the meanings of words may be differentiated with respect to their uses and to dispel the illusion that families of word-uses possess a single common feature that can be identified as the meaning of the word. Implicit in such an enterprise is the fact that such analyses do not lead to conclusions of the sort that we would normally expect from a work of philosophy. The therapy that Wittgenstein proposes as the cure for philosophy is that of showing how philosophical puzzlement may be dissolved by scrutinizing the forms of expression in language from which such puzzles arise in the hope that others may learn how to shift for themselves when philosophical bewilderment supervenes. His advice to his readers is this:

> If you are puzzled about the nature of thought, belief, knowledge and the like, substitute for the thought the expression of the thought, etc. The difficulty which lies in this substitution, and at the same time the whole point of it, is this: the expression of belief, thought, etc., is just a sentence – and the sentence has sense only as a member of a system of language; as one expression within a calculus (BB p.42a).

Once we appreciate the way in which our expressions of thought, belief and knowledge actually perform their office within a system of language then the compulsion to identify mysterious mental objects called 'thoughts', 'beliefs' and 'sense-data' is exorcised. Wittgenstein's concern is to bring language down to earth, not to reveal the essential nature of thought, belief and knowledge. Nor is his concern to show that certain forms of our expression are improper in their relation to the facts; that we ought not to say *this* but *that*. This is illustrated by his treatment of metaphysical propositions. He does not rule them out as meaningless because they are not empirically verifiable. Instead, he tries to show that they may be disguised statements about the grammar of a system of sentences and we are simply misled by 'the outward similarity between a metaphysical proposition and an experiential one' (BB p.55c). Another declared aim, which has an autobiographical component, is to remove the kind of bias 'which forces us to think that the facts *must* conform to certain pictures embedded in our language' (BB p.43c). The error here is to treat such pictures as pictures *of* reality when what we have done is to project on to the world certain features of our grammar.

Wittgenstein illustrates what he now sees the tasks of philosophy to be with an analogy concerning the arrangement of books in some sort of sequence in a library. Some of the greatest achievements in philosophy compare with taking up some books which appear to belong together and putting them on different shelves, 'nothing more being final about their positions than that they no longer lie side by side. . . . The difficulty in philosophy is to say no more then we know. E.g. to see that when we have put two books together in their right order we have not thereby put them in their final places' (BB pp.44d–45a).

In stark contrast with the *Tractatus*, which at the time of its publication he believed was the final solution of the problems of philosophy, the later philosophy makes no such claim. It would be wrong to draw the conclusion from the absence of philosophical theses in the later philosophy that Wittgenstein did not think that his investigations had no consequences. He certainly thought that his new methods led to the abolition of a great deal of traditional philosophy, even though he was at pains to deny that his work provided a final placement for things. The absence of such definite conclusions have led some interpreters of Wittgenstein to suppose that, because of this, criticism is disarmed. If there are no theses advanced how can there be any counter-theses? It is certainly true that the absence of definite theses, the openendedness of much of the discussion, the precise role of Wittgenstein's interlocutor and a literary style reminiscent of a policeman's notebook all conspire together to make interpretation and therefore criticism a task of great difficulty. This is not at all the same as accepting at face value the claim that Wittgenstein tells us only what we already know and that his investigations leave everything unchanged. The future development of philosophy in this century may well depend on calling this claim in question.

To what extent, if at all, is it appropriate to call the methods of the later philosophy empirical? In sharp contrast with the a priori logical structures of the *Tractatus* the later philosophy scrutinizes the applications of words in specific situations, appeals to the functions of natural or ordinary language, considers learning processes, proposes linguistic reconstructions and replacements and suggests experiments of various sorts. This represents an umistakeable shift towards a more empirical approach to language, but this change must not be exaggerated. Wittgenstein is not sketching a programme for the scientific study of language and his methods are not to be confused with those of science. He makes this explicit in examining what he calls 'our craving for generality' which arises from a misplaced preoccupation on the part of philosophers with the method of science.

Philosophers constantly see the method of science before their eyes, and are irresistably tempted to ask and answer questions in the way science does. This tendency is the real source of metaphysics and leads the philosopher into complete darkness. I want to say here that it can never be our job to reduce anything to anything, or to explain anything. Philosophy really is 'purely descriptive'. (Think of such questions as 'Are there sense-data?' and ask: What method is there of determining this? Introspection?)' (BB p.18c).

As a preparation for an understanding of what Wittgenstein thought philosophy was, we must first understand what he thought it was not. For example, the mistaken assimilation of philosophy with science has generated a host of mistakes and in particular to a tendency to construe expressions of sensations as descriptions of entities and to postulate the existence of 'thoughts', 'wishes', 'beliefs' and 'meanings'. The puzzlement that produces this situation is not that of the scientist who is troubled by the coarseness and naïvety of common-sense views. It arises out of a discomfiture or mental cramp induced by certain features of our notation (BB p.59a). Thus the asymmetry of the grammar of our temporal expressions with respect to an origin corresponding with 'now' inclines us to treat propositions about the future as not really propositions at all. The confusion is compounded if we regard this discovery as a kind of scientific statement about the nature of the future (BB p.109b). It is such pseudo-scientific methods applied to philosophy that led philosophers to search for and even identify a common essence of meaning of a word – the word 'good', for example – when an examination of concrete instances of its use would have prevented this and revealed the family of different meanings of the word. The search for essences was misconceived in that such essences are grammatical chimera and philosophers were looking in the wrong direction entirely. Instead of looking at reality they should have looked at language. The obsessional quest for the 'essence', or 'real nature', or 'definition' of knowledge led Socrates to dismiss as irrelevant, even for the purpose of a preliminary investigation, the enumeration of cases of knowledge (BB p.20a). 'We said that it was a way of examining the grammar (the use) of the word "to know", to ask ourselves what, in the particular case we are examining, we should call "getting to know". There is a temptation to think this question is only vaguely relevant, if relevant at all, to the question: 'What is the meaning of the word' to know'?' We seem to be on a side-track when we ask the question 'what is it like in this case' 'to get to know'?' But this question really is a question concerning the grammar of the word 'to know' and this becomes clearer if we put it in the form: 'What do we *call* 'getting to know'?' It is part of the grammar of the word 'chair' that *this* is what we call 'to sit on a chair', and it is part of the grammar of the word 'meaning' that *this* is what we call 'explanation of a meaning . . .' (BB pp.23d–24a).

The results of such investigations are not analogous to discoveries in the way that the demonstration of the existence of electrons or the phenomenon of radioactivity were discoveries. Philosophical problems are not solved by revealing entities and processes hidden from ordinary sight but rather are they dissolved by substituting one form of expression for another and considering those situations in which they are, and those in which they are not, at home. Clearly, there is a sense in which these are empirical exercises but to avoid the confusion of the methods of linguistic analysis with the methods of science it is best to describe them as Wittgenstein does as grammatical investigations.

The concept of grammar in the *Blue and Brown Books* is not restricted to a study of the traditional inflexional forms of language and the rules for their correct syntactical employment. The features of linguistic expressions in which Wittgenstein is interested are only marginally determined by the rules of grammar which are of concern to the grammarian and which we learn as children. What he means by grammar here is elucidated by a consideration of the circumstances in which words are used. This is brought out in the passage quoted above and one in the *Brown Book* where the word 'grammar' is followed by the parenthesis '(the use)' (BB pp.23d, 135c). Elsewhere he draws a distinction between syntactical and grammatical similarity when, for example, he points to the differences in grammar between statements about sense-data and statements about physical objects in spite of their outward or formal or syntactical similarity. Ignoring this distinction may mislead us into supposing that sense-data are 'new elements of the structure of the world, as though to say "I believe that there are sense-data" were similar to saying "I believe that matter consists of electrons"' (BB p.70c). When he wants to refer to the forms of our linguistic expressions he also uses on occasions the word 'symbolism' and writes of our being unable to 'rid ourselves of the implications of our symbolism' when we are misled by the outward similarities of such expressions as 'where does he go to when he goes out', and, 'where does the light go to when it goes out'? Plainly, spatial movement is a feature of the grammar of the first expression but not of the second. In such cases 'we are led into puzzlement by an analogy which irresistably drags us on' (BB p.108d). The difference in grammar between 'A has a gold tooth' and 'A has toothache' is obscured by the common sentence-form 'A has x'; it is this common form that prevents us seeing that they are not used analogously (BB p.53c). The place of ownership in the grammar of 'toothache' is the subject of a protracted examination by Wittgenstein. With respect to the *Tractatus*, propositional monism not only failed to elucidate sentences having the same form but further obscured their different grammars.

It is in connection with grammar that Wittgenstein devises a new picture analogy. Frequently, the grammar of certain linguistic expressions is associated with particular pictures (including, but not confined to, visual images) that are appropriate for some uses of the expressions but misleading for others. The picture of the mind as an epistemological container is appropriate and harmless when we talk of having or keeping things in mind but misleads us if we then try to locate the mind inside the head. He deals with a number of examples where 'the grammar of a word seems to suggest the "necessity" of a certain intermediary step, although in fact the word is used in cases in which there is no such intermediary step. Thus we are inclined to say: "A man *must* understand an order before he obeys it." "He must know where his pain is before he can point to it", "He must know the tune before he can sing it" and such like' (BB p.130e). This inclination arises from a picture which is suggested by the grammar of descriptions of physical processes. Such a picture is quite appropriate for the mechanical steps involved in a description of the following kind; the pedal moves the lever which rotates the arm that closes the valve. The appropriateness of that picture for *mental* processes is what Wittgenstein calls in question.

The remedy for these confusions is a grammatical investigation of these puzzling expressions that surveys their normal use, the circumstances of their use, the criteria for their correct use, how we learned their use and the appropriateness of the pictures associated with their use. We may then see, for example, that a feature like the necessity of certain connections between events are no more than a grammatical picture. Such investigations reveal that the characteristic of metaphysical problems is that 'we express an unclarity about the grammar of words in the *form* of a scientific question'. As, for instance, when we ask 'what is the object of a thought?' (Compare, 'what are the ultimate constituents of matter?') (BB p.35d–e).

Wittgenstein provides an illustration of a grammatical investigation and the sorts of problems it clears up in a passage in the *Blue Book* which is worth quoting in full:

> Our wavering between logical and physical impossibility makes us make such statements as this: 'If what I feel is always *my* pain only, what can the supposition mean that someone else has pain?' The thing to do in such cases is always to look how the words in question *are actually used in our language*. We are in all such cases thinking of a use different from that which our ordinary language makes of the words. Of a use, on the other hand, which just then for some reason strongly recommends itself to us. When something seems queer about the grammar of our words, it is because we are alternately tempted to use a word in several different ways. And it is particularly difficult to discover that an assertion which the metaphysician makes expresses discontentment with our grammar when the words of this assertion can also be used to state a fact of experience. Thus, when he says 'only my pain is real pain; this sentence might mean that the other people are only pretending. And when he says 'this tree doesn't exist when nobody sees it', this might mean: 'this tree vanishes when we turn our backs to it'. The man who says 'only my pain is real', doesn't mean to say that he had found out by the common criteria – the criteria, i.e. which give our words their common meanings – that the others who said they had pains were cheating. But what he rebels against is the use of *this* expression in connection with *these* criteria. That is, he objects to using this word in the particular way in which it is commonly used. On the other hand, he is not aware that he is objecting to a convention. He sees a way of dividing the country different from the one used on the ordinary map (BB pp.56b–57a).

It is useful here to tabulate the main characteristics of the later philosophy which were incorporated into the *Investigations*. These are mainly to be found in the *Blue Book* and include the following:

1. We must resist the temptation to look for some object which is the meaning of a word (1e).
2. A source of philosophical confusion is that the use of a substantive inclines us in all cases to look for an entity that corresponds to it (1d, 5b, 31c–d, 36b, 70c–d).

3. The notion that there are certain definite mental processes bound up with the working of language is a picture of an occult mechanism (3c–4a).

4. If anything can be said to constitute the life of a sign it is its *use* (4e).

5. Words with prima facie analogous grammars incline us to treat them analogously (7c, 53c).

6. Grammatical pictures that may be appropriate for some uses of an expression may persist and mislead us with respect to quite different uses, e.g., physical processes and mental processes (8c–9a, b, 16a, 64a, 66b).

7. The 'craving for generality' has its origins in such philosophical misunderstandings as:
   (a) looking for a common feature among all the entities subsumed under a general term (17c, 19d);
   (b) supposing the meaning of a word is an image or thing correlated to the word (18a);
   (c) treating words as though they were all proper names and then confusing the bearer of a name with the meaning of the name (18a);
   (d) a pre-occupation with the method of science (18c).

8. New expressions like 'unconscious toothache' and 'sense-data' may lead to the supposition that a new discovery has been made (23b, 47b, 55a).

9. Philosophy
   (a) neither explains nor reduces anything to anything but is purely descriptive (18c);
   (b) is a fight against the fascination which our forms of expression exert upon us (27d).

10. Philosophers
    (a) talk of analysing the meanings of words as though it were a kind of scientific investigation into what the word *really* means (27f–28a);
    (b) are puzzled because of the fascination which analogies between similar linguistic structures hold for us (26d);
    (c) do not have 'problems'; merely 'troubles' (46a);
    (d) have puzzles which are not *solved* but *cured* (58c–59a).

11. Conventions are the 'rock bottom' of language (24e, 57a).

12. 'Ordinary language is all right' (28c).

13. The meaning of a phrase is characterised by the use we make of it and is not a mental accompaniment to the expression (65b).

NAMES AND THE REFERENCE THEORY OF MEANING

Philosophical Investigations comprises the most authoritative treatment of what is commonly called the later philosophy of Wittgenstein that we have or ever will have. Although there are notes and remarks that came from his hand after he had written the *Investigations* none of them were revised with a view to publication as was the case with the bulk of the material found in his last published work. This is not to say that the later remarks are without value or do not impinge on points relevant to the *Investigations*. Nevertheless, the high water mark of Wittgenstein's later philosophy is to be found in Part I of the *Investigations*.

An examination of names and their place in various language systems leads Wittgenstein to an explicit rejection of a number of theses about names which were central to the *Tractatus*. These include the following:

(a) Naming is the essence, or bed-rock, or paradigm, of all lin-guistic activity.
(b) Names are logically primitive signs.
(c) Names stand for, represent, or mean the objects which they designate.
(d) The correlation of names with objects is the essential connec-tion between language and reality.
(e) Understanding the meanings of most words consists in the determination of their references.

In spite of variations in the status of objects and the nature of the name-object relation the theory of language which trades upon the above theses has a history which goes back to Plato, if not beyond. However, the account of naming with which Wittgenstein opens the *Investigations* is taken neither from Plato nor the *Tractatus* but from St Augustine's *Confessions*. In this work Augustine gives a kind of autobiographical account, which he generalises, of how we learn the names of objects such that as a result of hearing 'words repeatedly used in their proper places in various sentences' we learn to speak the language. According to Wittgenstein, this is a 'particular picture of the essence of human language' and he comments; 'In this picture of language we find the roots of the following idea: every word has a meaning. This meaning is correlated with the word. It is the object for which the word stands' (PI 1). He recognises that there are areas of language in which words may be said to stand for, or to mean, an object but although this concept of meaning 'has its place in a primitive idea of the way language functions' it is also 'the idea of a language more primitive than ours' (PI 2). It sets out to describe a system of communication and abtracts from language certain features which are appropriate primarily to the names of things and people's names and leaves many of the remaining kinds of words used in a complex language as 'something that will take care of itself'. The elevation of the naming of things to the status of the essence or bed-rock of language is for Wittgenstein the prime example of the adoption of a picture of one feature of language as a picture of the whole.

His initial examination of this picture takes the form of the invention of a model language-game; an example of a primitive system of communication 'for which the description given by Augustine is right'. The object of this invention is to provide a simple working model of a naming situation so that we might grasp clearly the functions of naming activities. This is an important illustration first worked out in detail in the *Brown Book* – although there are references to it in earlier writings (cf. PG 19) – and refined and repeatedly invoked in the *Investigations*. The purpose of this language-game is to serve as a means of communication between a builder A and an assistant B so that when A calls out a word in this language B brings the object corresponding to it. The entire vocabulary consists of the four words 'block', 'pillar', 'slab' and 'beam'. The first result of this investigation is to emphasise that Augustine's description of naming is quite appropriate for this model but 'not everything we call language is this system' (PI 3). Putting this another way, what is wrong with Augustine's–and the early Wittgenstein's–theories of meaning is that they idealise a particular linguistic activity into a paradigm representative of a multiplicity of other quite different activities. This is the classic illustration of Wittgenstein's conviction that the major source of philosophical errors lies in the attribution of features peculiar to a particular language-game to others designed for very different purposes. The compulsion that drives us to do this is our craving for generality.

His second point regarding Augustine's description of names and language is that his theory of learning is circular because he describes the learning of human language as if the child came into a strange country and did not understand the language of the country; that is, as if it already had a language only not this one. Or again: as if a child could already *think*, only not yet speak. And 'think' would mean here something like 'talk to itself' (PI 32).

Wittgenstein consistently rejects appeals to some kind of inner language in which we think before we speak, either as children learning language or as adults in which the mental language is both a shadow and a cause of the spoken language. His picture of language-learning is that children copy certain practices in a social setting so that learning the names of things is acquiring the mastery of a particular technique.

The invention of language-games is invoked because he thinks that simple language models will make plain what more complex examples tend to obscure. The appeal to such models in the *Blue Book* is accompanied by some words of explanation which throw light on them. Language-games are ways of using signs which are simpler than those in which we use the signs of ordinary language. They include those forms of language with which a child begins to make use of words and also invented models of more primitive forms, like the presentation to a grocer of the words 'six apples' written on paper. Studies of problems like truth and falsity, the relationships between propositions and reality, and the use of assertions, assumptions and questions will all be enhanced by the consideration of simple language-games that are free from the complications and confusions of more complex situations.

> When we look at such simple forms of language the mental mist which seems to enshroud our ordinary use of language disappears. We see activities, reactions, which are clear-cut and transparent. On the other hand, we recognise in these simple processes forms of language not separated by a break from our more complicated ones. We see that we can build up the complicated forms from the primitive ones by gradually adding new forms (BB 17).

The belief that the serial addition of language-games will merge without break into the complicated forms of ordinary language represents a craving for generality that ought to arouse our suspicions.

In the *Investigations* he specifies three senses in which he uses the expression language-game. It is to be used of:

1. Invented models like that of the system of communication employed by the builder and his assistant.
2. Activities such as the naming of objects, the repetition of names and actual word-games like ring-a-ring-a-roses by means of which children learn their native language.
3. Language situations in their entirety; i.e. the words and context of actions, habits and customs in which they are employed (PI 7).

What the investigation of language-games is intended to show is that the actual uses of words are as multifarious as the uses of different tools and to say that 'every word in language signifies something', or, 'learning language consists in giving names to objects' is to ignore this multiplicity of different functions (PI 13, 26). Not only do words differ in their functions but also they may derive their significance from the situations in which they are employed and in which, as it were, they are at home. An important consequence of this is that it is an error to suppose that the meaning of a word is a constant which remains the same in all the circumstances of its uses. So far as names are concerned, 'naming something is like attaching a label to a thing' and 'this is preparatory to the use of a word' (PI 26).

Implicit in the account of language given by Augustine is the idea that the name of an object is unambiguously communicated by an ostensive definition. That is to say, by pointing to an object and at the same time uttering its name. A variant on this idea is Russell's suggestion that 'this', accompanied by an appropriate ostensive gesture, constitutes 'this' as the only genuine logical name. Wittgenstein characterises this suggestion as a 'queer conception' due to 'a tendency to sublime the logic of our language'. 'We call very different things "names", and the word "name" is used to characterise many different kinds of use of a word, related to one another in many different ways – but the kind of use that "this" has is not among them' (PI 38, 45). It is true that in giving an ostensive definition we may point to an object and utter a name and we may also use the ostensive gesture and say the word 'this'. However, the similarity of the gestures should not mislead us into thinking of 'this' as a name. 'It is precisely characteristic of a name that it is defined by means of the demonstrative expression "That is N" (or "that is called N"). But do we also give the definitions: "That is called 'this' ", or "This is called 'this' "?' (PI 38).

Wittgenstein traces the idea that there is something fixed and constant about '*the* relation between name and thing' as due to the curious malady which impels philosophers to stare at an object and repeat its name innumerable times in the hope of uncovering this relationship. Such superstitious occult processes enter the moment a word, in this case a name, is disengaged from normal use. In his classic phrase: 'Philosophical problems arise when language goes on holiday'.

Precisely what is the issue between Russell and Wittgenstein here? Russell writes:

> 'This' denotes whatever, at the moment when the word is used, occupies the centre of attention. With words which are not egocentric, what is constant is something about the object indicated, but 'this' denotes a different object on each occasion of its use: what is constant is not the object denoted, but its relation to the particular use of the word. Whenever the word is used, the person using it is attending to something and the word indicates this something. When a word is not egocentric there is no need to distinguish between different occasions when it is used, but we must make this distinction with egocentric words, since what they indicate is something having a given relation to the particular use of the word.[2]

Thus, Russell makes an important distinction between egocentric and indicative words. In the case of indicative words what is constant is something about the *object* indicated by the word; in the case of egocentric words what is constant is something about the *use* of a word on a particular occasion. He elaborates on this in his brief and little-noticed reply to P. F. Strawson's treatment of the theory of descriptions in the latter's celebrated paper 'On Referring'. Russell remarks that there are 'descriptive phrases from which egocentricity is wholly absent' and that in such cases considerations of use on a particular occasion are irrelevant. He asks for an analysis of the kind Strawson offered of descriptive phrases to be applied to such examples as 'the square root of minus one is half the square root of minus four'. In this example there are no egocentric words but 'the problem of interpreting the descriptive phrase is exactly the same as if there were'.[3] He continues

> It is of the essence of a scientific account of the world to reduce to a minimum the egocentric element in an assertion, but success in this attempt is a matter of degree, and is never complete where empirical material is concerned. This is due to the fact that the meaning of all empirical words depend ultimately upon ostensive definitions, that ostensive definitions depend upon experience, and that experience is egocentric. We can, however, by means of egocentric words, *describe* something which is not egocentric; it is this that enables us to use a common language.[4]

Russell argues that there are 'two problems, that of descriptions and that of egocentricity' and alleges that Strawson has assumed them to be the same and offered a solution only to the egocentric problem.[5]

This account of language, particularly its alleged relationship with logically private experience, is a crucial difference between Russell and the later Wittgenstein. Russell advocates a phenomenalist thesis to the effect that empirical descriptions are constructed essentially and ineradicably from egocentric or private experience. Nevertheless, he held that the problems of descriptions and egocentricity or logical privacy are separable and the egocentric component of descriptions makes no difference in their analysis which is the same as for completely non-egocentric descriptions. The reason for this, Russell thinks, is that descriptions describe something which is not itself egocentric and it is this fact that makes common language possible. The gap between logically private experience and common language is bridged by ostensive definitions. Hence the importance of 'this' as the only genuine logical name, for 'this' not only names the private experience (whatever occupies the centre of attention of the user) but, accompanied by an appropriate gesture of pointing, is an integral part of an ostensive definition that enables us to translate 'this' into a common-language description. In this respect Russell would agree with Wittgenstein that naming was like attaching a label preparatory to the use of a word except that he would say that initially the label is 'this'. Wittgenstein's criticism that the characteristic of a name is that it can be defined by 'This is N' and we do not say, 'This is "this"' does not answer Russell's point. Russell's 'this' names the logical subject of the sentence – whatever engages the attention at the time – not its grammatical subject. In the sentence 'This is N' (or 'This is called N'), 'this' is a logical name denoting a private experience and coupled with an appropriate ostensive gesture gives the grammatical name 'N' as its equivalent in common language. Ostensive definition is Russell's escape route from logically private experience to public discourse. One of the central concerns of the *Investigations* is an examination and repudiation of this phenomenalist account in favour of a view of language entirely purged of logically private components. According to Russell, language represents reality through the medium of private mental events and the weakness of his notion of ostensive definitions is that we are never really sure whether these point *outwards* or *inwards*. According to Wittgenstein, language represents reality through the conventions, customs and habits of those who use the language. It is essentially a social phenomenon, a shared form of life. Hence, Wittgenstein's use of the concept language-game to include both language *and* the activities of which it forms part.

Russell's analysis presupposes that an ostensive definition unambiguously determines the relationship between an object and its name. Wittgenstein questions this when he asks, is an object a 'this' until it receives a name in the 'baptismal ceremony' of ostensive definition? Does this ritual subsequently fix the meaning of a name? If I point to a person and name him someone else 'might equally well take the name of a person, of which I give an ostensive definition, as that of a colour, of a race, or even of a point of the compass. That is to say: an ostensive definition can be variously interpreted in *every* case' (PI 28). Consider the language-game used by the builder and his assistant. To point to an object and say 'slab' might be taken to mean 'bring it', 'remove it' 'smash it' or 'worship it' or almost anything besides the name. If we imagine a comprehensive set of ostensive gestures which systematically rule out all these possible interpretations and indicates unambiguously that 'slab' is a *name*, then the question arises, a name of what? Does it name the shape, or texture, or colour or the particular characteristics of that piece of stone and no other?

Wittgenstein's point is not to deny that an ostensive definition may help to explain the use or meaning of a word but it does so only 'when the overall role of the word in language is clear' (PI 30). If we ostensively define 'two' in the sentence, 'This number is called "two"', then 'the word "number" here shows what place in language, in grammar, we assign to the word'. The important point is that the post at which the ostensively defined word is stationed is already marked out in language – in this example by the word 'number'; it is not the ostensive definition that marks it out (PI 29). Even in a primitive language-game consisting of only four words the successful employment of the word 'slab' presupposes an already established practice. It is the established practice of ordinary language that makes credible the workings of the model, not the other way round. For these four words to function as a system of communication the builder must have been able to say to his assistant. 'When I call out "slab" I want you to bring this type of stone.' Ostensive definition is an illustrative aid to the meaning of a word whose role is *already fixed* by its place in language: 'Only someone who already knows how to do something with it can significantly ask a name' (PI 31).

He considers another possibility. If pointing to an object is insufficient to determine whether we are intending to refer to its shape, texture, colour or number, are there any 'characteristic experiences' which in conjunction with an ostensive definition will exclude such ambiguity? For example, pointing to the shape of an object might be accompanied by the characteristic process of tracing the outline with one's eyes or fingers, and this would establish that what was intended was the shape and not, say, the colour. In such a case, how would we know that what was meant was the shape and not the texture? The accompaniment of the most expressive characteristic experiences is still insufficient to uniquely determine the reference of an ostensive definition or precisely what we meant by the name we uttered when pointing. As regards the characteristic experience of pointing to a shape by following the outline with one's fingers or eyes as one points; 'But *this* does not happen in all cases in which I "mean the shape", and no more does any other one characteristic process occur in all these cases' (PI 35). That there are characteristic experiences that occur often, though not always, in pointing to the shape or to the number is not disputed but 'do you also know of an experience, characteristic of pointing to a piece in a game *as a piece in a game*? All the same one can say: "I mean that this *piece* is called the "king", not this particular bit of wood I am pointing to"' (PI 35). The significance of the 'king' in chess is not fixed by a definition, ostensive or otherwise, but by its role in the game. Similarly with words, including names; their meanings are not fixed by hierarchies of definitions standing one behind the other – a is b, b is c, . . . m is n . . . – but by their uses in various language situations.

Of course, when all other routes are closed we can always retreat into the labyrinth of the mind; 'because we cannot specify any *one* bodily action which we call pointing to the shape (as opposed, for example, to the colour), we say that a spiritual (mental, intellectual) activity corresponds to these words' (PI 36). The spiritualisation of ostensive definition is complete when we interpret what we mean by it as referring to a mental process. To this Wittgenstein replies:

> Can I say, 'bububu' and mean 'if it doesn't rain I shall go for a walk'? It is only in a language that I can mean something by something. This shows clearly that the grammar of 'to mean' is not like that of the expression 'to imagine' and the like (PI p.18n).

The grammar of 'to mean something by something' is not a mysterious mental act but a rule of translation; i.e. both 'somethings' are located in language.

The grammar of meaning, particularly the relation of the meaning of a name to ostensive definition, is summed up by Wittgenstein like this;

> For a *large* class of cases – though not for all – in which we employ the word 'meaning' it can be defined thus: the meaning of a word is its use in the language. And the *meaning* of a name is sometimes explained by pointing to its bearer (PI 43).

The relation between a name and the object that bears the name brings up the notion of correspondence which Wittgenstein examines afresh. The *Tractatus* traded heavily on a notion of correspondence according to which names *mean* the elements with which they correspond. This relationship of correspondence is what connects language and reality. Wittgenstein now objects to this argument; 'the word "meaning" is being used illicitly if it is used to signify the thing that corresponds to the word. That is to confound the meaning of a name with the *bearer* of the name'

(PI 40). Thus, the semantic route to ontology trades on an illicit transition from name to bearer of the name.

He also scrutinises the concept of primary elements as entities which cannot be described but only named and, taking Plato's version of this doctrine, invents a model language-game 'for which this account is really valid'. We are to imagine an arrangement of red, green, white and black squares and also that 'the words of the language are (correspondingly) "R", "G", "W", "B" and a sentence is a series of these words' (PI 48). Each coloured square represents a primary element, each name corresponds to an element and a sentence is a complex of names descriptive of an arrangement of elements. In a language-game of this kind it seems natural to call the elements 'simples' but under other circumstances we could say that each square is composite consisting, for example, of a shape and a colour. 'Does it matter which we say, so long as we avoid misunderstandings in any particular case?' (PI 48). So much for logical atoms! He then considers what is meant by saying:

> that we cannot define (that is describe) these elements, but only name them. We might say in a limiting case where a complex consists of only one square that 'its description is simply the name of the coloured square'. Here we might say . . . that a sign, 'R' or 'B', etc., 'may be sometimes a word and sometimes a proposition'. He regards this type of argument as leading 'to all kinds of philosophical superstition' because 'whether it is a word or a proposition depends on the situation in which it is uttered or written'. His conclusion is that 'naming and describing do not stand on the same level: naming is a preparation for a description. Naming is not so far a move in the language-game – any more than putting a piece in its place on the board is a move in chess. We may say: *nothing* has so far been done, when a thing has been named. It has not even *got* a name except in the language-game. This was what Frege meant too, when he said that 'a word had meaning only as part of a sentence' (PI 49).

Plato, Russell and the early Wittgenstein shared a common error in treating names as descriptions of bare particulars and thereby confused two different linguistic activities, naming and describing.

Wittgenstein completes his rejection of logical atomism when he investigates what it means to say that 'we can attribute neither being nor non-being to elements'. He considers an analogous case based on the standard metre, which was then in Paris, of which 'one can neither say it is one metre long, nor that it is not one metre long'. But this is not the ascription of some extraordinary property to it; it only marks 'its peculiar role in the language-game of measuring with a metre rule'. If we had standard colour samples preserved with the standard metre 'then it will make no sense to say of this sample that it is of this colour or that it is not'. 'This sample is an instrument of the language used in ascriptions of colour. In this language-game it is not something that is represented, but is a *means* of representation.' Analogously, for Plato's 'primary elements', Russell's 'individuals' and Wittgenstein's 'objects', what looked as if it *had* to exist is merely part of the language. 'It is a paradigm in our language-game; something with which comparison is made. And this may be an important observation; but it is none the less an observation concerning our language-game – our method of representation' (PI 50).

The statement 'the standard metre is one metre in length' is not an experiential proposition but a tautology of the form $p = p$ or $p \supset p$. In the *Tractatus* he said of tautologies that they lack sense but they are not nonsensical; they are part of the symbolism (like $\supset$ in arithmetic (4.461–4.4611). A tautology tells us nothing about the world because 'it does not stand in any representational relation to reality' (4.462–4.463). Nevertheless, 'there are certain cases in which one is tempted to use expressions of the form "a = a" or "p ⊃ p" and the like. In fact this happens when one wants to talk about prototypes, e.g., about proposition, thing etc.' (5.5351). The prototype of the *Tractatus* has developed into the paradigm of the *Investigations*. A paradigm is not a representation of anything in the world but constitutes a method of representation. They are the frames of reference which we devise for the description of reality and confusion follows when we interpret our own paradigms as themselves disclosures of reality. The ontology of the *Tractatus* is the result of just such a confusion. The existence of unanalysable objects is not a feature of reality but a feature of a chosen paradigm or method of representation. In the *Tractatus* Wittgenstein projected on to reality the shadows of his own paradigm and its objects were the images of his own grammar.

Finally in this section, I wish to draw attention to what seems to be an interior weakness in Wittgenstein's notion of a language-game. According to the *Blue Book*, a language-game is a primitive form of language from which, without a break, we can build more complicated forms by adding new ones (BB p.17). In the *Investigations* the four-word system of communication used between a builder and his assistant is conceived 'as a complete primitive language' (PI 2). This not a particularly perspicuous example for a number of reasons. That the words 'block', 'pillar', 'slab' and 'beam' are names of objects we know from their use in ordinary language. But this it not how they are used in the language-game where they function as commands; i.e. 'slab' means 'bring me one of those pieces of stone'. Within the language-game itself, if 'slab' is a name at all it is a name of an *activity* and this is not a felicitous example of what Augustine meant by naming an *object*. The example does not illustrate Augustine's idea at all, but rather Wittgenstein's own conviction that naming is a preparation for use and on its own is empty. The words of the language-game are used in two senses; first, as names of objects (which comes from the grammar of their ordinary-language use) and second, as commands (which comes from the grammar of the language-game). This more or less complex conflation of different grammars is neither 'primitive' nor is it 'complete'. It is not complete because it presupposes an acquaintance with ordinary language through which the builder and his assistant known that 'block', 'pillar', etc. are names which are then used as truncated commands to act in certain ways with respect to the objects so named. It cannot be supposed that within the limits of the language-game the builder taught his assistant these names by means of ostensive definitions in view of the ambiguities alleged to pertain to this procedure. There is nothing in the language-game, nor are there any characteristic gestures, that will determine the name of an object *as* the name of an object. The activities of the builder and his assistant do not help us here either; they are only elaborate forms of characteristic gestures. What makes clear the role of a name is its grammatical station and no such station exists within Wittgenstein's primitive language-game. N. Malcolm remarks; ' "Slab-Beam" does not presuppose any previous understanding of language: it could be 'a complete primitive language'.'[6] This is certainly what Wittgenstein intended, but both Malcolm and Wittgenstein himself have overlooked the circularity of Wittgenstein's argument here. This language-game can be regarded as complete, i.e., it does not presuppose any previous understandings of language, only if ostensive definition is sufficient to determine the names of the four objects concerned. Since this is what Wittgenstein denies, then the names are fixed by the grammar of ordinary language which does presuppose a previous understanding of language and conflicts with the notion of completeness. Wittgenstein is landed with another version of the chicken and the egg controversy; which comes first, the name or its station, the use or the grammar?

He recognises this dilemma in an interesting passage in *Philosophical Remarks*.

> If I explain the meaning of a word 'A' to someone by pointing to something and saying 'This is A', then this expression may be meant in two different ways. Either it is itself a proposition already, in which case it can only be understood once the meaning of 'A' is known, i.e., I must leave it to chance whether he takes it as I meant it or not. Or the sentence is a definition. Suppose I have said to someone 'A is ill', but he doesn't know who I mean by 'A', and I now point at a man, saying 'This is A'. Here the expression is a definition, but this can only be understood if he has already gathered what kind of object it is through his understanding of the grammar of the proposition 'A is ill'. But this means that any kind of explanation of a language presupposes a language already. And in a certain sense, the use of language is something that cannot be taught, i.e., I cannot use language to teach it in the way in which language could be used to teach someone to play the piano – and that of course is just another way of saying: I cannot use language to get outside language (PR 6 p. 54).

The attempt to construct a language-game which is primitive and complete seems to be another way of trying to get outside language.

This difficulty did not escape Wittgenstein's notice and he comments on it in notes comprising *Remarks on the Philosophy of Psychology*.

> *Under what circumstances* would one really call the sounds of the builder, etc. a language? Under *all* circumstances? Certainly not! Was it wrong then to isolate a rudiment of language and call it language? Should one perhaps say that this rudiment is a

language-game only in the context of the whole that we usually call our language?[7]

Unfortunately, perhaps significantly, Wittgenstein does not address himself to this question. Instead he goes on to emphasise again that the surrounding of the language-game 'is not the mental accompaniment of speech'. That associated with a primitive language-game 'there is such a thing as "primitive thinking" which is to be described via primitive *behaviour*' (RPPII p.39, §204–5; cf Z pp. 98–9). But Wittgenstein himself points out that primitive behaviour, such as gestures of ostensive definition, may be variously interpreted and therefore is insufficient to give meaning to the builder's language-game in isolation from the rest of language.

MEANING AND ANALYSIS

According to Russell's theory of definite descriptions, ordinary proper names are truncated or telescoped descriptions which may replace them when they occur in existential propositions. Ordinary proper names are not to be confused with logically proper names which stand for particulars that can only be named; their meanings derive from their denotations without the interposition of descriptions. On the other hand, ordinary proper names have meanings that can only be elicited by first analysing them into their equivalent descriptions. For example, the name Romulus is a truncated description and stands for the person who killed Remus and founded Rome, etc. 'Any proposition about Romulus really introduces the propositional function embodying the description, as (say) 'x was called "Romulus" . . . and when you say "Romulus did not exist", you mean that this propositional function is not true for one value of x'.[8]

Thus, the relation of *denoting* or *standing for* an object can only be attributed to logically proper names and not ordinary proper names. It was this that enabled Russell to offer a solution for a puzzling problem connected with proper names which had long proved troublesome. If we suppose that the meaning of a proper name is the entity it denotes or stands for, what are the meanings of those names that stand for non-existent entities? It seems absurd to dismiss as meaningless every proposition referring to Odysseus, or the present king of France, or the round square, because no objects exist with which these names correspond. This has been the point at which for two millennia all correspondence theories of names have lapsed into incoherence. Russell avoided this difficulty altogether by analysing proper names into a logically equivalent descriptive form consisting of a conjunction of propositions at least one of which was an existential proposition. In the event that the person, or thing named, does not exist then the existential proposition is false. If the existential proposition is false then the whole conjunction of propositions is also false and, therefore, the proper name which is logically equivalent to this conjunction is false and not meaningless.

Wittgenstein embodied this feature of Russell's theory of descriptions in the *Tractatus* with respect to propositions that mention non-existent entities. 'A complex can be given only by its description, which will be right or wrong. A proposition that mentions a complex will not be nonsensical, if the complex does not exist, but simply false' (3.24).

In the *Investigations* he returns to a fresh consideration of Russell's theory of descriptions with particular reference to its consequences for the meanings of names.

> We may say, following Russell: the name 'Moses' can be defined by means of various descriptions. For example, as 'the man who led the Israelites through the wilderness', 'the man who lived at that time and place and was then called "Moses"', 'the man who as a child was taken out of the Nile by Pharaoh's daughter' and so on. And according as we assume one definition or another the proposition 'Moses did not exist' acquires a different sense, and so does every other proposition about Moses (PI 79).

The meaning of 'Moses' varies with respect to the different descriptions we entertain. Russell, too, recognised that the definition of a proper name by different descriptions entailed that the name has different meanings depending on which description one has in mind when using the name. Over the significance of this fluctuation in meaning Russell and Wittgenstein part company. Russell deplores the unfortunate ambiguities that this involves for ordinary language but concludes that an unambiguous language would be largely private to the speaker and so make ordinary communication difficult and, in some areas of discourse, impossible.[9] Wittgenstein, on the other hand, goes on;

when I make a statement about Moses, – am I always ready to substitute some *one* of these descriptions for 'Moses'? I shall perhaps say: By 'Moses' I understand the man who did what the Bible relates of Moses, or at any rate a good deal of it. But how much? Have I decided how much must be proved false for me to give up my proposition as false? Has the name 'Moses' got a fixed and unequivocal use for me in all possible cases? – Is it not the case that I have, so to speak, a whole series of props in readiness, and am ready to lean on one if another should be taken from under me and vice versa?

Consider the statement, 'N is dead'. The meaning of the name 'N' may be given by a series of descriptions such that a definition of 'N' could be 'the man of whom all this is true'. Suppose that one of these descriptions proved to be false – would we then be prepared to declare the original proposition 'N is dead' to be false? Would we not simply change our definition of the name?

And this can be expressed like this: I use the name 'N' without a *fixed* meaning. (But that detracts as little from its usefulness, as it detracts from that of a table that it stands on four legs instead of three and so sometimes wobbles.) Should it be said that I am using a word whose meaning I don't know, and so am talking nonsense? – Say what you choose, so long as it does not prevent you from seeing the facts. (PI 79).

This lack of fixed meanings for names – and many other kinds of words – is not a deplorable ambiguity which can only be eliminated the closer we approximate to a strict calculus of language. Ordinary language itself offers any number of props which will support us when a particular prop gives way without or needing to have recourse to an ideal and permanent foundation. Wittgenstein's attitude to the theory of descriptions is that it is one way among others via which we may escape from confusions generated by the names of non-existent entities. However, it is not the unique and inviolable solution of these problems. It is not unique because there are many ways of construing the meaning of statements like 'Moses did not exist' by no means all of which are existentially puzzling. It is not inviolable because the falsity of one proposition of the conjunction of descriptions that are held to be logically equivalent to 'N' would not necessarily make us declare that the statement 'N is dead' was false. There are other options open to us and, furthermore, these are available within the field of ordinary language. When the table wobbles cutting the legs to equal lengths may seem an ideal solution, but a wad of paper can serve a similar purpose and, when the floor is uneven, is a better one.

Wittgenstein's dislike of this kind of analysis is not confined to the theory of descriptions but extends to everything that was embraced by the expression 'logical analysis'. It will be recalled that this was the tool by which, in principle, complex sentences could be resolved into their constituent simple propositions and must rank as the most discussed and least used instrument in the history of philosophy. In spite of the fact that the instrument did not work it was immensely important because of the tacit assumption that questions about the meanings of words were answerable by processes of analysis. It is for this reason that Wittgenstein subjects logical analysis itself to a grammatical investigation. In the model language-game used by the builders we may suppose that the word 'slab' has the same meaning as 'bring me a slab', but the shorter expression is not an analysed or logically primitive form of the longer one which brings out its meaning in some mysterious way. Perhaps we are inclined to say that 'slab' *really means* 'bring me a slab', but 'why should I translate the call 'slab' into a different expression in order to say what someone means by it?' (PI 19). There are no more grounds for regarding the first expression as a shortened form of the second than for regarding the second as a lengthened form of the first, and that means that we cannot identify one of them as logically primitive. 'To imagine a language means to imagine a form of life' and what 'slab' *really means* in this language-game is made clear in the form of life of the builders.

Wittgenstein's interlocutor treads familiar ground when he observes that 'the shortened and unshortened sentence have the same sense'. Can we not isolate this sense, as it were, and represent what these sentences have in common in symbols just as the original sentences are expressed in symbols. If neither sentence is an analysed form of the other then can we not express the analysed form in a notation which perspicuously represents this sense in a proposition? This gambit is declined: 'But doesn't the fact that sentences have the same sense consist in their having the same use?' (PI 20). That remark is a watershed in modern philosophy and marks the final divergence of Russell and Wittgenstein.

The investigation proceeds with a consideration of a proposed analysis of 'my broom is in the corner'. He asks; 'is this really a statement about the broomstick and the brush?' Certainly the sentence can be replaced by a statement giving the positions of the stick and the brush but what is meant by calling this statement 'a further analysed form of the first one'? What he is denying is that there is a hidden meaning in the original statement which analysis reveals such that we 'understand the further analysed sentence better'. In fact, the analysed form achieves no more than the ordinary one and 'in a roundabout way'. 'True, the broom is taken to pieces when one separates broomstick and brush; but does it follow that the order to bring the broom also consists of corresponding parts?' (PI 60). The separability of a thing is no ground for supposing the separability of statements made about the thing. The sources of philosophical errors are not only linguistic and from the structure of things we can draw misleading analogies about the structure of language. The idea of a name as that which signifies an element of reality remaining the same throughout change is a picture whose appropriateness derives from the construction of a chair from component parts (cf. PI 59).

All this leads Wittgenstein to what he calls, rightly, 'the great question that lies behind all these considerations'. If analysis is not the explication of meaning nor is an 'analysed form logically more fundamental than any other', what is the essence of language and where is it to be found? What about that part of the *Tractatus* which gave the 'most headache, the part about the *general form of propositions* and of language'? (PI 65). His answer to these questions is now historic:

> Instead of producing something common to all that we call language, I am saying that these phenomena have no one thing in common which makes us use the same word for all – but that they are *related* to one another in many different ways. And it is because of this relationship, or these relationships, that we call them all 'language'.

He explains these relationships in terms of his celebrated analogy of games. According to N. Malcolm the idea that in language we play games with words first struck Wittgenstein when he was passing a field where a game of football was in progress.[10] This incident may be Wittgenstein's first conscious recollection of the game analogy but a discussion of the game of chess as analogous to the rules of arithmetic is to be found in the writings of Frege.[11] The interlocutor might well have objected – 'surely, there must be something common to what we call games too?'.

> Don't say: 'There –must be something common, or they would not be called "games"' – but *look and see* whether there is anything common to all. . . . And the result of this examination is: we see a complicated network of similarities overlapping and criss-crossing: sometimes overall similarities, sometimes similarities of detail. I can think of no better expression to characterise these similarities than 'family resemblances': for the various resemblances between members of a family: build, features, colour of eyes, gait, temperament, etc. etc., overlap and criss-cross in the same way – And I shall say: 'games' form a family (PI 66–7).

He finds the analogy between games and language peculiarly apt precisely because the concept 'game' is inexact and not everywhere circumscribed by rules – a concept with blurred edges, as it were. And a concept with blurred edges, unlike a blurred concept, is not unusable.

Thus there is no common feature, or essence, or general propositional form, underlying and underwriting language; this is the most crucial of all philosophical superstitions and the most prolific generator of confusions. What now becomes clear is that at the heart of Wittgenstein's grammatical investigations is the repeated invocation of the analogies of games, family resemblances and pictures which make them so distinctive and mark them off from a scientific enquiry into language. Their object is not the discovery of new facts about language or the learning of language but the loosening of the shackles and reduction of the fascination that certain of our forms of expression impose upon us. The role of grammatical investigations is not explanatory but therapeutic.

Finally, Wittgenstein deals with the idea that to analyse a sentence is to explain its meaning in the most fundamental way possible. This is the core of logical atomism; analysis is the satisfaction of the demand for ultimate explanations of the meanings of words. Supposing someone does not understand the meaning of the name 'Moses' and this is explained by saying 'he was the man who led the Israelites out of Egypt'. 'But similar doubts to those about "Moses" are possible about the words of this explanation (what are you calling "Egypt", whom the "Israel-ites" etc.?). Nor would these questions end when we got down to words like "red", "dark", "sweet"' (PI 87). Were we able to reach the 'fully analysed' form of a sentence whose meaning we want explaining the demand for explanation can be significantly renewed and the need for it remain. Knowing the logically simple components of a sentence is no guarantee that we will understand its meaning any better. The interlocutor objects: 'But then how does an explanation help me to understand, if after all it is not the final one? In that case the explanation is never completed; so I still don't understand what he means, and never shall!' To this Witt-genstein replies; 'an explanation may indeed rest on another one that has been given, but none stands in need of another – unless *we* require it to prevent a misunderstanding'. Explanations do not form a hierarchy ascending from an ultimate or final explanation which is found in the fully analysed version of the sentence in need of explanation. What counts as the explanation of the mean-ing of a sentence is not some process of analysis but 'whatever serves to remove or arrest a misunderstanding'. The notion of a 'final explanation' which is proof against all doubt and misunder-standing is a myth generated by the peculiar picture of meaning characteristic of logical atomism.

Analysis as conceived in logical atomism is a product of at least four mistakes:

1. *Logical* – that sentences are truth-functional combinations of elementary propositions.
2. *Linguistic* – that the meanings of sentences having equivalent uses may be represented in common propositional forms.
3. *Empirical* – that because material things are separable into component parts our statements about them are comparably structured.
4. *Epistemological* – that elementary propositions describe sense-data (Russell's version) or represent reality (Wittgenstein's version) and whose elucidation constitutes the ultimate explanation of questions of meaning.

It has also been remarked that half a century of logical analysis has failed to produce a single convincing example of a sentence transmuted into a fully analysed propositional form. Wittgen-stein's rejection of logical atomism entails, among other things, that the central thesis of the *Tractatus* that fundamentally ordinary language is in order as it stands is deprived of its justification. As a result, the thesis must either be modified or abandoned or else a new kind of justification must be offered. In fact, of course, the main outlines of this new justification are already beginning to emerge – although Wittgenstein would not care for the word 'justification' as a description of what he is about.

6

The Grammar of Mathematics

THE FOUNDATIONS OF MATHEMATICS

In order to obtain an overview of Wittgenstein's thinking about mathematics it is necessary to examine two principal sources of material. The first is *Remarks on the Foundations of Mathematics* which consist of writings belonging to the period 1937–45 when he was also working on Part I of the *Philosophical Investigations*. The second source is a publication which is a valuable addendum to *RFM* entitled *Wittgenstein's Lectures on the Foundations of Mathematics*. This work consists of a conflation of notes taken by four of Wittgenstein's students who attended his lectures at Cambridge in 1939, skilfully edited by Cora Diamond. Valuable material on this subject from an earlier stage in his thinking is to be found in the notes of Wittgenstein's lectures at Cambridge edited by D. Lee and A. Ambrose respectively.

The interpretation and assessment of Wittgenstein's views on mathematics is complicated by his own notoriously difficult and inimitable style of philosophising together with the fact that many of his would-be interpreters have chosen to revile what they do not understand. No other aspect of his thought has been the subject of such hostility and misinterpretation as the object of his enquiries into mathematics. His aim is best expressed in a remark found in a box of slips cut from his own typescripts and subsequently published under the title *Zettel*. 'On mathematics: "Your concept is wrong – However, I cannot illumine the matter by fighting against your words, but only by trying to turn your attention away from certain expressions, illustrations, images, and *towards* the *employment* of the words"' (Z 463). His concern with mathematical propositions is not with their role qua mathematics but with the penumbra of explanations, justifications, grammatical pictures, analogies, images, resemblances and assimilations with experiential propositions which surrounds their actual use in the activities of counting, calculating and proving. The intention is to expose the grammatical sources of the misleading accounts of mathematical propositions given by logicists, realists, finitists, formalists and intuitionists alike and by exposing abolish them. These are not mathematical but grammatical investigations which exhibit the fluctuation and fluidity of our ways of talking about various mathematical activities.

The problems arise not from mathematics but from what Cantor, Dedekind, Frege, Hardy, Hilbert, Gödel and (particularly) Russell have written in explanation of mathematics or in attempting to provide it with foundations. The aim is to show, for example, the lack of fit between what we actually do when we calculate and what mathematical philosophers have alleged in explanation or justification of what we do. Consequently, Wittgenstein sees his task as that of dispelling misunderstandings by posing questions, suggesting exceptions, considering alternatives, proposing counter-examples, dissolving pictures, devising intermediate cases and breaking down intuitively accepted distinctions. From this fundamentally grammatical investigation it is mistaken to try and distil a philosophy of mathematics. Disputants over whether or not Wittgenstein was a finitist or a formalist or an intuitionist have missed the universality of his rejection of mathematical philosophy. As Wittgenstein observed in one of his Cambridge lectures:

> We want to see the absurdities both of what the finitists say and of what their opponents say – just as we want in philosophy to see the absurdities both of what the behaviorists say and of what their opponents say. Finitism and behaviourism are as alike as two eggs. Both sides of such disputes are based on a particular kind of misunderstanding – which arises from gazing at a form of words and forgetting to ask yourself what's done with it, or from gazing into your own soul to see if two expressions have the same meaning and such things.

And again he remarks:

> Intuitionism comes to saying that you can make a new rule at each point. It requires that we have an intuition at each step in calculation, at each application of a rule; for how can we tell how

a rule which has been used for fourteen steps applies at the fifteenth? — And they go on to say that the series of cardinal numbers is known to us by a ground-intuition — that is, we know at each step what the operation of adding 1 will give. We might as well say that we need, not an intuition at each step, but a *decision*. Actually there is neither. You don't make a decision: you simply do a certain thing. It is a question of a certain practice. Intuitionism is all bosh — entirely. (LFM 111, 237).

To try and classify Wittgenstein as a logicist, realist, finitist, formalist or intuitionist is to ignore his rejection of generality and consequently his rejection of the idea that mathematics has a uniform grammar. There is no grammar of mathematics; only grammars. Associated with the different activities and different grammars of mathematics are various conceptual pictures which seem appropriate for some of these activities and misleading for others. Are these pictures concomitants of the activities of counting and calculating or are they projections of the grammar of what we say in explanation of these activities? This is the most fundamental of the questions about mathematics posed by Wittgenstein.

The logicist thesis, the specific formulation of which by Russell and Whitehead created the philosophical environment of the early Wittgenstein, sought to derive the grammar of mathematics from the propositions of logic. The objective of this programme is rejected by Wittgenstein in his remark, 'It is my task, not to attack Russell's logic from within, but from without. That is to say: not to attack it mathematically — otherwise I should be doing mathematics — but its position, its office' (RFM p.383). Its office was that of providing a foundation for mathematics in logic, free from the vicious-circle paradox that Russell had detected in Frege's version of logicism. Frege's view of mathematics was an amalgam of Platonism and logicism and his analysis of the foundations of arithmetic arrived at the conclusion that

Arithmetic thus becomes simply a development of logic, and every proposition of arithemetic a law of logic, albeit a derivative one. To apply arithmetic in the physical sciences is to bring logic to bear on observed facts; calculation becomes deduction. . . . The laws of number . . . are not laws of nature . . . ; they are laws of the laws of nature.[1]

Frege's definition of number treated the proposition 'the same number belongs to the concept F as to the concept G' as equivalent to 'the extension of the concept "equal to the concept F" is identical with the extension of the concept "equal to the concept G"'.[2] Using the Russellian notation for quantification this means that for every concept ϕ there was a class x(ϕx) as its extension and that

$$(x)(\phi x) = (x)(\psi x) . \supset . (x)(\phi x \equiv \psi x)$$

Thus, something belongs to a class when it falls under the concept whose extension the class is and from one concept's coinciding in extension with another concept we can infer that any object that falls under the one also falls under the other. But consider the class of men. It is clear that the class of men is not a man and that here we have the concept; class that does not belong to itself. The extension of this concept is the class of classes that do not belong to themselves.

This leads straight to Russell's paradox or, as Wittgenstein sometimes calls it, Russell's contradiction. The opacity, to put it no stronger, in Frege's notion of classes and their extensions was problematical for his definition of number in particular and his attempt to derive arithmetic from logic in general. Russell took this problem of the self-membership of classes to be a particular example of the vicious-circle paradox characteristic of all self-referential expressions. Accordingly, if Frege's programme of founding mathematics on logic was to be carried through this paradox had to be eliminated and this was the specific role of Russell's theory of logical types. The synthesis of propositions, functions, classes stratified into hierarchies of logical types and certain extra-logical theses, like the axiom of infinity, became the magnum opus of logicism known as *Principia Mathematica*.

Consistently with his life-long aversion for the theory of logical types Wittgenstein wondered what the fuss was all about. To the interlocutor's question; 'But you can't allow a contradiction to stand!' Wittgenstein replies, characteristically, 'Why not?' To the further rejoinder, '"Contradiction destroys the calculus"' he continues; 'What gives it this special position? With a little imagination, I believe, it can certainly be shaken' (RFM 370, 376). Frege's arithmetic may be like measuring with a soft ruler but it is still a system of measurement – compare the pace and the metre as standards of measurement.

Wittgenstein's principal objection to the logicist thesis that mathematics is founded on logic was that the creation of such an ediface was unnecessary.

> What does mathematics need a foundation for? It no more needs one, I believe, than propositions about physical objects – or about sense impressions, need an *analysis*. What mathematical propositions do stand in need of is a clarification of their grammar, just as do other propositions. The *mathematical* problems of what is called foundations are no more the foundation of mathematics for us than the painted rock is the support of a painted tower (RFM p.378).

Wittgenstein's concept of mathematics is modelled on his concept of natural language. Just as language derives its significance from our forms of life so too does mathematics. What gives sense to propositions is their use and what gives sense to our calculi are their applications. Frege held that what raised arithmetic from a game to a science was applicability. But their respective notions of applicability must not be confused. For Frege the applicability of the truths and relations of mathematics was to a class of logical objects such that mathematics had the character of discovery. To draw a line in geometry was to trace a connection that was already there. To follow a rule, such as that for the expansion of a numerical series, was to proceed along a set of steps whose nature and direction were determined by the rule. For Wittgenstein the applicability of mathematics was to human activities such as counting, adding and calculating all of which were inventions rather than discoveries. Following a rule was inseparable from interpreting it and as a rule may be variously interpreted the feeling of compulsion, of being determined, arose from a particular, though not a vacuous, picture of following a rule.

A most important principle implicit in Wittgenstein's examination of both language and mathematics is his rejection of the sort of generality utilised by philosophers such as Frege and Russell. His analyses of many different examples are specifically designed to counter this craving for generality that he saw as the source of so much mistaken philosophy. He sets his face against the idea that the activities of mathematics may be generalised and justified in terms of something else. This underlies Russell's definition of number, for example, 'which we expect to tell us *what* a number *is*.

The difficulty with this explanation in terms of something else is that the something else may have an entirely different grammar' (Ambrose pp.29–30). This remark illustrates a criticism directed against the entire logicist programme of both Frege and Russell. In the writings of Frege and in *Principia Mathematica* the grammar of arithmetic is translated into something else, namely, the grammar of classes, correlations, functions, arguments, propositions, logical constants and the logical operations of conjunction, disjunction, negation and material implication. This is what Wittgenstein called 'the curse of Russell's prose in mathematics' (RFM 408). Russell took for granted that each of these concepts comprised a uniform class of instances or operations and Wittgenstein sought to call this in question by devising examples illustrating important grammatical differences within each of these classes of instances and operations. The attempt to define number overlooked the fact that while we call cardinal numbers, irrationals and real numbers all *numbers* they have utterly different grammars. According to Wittgenstein, we should not ask about the definition of number; we should get clear about the grammar (cf. Ambrose 117, 127, 164). Wittgenstein concedes that he seems to be saying that every proposition is different and thus denying the generality of mathematics and arithmetic as though we have many arithmetics. But the generality of the ordinary arithmetic we learned at school is not in the least threatened. This becomes clear if we look at the way arithmetic is *applied*. Arithmetic is a calculus and is related to its application in roughly the same way as a paradigm is to what it is a paradigm of. Arithmetic is learned by counting beads on an abacus or using physical objects for illustration. Later we learn to operate the calculus without reference to any particular objects.

> But this is not because arithmetic is 'general'. Arithmetic is like an instrument box – like a box of joiner's tools – and we can be taught the use of the instruments. . . . Arithmetic is not taught in the Russellian fashion, and this is no inaccuracy. We do not begin arithmetic by learning about propositions, and functions, nor with the definition of number. And this is not because children cannot understand these things. The way we learn arithmetic is the proper way (Ambrose, p.127).

We cannot be content with Wittgenstein's distinction between the calculus and its application as an account of the generality of arithmetic which may be operated as a calculus independently of any of its applications. I do not think Wittgenstein was content with this either, any more than he could have been with the homely illustration of arithmetic as a box of joiner's tools, for, unlike arithmetic, tools can only be used when they are applied. Having regard to the fact that none of us would wish to defend all utterances recorded by our students, without impugning their accuracy, it is possible to see what Wittgenstein was driving at. The generality of the concepts used by Frege and Russell may be variously classified in quite different ways and lack the uniformity that they attributed to them as the logically secure foundations of mathematics. What Wittgenstein is denying is that mathematics and logic are one building with logic as the foundation. 'Russell's calculus is one calculus among others. It is a bit of mathematics' (Ambrose, p.13). The idea that Frege and Russell had that there was *one* fundamental calculus, namely logic, on which any other calculus could be based is mistaken.

> The idea that logic gives the general form of a mathematical statement breaks down when one sees there is no such thing as one idea of a proposition, or of logic. One calls lots of things propositions. If one sees this, then one can discard the idea Russell and Frege had that logic is a science of certain objects – propositions, functions, the logical constants.

Wittgenstein goes on with some remarks which are of interest with respect to contemporary discussion of many-valued logics as alternatives to classical logic and which illustrate the purpose of devising language-games.

> I am not taking the view of C. I. Lewis and the Warsaw schools that there are many different logics. In speaking of more than one logic I am not referring to non-Aristotelian logics such as the three-valued logic in which propositions had three possibilities instead of two, T, F, and Possible. There is great danger in making up such a game, unless taken as a game. The value of such games is that they destroy prejudices; they show that 'it need not always be this way'. But if this latter is said as though it were a statement of science (like 'You think all rats are like this, but there are others'), then the 3-valued system, for

example, might appear to be an *extension* of logic, representing a discovery (Ambrose 138–9).

Wittgenstein asserts that an incredibly ambiguous grammar of generality is concealed by the notation in Russell's calculus. The notation '(x)fx' is taken to mean 'for all things so-and-so is the case', but this 'needs to be examined in each instance for sense'. Similar considerations apply to the use of predicates in the calculus and Wittgenstein alleges that Russell's use of (∃x)fx and (x)fx simply selects from language a particular use of 'predicate', 'some' and 'all' from a variety of different uses and generalises this into the real or correct use (LFM 167—8, 268–70; Ambrose 68–9, 125). Russell might be defended here by pointing out that he was well aware of the ambiguous grammar, or, as he preferred to put it, the abominable syntax of ordinary language. By writing '(x)' instead of 'all' and '(∃x)' instead of 'some' or 'any' he is using a notation in a strictly defined calculus that avoids these ambiguities or abominations. Wittgenstein's point, however, is that this can only be maintained at the expense of the generality of the claim that Russell's calculus gave the general form of propositions. According to him, both (x)φx = φa.φb.φc – and (∃x)φx = φaVφbVφc – 'are a translation from our language: they do not remove the ambiguities of our use of "some" or "all" in language' (Lee 90). He further alleges that there is ambiguity within the notation of the calculus quite apart from that incorporated by transfer from ordinary language. In both '(x)fx' and '(∃x)fx' Russell takes the 'x' inside the bracket to stand for a *thing* so that 'I met a man' = 'I met a thing which is a man'. Can one talk of a *thing* which is a man? The 'x' inside the bracket stands for men not things. Wittgenstein concedes that reducing 'I met a man' to 'There is an x such that I met x.x is a man' was a way of writing generality that called attention to the distinction between 'I met a man' and 'I met Smith', but in other ways was enormously misleading. Firstly, the ordinary sentence is not explained by reducing it to the calculus form because this still leaves the use of 'x' unexplained. Secondly, Russell's use of 'man' as a predicate is a curious and atypical example of the way predicates are used in our language. 'Whoever says "Socrates is a man"? I am not criticising this because it does not occur in practical life. What I am criticising is the fact that logicians do not give these examples any life' (Ambrose 124–5). The logic of Frege and Russell describes the use of langauge in a vacuum and what Wittgenstein held to be 'the basic evil of Russell's logic, as also of mine in the *Tractatus*, is that what a proposition is is illustrated by a few commonplace examples, and then presupposed as understood in full generality' (Ambrose 99, RPP I 38). The tendency to describe the use of language in a vacuum is illustrated by Russell's discussion of '-f(f)', which, according to Wittgenstein, simply lacks any application, and hence meaning (RFM 367).

Wittgenstein is also critical of Russell's introduction of symbols for relations of two or more terms on the grounds of a mistaken notion of generality and, more particularly, the assimilation of the exemplification of relational terms with the discovery of phenomena. Russell's underlying objective was the building up of a logic to apply to all eventualities as though to say 'love is a 2-termed relation' is to announce a discovery, a natural phenomenon that fitted the relational scheme without which it would be empty.

> It is absurd to look at 13-termed relation as empty until we have found a 13-termed phenomenon, for the calculus we make with these words does not receive any *content* from what is found: it remains a calculus. Russell thought that in treating foundations he had to arrange for the *application* of arithmetic, for example, to functions. One could not talk about 3 apart from some type of function, so one would need to classify functions. Number is a property of a function. Russell and F. P. Ramsey thought that one could in some sense prepare logic for the possible existence of certain entities, that one could construct a system for welcoming the results of analysis. . . . Constructing a relation does not depend on finding a phenomenon. Discovering a word-game is different from discovering a fact (Ambrose 142–3).

Frege and Russell rest their theory of cardinal numbers on the fundamental notion of correlation which is introduced via the idea of being equal in number. This was achieved through a notion of similarity or one-to-one correlation. Two classes were said to be equal in number if their extensions were correlated 1–1. Russell said that the number 2, for example, is the class of all classes that *are* correlated 1–1 to the prototype and not that it is the class that *can be* 1–1 correlated. Wittgenstein objects that there is a difference between the criteria *'can be* 1–1 correlated' and *'are* 1–1 correlated'. Are we to say that two classes have the same number when they have not been 1–1 correlated? We can say that classes are equal in number if they *can be* correlated provided we give instructions for telling how we find whether they can be. However, Russell's criterion for sameness of number, namely that the classes concerned *are* 1–1 correlated, is peculiar for no correlation seems to be made. Russell's way out of this difficulty was to say that no actual correlation need be made since two things are always correlated with two others by identity. For there are two functions, the one satisfied only by a, b and the other only by c, d, namely, $x = a.V.x = b$ and $y = c.v.y = d$. By substituting a for x and c for y we have $a = a \ V \ a = b$ and $c = c.V.c = d$. We can then construct a function satisfied only by the pairs ac and bd, that is, a function correlating one term of one group with one term of the other, namely, $x = a.y = c.V.x = b.y = d$, or the function, $x = a.V.y = d : x = b.V.y = c$. 'These correlate a with c and b with d by mere identity when there is no correlation by strings or other material correlation' (Ambrose 149–50; PG 355–8).

To this Wittgenstein objects that the sense of ordinary physical correlation as exemplified by placing cups and saucers one on the other and the sense of Russell's correlation by identity have different grammars. To say of cups and saucers that they are not correlated in this way does not mean that they cannot be correlated in another way. The peculiar property of Russell's correlation is that if correlation by identity does not hold, no other correlation could hold. With physical correlation, but not correlation by identity, what counts as a 1–1 correlation may be variously interpreted. Russell's correlation by identity invokes possible, not actual, correlations and possible here means logically possible. 'Where is the phenomenon of possibility to be looked for? Only in the symbolism we use. The essence of logical possibility is what is laid down in language' (Ambrose 159, 162). Wittgenstein criticises Russell for putting the cart before the horse with respect to his account of similarity or having the same number. We certainly could check our calculations by making actual physical correlations. It is easy to check $3 + 4 = 7$ by means of drawing lines and making one-to-one correlations but we don't do the same with 3 billion + 4 billion = 7 billion. Furthermore, if for large numbers we added and got one result and then correlated and got a different result we would trust the addition rather than the correlation. 'This is all I'm saying. We already have a calculus and we don't check up on it by some other method. Instead, if anything disagreed with this calculation we should reject it' (LFM 286).

Wittgenstein also finds Russell's notation puzzling because it makes identity to be a relation between two things. It suggests that there is such a proposition as x = x which seem to bring two objects, or an object and itself, into relation. Russell's notation, for example, '(∃x.y)fx.fy, is about the *things* referred to by x and y but 'x = y' is taken to assert that the *sign* 'x' means the same as the *sign* 'y'. Why this shift from things to signs? In the case of x = x what is it that tempts us to suppose that it is a fundamental truth that a thing is identical with itself – that this chair is identical with itself? 'There is no finer example of a useless proposition' (Ambrose 146–7; PI 216).

We have no need of a definition of number, and it was only thought that we do because 'number' is a substantive which was regarded as denoting a thing with which mathematics deals. Russell's account of *having the same number* makes it appear to entail a correlation, a correlation of classes by an ethereal relation. This relation is really a chimera, and to say that classes are so correlated gets us no further than saying they have the same number. We cannot discover the logical correlation in any other way than by discovering whether they have the same number. If one asks what is the fundamental criterion for the possibility of 1–1 correlation, it is that they have the same number! Russell's definition of number is futile (Ambrose 162–3; cf. also pp.205ff).

MATHEMATICS AND REALITY

The idea that mathematics creates essences, or to put this less exotically, to say that mathematical grammars are paradigms invented for particular purposes, encounters its most serious objection from the correspondence between mathematics and reality. Surely this correspondence is not fortuitous and we must regard the grammar of mathematics as in some way structured by reality. As we have previously noticed, this conviction was crucial to Frege's account of mathematics and his reaction to formalism gave rise to the celebrated aphorism; 'it is applicability alone which elevates arithmetic from a game to the rank of a science'.[3] This is the first step on a slippery slope which landed Frege in the position of maintaining that mathematical objects were ontological entities.

Without wishing to nail Frege's colours to the mast, many philosophers have felt that some applications of mathematics lend credence to Kant's claim that arithmetic and geometry comprise bodies of synthetic −a priori propositions. There is a kind of correspondence between the development of the natural number series in arithmetic and our experience of the succession of events in time. It is the case that (for small distances) the projections and methods of triangulation of Euclidean geometry correspond with empirical measurements of spatial arrangements of things in the world. As every physicist knows, the demonstration of a correspondence between events and mathematical relationships counts not only as an explanation of those events but provides a basis for the prediction of phenomena. In some cases these predictions may be made before the experimental verification of the phenomena. The mathematical intervals of the periodic table of the elements allowed us to infer some, at least, of the properties of certain elements prior to their discovery. The distinguished Japanese physicist Yukawa, on the basis of a new mathematical theory of nuclear forces, predicted the existence of mesons that have masses in a range intermediate between those of the electron and the proton. It was two years after this prediction that one type of meson was discovered among cosmic rays. One can sympathise with those who feel that in one form or another mathematical realism is forced upon us. I.e. that the essential structure of mathematics is fixed and determined by the structure of reality; the world has a mathematical form.

The most extreme version of mathematical realism was developed by the Pythagorean school who held that the world was actually constructed out of points, lines and planes. This view generated a great deal of conceptual confusion arising from the identification of mathematical points (which have no magnitude) with material points (which do have magnitude). Examples of this confusion range from attempts to find a material counterpart to the grammatical rule that an infinity of points may be interposed between any given two points on a line, to arguments about the number of angels that can balance on the point of a pin. Pythagorean realism is no longer a living option for us and more sophisticated accounts of the relations between mathematics and reality have been formulated.

These received a severe blow when it was discovered that

Euclidean and Reimannian geometries, although mutually incompatible due to the adoption of different parallels postulates, *both* had applications to the world. Nevertheless, it is quite understandable that the tendency to describe mathematics as a body of synthetic a priori propositions is a recurring illness among philosophers and mathematicians. G. H. Hardy, for example, wrote of mathematical theorems that they 'are, in one sense or another, however elusive and sophisticated that sense may be, theorems concerning reality . . .'[4] (cf.LFM 239 and note). Wittgenstein's view of this is interesting;

> Professor Hardy says: Goldbach's theorem (that every even number is the sum of two primes) is true or false depending upon the mathematical facts; it is not a matter of rules or convenience; it is a theorem concerning reality. How would you defend this? I said (in reply to Hardy's idea of a world of mathematical entities that the mathematician looks into) that the mathematician is a man who builds roads, or invents new ways of thinking (LFM p.139).

But how does reality connect with these inventions? His answer is characteristically paradoxical:

> If you say, 'Mathematical propositions say something about a mathematical reality' – which expresses a natural tendency – a result of that tendency would be roughly this: We say certain things about animals. These are propositions we all know, and propositions about exotic animals, which have a certain charm. If you have the idea that mathematics treats of mathematical entities, then just as some members of the animal world are exotic, there would be a realm of mathematical entities that were particularly exotic – and therefore particularly charming. . . . If you say that mathematical propositions are about a mathematical reality – although this is quite vague, it has very definite consequences. And if you deny it, there also queer consequences – for example, one may be led to finitism. Both would be quite wrong. There is a *muddle* at present, an unclarity (LFM 140–1).

Although Wittgenstein understands the tendency to say that mathematics is about reality he does not wish to affirm or deny this claim. Still less is he prepared to choose between the alternatives, either mathematics is about reality or it is about marks on paper, since he regards both positions as based on misunderstandings (cf. LFM 112). Here again, Wittgenstein's discussion of this problem is not intended to solve it but to dissolve it. We might consider the world as created with certain mathematical properties, for example, and say that in the game of chess 'it's a mathematical reality that he can't mate with two pawns'. Pressed further, we might say that mating with two pawns has no counterpart in the real world, unlike mating with a queen and a pawn. 'But what is its counterpart in the shadow world? What stands for the number 3 in the shadow world? Not 111, or three apples. You can't think. You could imagine a realm of spider-web lines, etc., a space somewhere in heaven reserved for Euclidean geometry. All points would be connected by straight lines – but would all straight lines be bisected? All constructions be done? But you would imagine the shadow world to consist simply in a copy of Euclids' *Elements*. There is no need to project the thing into a universe of its own' (LFM 149). Wittgenstein continues his examination of the notion of mathematical propositions corresponding to reality using Hardy as his stalking-horse, in spite of the fact that Hardy does not actually speak of a correspondence to reality (LFM 239 note). The point of this examination is to show that Hardy is comparing mathematical propositions with the propositions of physics and that such a comparison is grossly misleading. On the other hand, one might say that mathematical propositions correspond to reality in order to emphasise that there are some mathematical propositions which we affirm – which 'is harmless but meaningless'. Or we might be calling attention to the fact that they don't correspond to *moods* or combating the idea that mathematics is 'something vague which goes on in the mind' or that it is about scratches on a blackboard. The sense in which there is a correspondence between mathematics and reality is expressed by Wittgenstein in the following notes from his lecture which are best given in full.

If you say, 'Some reality corresponds to the mathematical proposition that 21×294', then I would say: Yes, reality, in the sense of experiential (empirical) reality *does* correspond to this. For example, the central reality that we have methods of representing this so that it can all be seen at a glance. In such a case as 21×14 nothing is easier than to lay out 21 rows of 14 matches and then count them; and then there is no doubt at all that *all of us* would get the same result. This is an experiential result; and it is immensely important. . . . We have certain words such that if we were asked, 'what is the reality which corresponds?' we should all point to the same thing – for example, 'sofa', 'green', etc. But 'perhaps', 'and', 'or', 'two', 'plus' . . . are quite different. If a man asks, 'Does no reality correspond to them?' what should we say? How should we explain this feeling that there is a reality corresponding to these words too? He means, 'Surely we have some use for them'. And that is obviously true. . . . So with these words 'and', 'or', etc., we can say that the reality which corresponds to them is that we have a use for them.

What I want to say is this. If one talks of the reality corresponding to a proposition of mathematics or logic, it is like speaking of a reality corresponding to these *words* – 'two' or 'perhaps' – more than it is like talking of a reality corresponding to the sentence 'It rains'. Because the structure of a 'true' mathematical proposition or a 'true' logical proposition is entirely defined in language; it doesn't depend on any external fact at all, I don't say: 'No reality corresponds'. To say 'A reality corresponds to $2 + 2 \times 4$' is like saying a reality corresponds to a rule, which would come to saying: 'it is a useful rule, *most* useful – we couldn't do without it for a thousand reasons, not just *one*.'

You might say: Mathematics and logic are part of the apparatus of language, not part of the application of language. It is the whole system of arithmetic which makes it possible for us to use '900' as we do in ordinary life. It prepares '900' for the work it has to do. In this sense, mathematical propositions do not treat of numbers. Whereas a proposition like 'There are three windows in this room' *does* treat of the number 3 . . . a mathematical proposition is not *about* its constituents in the sense in which 'The sofa is in this room' is about the sofa (LFM 246, 248–50, 254).

To say that arithmetic and geometry are bodies of synthetic *a priori* propositions or that the structure of the world determines the grammar of mathematics puts things the wrong way round. When mathematics and reality correspond it is because we project on to the world certain features of the grammar of our mathematical paradigm such that, in a sense, the world is a grammatical construction. In Newtonian physics the concept of a particle as a point mass of negligible volume is the ontological counterpart or projection on to the world of the concept of the mathematical point which has position but no magnitude. The mathematical point cannot be an item of experience and the relationship of the particle to experience is through abstraction and idealisation. The fact is that the Newtonian concept of a particle which is completely described by specifying the spatio-temporal coordinates of its position and momentum represents a material projection of the mathematical point and as such is a convenient fiction. In the same way, Newtonian space is a projection of the relationships between points, lines and planes that are a characteristic of the grammar of Euclidean geometry. What had the character of a discovery of the correspondence between Newtonian reality and Euclidean geometry is in fact a requirement of a particular method of projection according to which we fashion reality in the shape of our chosen paradigm. It is hardly surprising, therefore, that the Newtonian characterisation of reality as particles moving about in the void failed to account for the totality of human experience and that the concept of a particle collapsed in the face of phenomena that led to the formulation of quantum mechanics. We now find ourselves having to oscillate between two mutually incompatible pictures of reality arising from the different grammars of the mathematics of particles and waves respectively. A feature of the grammar of Newtonian mechanics is that of strict determinism, whereas the grammar of quantum mechanics has the feature of indeterminacy for sub-atomic phenomena. To ask whether the world really is determined or indeterminate is to fail to see that what we have here is only a grammatical conflict. It is some comfort to know that the tendency to become enslaved by our grammatical categories is an occupational hazard for others besides philosophers.

Newton's law of universal gravitation, that every particle of matter behaves as if it attracted every other particle in the universe with a force directly proportional to the product of their masses and inversely proportional to the square of the distance between them, is an excellent rule of thumb device for explaining and predicting the behaviour of the moon and the planets in orbit and the phenomenon of oceanic tides on earth. The projection of the grammar of this mathematical relationship on to reality created a picture of a mechanical force acting instantaneously through space that was frankly incredible to Newton himself. In one of his letters he wrote:

> That gravity should be innate, inherent and essential to matter, so that one body may act upon another at a distance through a vacuum, without the mediation of anything else, by and through which their action and force may be conveyed from one to another, is to me so great an absurdity that I believe no man who has in philosophical matters a competent faculty of thinking can ever fall into it.[5]

Berkeley complained that Newton misused the words 'gravity' and 'force' and by introducing force acting instantaneously at a distance throughout space as the cause or principle of motion (or acceleration) introduced an 'occult quality' into physics (De Motu 6). The invention subsequently of a mechanical aether as an all-pervading medium through which this force is transmitted invoked one grammatical phantom to explain another.

The projection of the grammar of Riemannian geometry on to the world in Einstein's general theory of relativity results in a very different picture of reality from that of Newton's use of Euclidean geometry. Mass, length and time are not the absolute values of the Newtonian system but vary with respect to a co-ordinate system and motion. The concept of an object loses its traditional properties and the boundaries between material bodies and space are not sharply defined. The idea of gravitation as a mechanical force of mutual attraction through space is abandoned and gravity becomes a Riemannian metric property of space–time. The projection of gravity as Riemannian curvature of space–time, in spite of its brilliance and fertility, suffers from the same defect characteristic of other extrapolations of mathematical grammar, namely, as a picture of reality it is partial and incomplete. The phenomenon of electromagnetism has resisted all efforts so far to produce a unified field theory such that electromagnetism and gravity alike are capable of a geometrical interpretation. Electrified and magnetised bodies have still to be conceptualised as acted on by forces. This seems to be another example, like that provided by classical and quantum mechanics, of our need to retain incompatible pictures of reality. Philosophers may dislike the apotheosis of grammatical conflict implicit in Bohr's principle of complementarity and long for a super-mathematical grammar whose projection as a model of reality does not fail us at some point. Whether or not this possibility can be realised remains to be seen and for the moment we have to work with a variety of pictures of the world that are incomplete and incompatible. Paradox and modern mathematical physics are inseparable.

The problem for mathematical realists, like Frege, now becomes explicit. According to this view, the applicability of mathematics is evidence of a correspondence with reality such that the structures of mathematical grammars are determined by the structure of the world. But we now have instances of mutually inconsistent grammars – e.g. Euclidean and Reimannian geometries – both of which have been found to have applications to the world. This appears to be a fatal objection to all forms of mathematical realism. What I have argued for might be called mathematical idealism inasmuch as it inverts the realist thesis. That is, that mathematical grammars are inventions whose applications consist of interpretations of reality according to particular paradigms and that is all that is meant by asserting a correspondence between mathematics and the world.

Frege was well aware of the threat to mathematical realism posed by non-Euclidean geometries and this explains the violence of his rejection of any alternative to Euclid. There is a little-noticed passage in his Posthumous Writings which is very revealing here:

> No man can serve two masters. One cannot serve both truth and untruth. If Euclidean geometry is true, then non-Euclidean geometry is false, and if non-Euclidean geometry is true, then Euclidean geometry is false.
>
> If given a point not lying on a line one and only one line can be drawn through that point parallel to that line then, given any line 1 and point P not lying on 1, a line can be drawn through P parallel to 1 and any line that passes through P and is parallel to 1 will coincide with it.
>
> Whoever acknowledges Euclidean geometry to be true must reject non-Euclidean geometry as false, and whoever acknowledges non-Euclidean geometry to be true must reject Euclidean geometry.
>
> People at one time believed they practised a science, which went by the name of alchemy; but when it was discovered that this supposed science was riddled with error, it was banished from among the sciences. Again, people at one time believed

they practised a science, which went by the name of astrology. But this too was banished from among the sciences once men had seen through it and discovered that it was unscientific. The question at the present time is whether Euclidean or non-Euclidean geometry should be struck off the role of the sciences and made to line up as a museum piece alongside alchemy and astrology. If one is content to have only phantoms hovering around one, there is no need to take the matter so seriously; but in science we are subject to the necessity of seeking after truth. There it is a case of in or out! Well, is it Euclidean or non-Euclidean geometry that should get the sack? That is the question. Do we dare to treat Euclid's elements, which have exercised unquestioned sway for 2000 years, as we have treated astrology? It is only if we do not dare to do this that we can put Euclid's axioms forward as propositions that are neither false nor doubtful. In that case non-Euclidean geometry will have to be counted amongst the pseudo-sciences, to the study of which we still attach some slight importance, but only as historical curiosities.[6]

In fairness to Frege it should be pointed out that these remarks were written between 1899 and 1906 and, hence, were before the spectacular physical interpretation given to Reimannian geometry by Einstein in the general theory of relativity. Nevertheless, Frege's view is no longer tenable.

Wittgenstein's position with respect to Euclidean geometry is made clear by the following remarks.

Euclidean geometry is a part of grammar. It is a convention of expression and so part of grammar. (Minkowski accounts for the result of the Michelson-Morley experiment by a new geometry, Fitzgerald by contraction. These are merely two expressions of the same fact; we can adopt either, unless a decisive experiment is possible between them) (Lee 8).

Geometry does not treat of cubes but of the grammar of the word 'cube', as arithmetic treats of the grammar of numbers. The word 'cube' is defined in a geometry, and a definition is not a proposition about a thing. If we alter the geometry we alter the meaning of the words used, for the geometry constitutes the meaning. ... Geometrical propositions say nothing about cubes, but determine which propositions about cubes make sense and which do not. This comment suggests the relation between mathematics and its application, i.e., between a sentence giving the grammar of the word and an ordinary sentence in which the word figures. . . . There is one sort of mistake that it is important to look at because of its pervasiveness. This is that the real cube and the geometrical cube are comparable. Geometry is not a physics of *geometrical* straight lines and cubes. It constitutes the meaning of the words 'line' and 'cube'. The role the cube plays in its geometry is the role of a *symbol*, not that of a solid with which inaccurate real cubes are comparable (Ambrose 51).

Geometry and arithmetic consist of nothing but rules of symbolism comparable to the rule which lays down the unit of length. Their relation to reality is that certain facts make certain geometries and arithemetics practical (Ambrose 84).

Can there be true propositions in the language of Euclid, which are not provable in his system, but are true? – Why, there are even propositions which are provable in Euclid's system, but are *false* in another system (RFM 118).

Current thinking about mathematics has moved in the direction of Wittgenstein and against Frege.

THE NOTION OF NECESSITY

The view of the axioms of mathematical systems as necessary truths because they are based on laws of thought, or are self-evident, or correspond with reality, is much less fashionable than it was. Kant's view of Euclidean geometry as a set of synthetic *a priori* propositions descriptive of the properties of physical space has not survived the development of non-Euclidean geometries and the dethronement of the Newtonian concept of absolute space. As Wittgenstein points out, what is important with respect to axioms is not their self-evidence or their attachment to reality but our acceptance of them as parts of speech to which we assign a particular function (RFM 223ff). However, having accepted our axioms and formulated our rules of transformation are we not compelled to accept as logically necessary the theorems derived from them? Surely, the axioms and the rules of procedure once adopted determine the steps to be followed in drawing logical inferences such that we must follow these steps if we wish to draw correct inferences? This view of logical inference has dominated mathematics and logic from Euclid and Aristotle to Frege and Russell and still has its adherents today. Wittgenstein on the other hand, ascribes to the peculiar use in mathematical logic of the verbs 'to follow' and 'to infer' the idea that 'following is the existence of a connexion between propositions, which connexions we follow up when we infer' (RFM 44). For example, in *Principia Mathematica* one proposition follows from another if one can be derived from the other in a proof or if it can be justified by a fundamental law of logic. Since 'what is implied by a true premiss is true' we are justified in inferring the proposition $\vdash q$ from $\vdash p \supset q$.p. This idea is even more explicitly formulated by Frege who thought that the straight line which connects any two points in Euclidean geometry 'is really already there before we draw it', as though our drawing it is like tracing it (RFM 45). This picture of inference as following steps which are already laid out in advance and which are justified by laws of logic is not substantiated by what we actually do when we infer, namely, 'That in some language-game we utter, write down (etc.) the one proposition as an assertion after the other; and how can the fundamental law of logic justify me in *this*?'

Russell's claim in *Principia Mathematica* that inference is justified by a fundamental law of logic is made because he wishes to establish the *correctness* of the processes of inference employed. If the criterion of correctness of inference is some fundamental law of logic what criterion of correctness do we use to establish this law? If, in order to avoid an infinite regress, we appeal to self-evidence in justification of the law then we might as well apply this criterion direct to the rule of procedure in inference. If self-evidence is sufficient for the law it is sufficient for the rule as well. The rule stands in no need of further justification for

it is really only a piece of information that in this book only *this* move from one proposition to another will be used (as it were a piece of information in the index); for the correctness of the move must be evident in its own place; and the expression of the 'fundamental law of logic' is then the *sequence of propositions* itself (RFM 44–5).

The sense of being fundamental is something given by the system of propositions, like the adoption of a system of measurement and the correctness of propositions within the system is like the correctness of particular measurements within the chosen paradigm. To try and justify the paradigm by identifying it with 'a fundamental law of logic' is an example of a grammatical misunderstanding.

Quite apart from the importance of these remarks as a rejection of the picture of logical necessity drawn in the *Tractatus* they also clearly illustrate the later Wittgenstein's method of treating philosophical problems in a way that seeks their dissolution rather than their solution. Repeatedly he draws attention to the fact that a particular picture may present itself to us arising from a peculiar use of certain words that seems appropriate when we are doing philosophy; in the present context the verbs 'to follow' and 'to infer'. In this case the picture suggests that inferring is the following of steps linking propositions that are laid out in advance and from which we cannot deviate if we are to infer correctly. To break the hypnotic fascination and persuasiveness of this picture 'it is necessary to look and see how we carry out inferences in the practice of language; what kind of procedure in the language-game inferring is' (RFM 43). Another misleading picture of inference is to call it a mental process, as though 'inferring is a peculiar activity, a process in the medium of the understanding, or as it were a brewing of the vapour out of which the deduction arises'. Wittgenstein treats as misleading those pictures which purport to depict either the structure of reality or inner processes of understanding and commends the therapeutic and exorcist functions of an examination that he calls a grammatical investigation. It is this type of examination that reveals that 'there is nothing occult about this process: it is a derivation of one sentence from another according to a rule; a comparison of both with some paradigm or other, which represents the schema of the transition' (RFM 39).

Inevitably Wittgenstein's interlocutor objects: 'But doesn't e.g., "fa" have to follow from "(x).fx" if "(x).fx" is meant in the way we mean it?' (RFM 41). Our regular use of the word "all" inclines us to say 'From "all" if it is meant *like this, this* must surely follow!' Wittgenstein retorts; 'No, it isn't true that it *must* – but it *does* follow: we *perform* this transition' (RFM 42). The regularity of such a transition is not an index of its necessity but of our agreement in practice. But surely, if you mean '(x).fx' you also mean 'fa' and if you meant 'fa' then the step has been taken in the mind before you utter or write it? Putting this another way, if you did not mean 'fa' when you meant '(x).fx' then you did not understand '(x).fx'. In short, the assertion of '(x).fx' and the denial of 'fa' is a contradiction such that if you assert '(x).fx' you *must* also assert 'fa'. Wittgenstein deals with this argument in a passage in the *Investigations* when he writes:

> Is it correct for someone to say: 'When I gave you this rule, I meant you to . . . in this case'? Even if he did not think of this case at all as he gave the rule? Of course it is correct. For 'to mean it' did not mean: to think of it. But now the problem is: How are we to judge whether someone meant such and such? The fact that he has, for example, mastered a particular technique in arithmetic and algebra, and that he taught someone else the expansion of a series in the usual way is such a criterion. 'When I teach someone the formation of the series . . . I surely mean him to write . . . at the hundredth place?' Quite right; you mean it. And evidently without necessarily even thinking of it. This shews you how different the grammar of the verb 'to mean' is from that of 'to think'. And nothing is more wrong-headed than calling meaning a mental activity! (PI 692–3).

This passage succinctly expresses the purport of what Wittgenstein is feeling his way towards in *RFM*. When applying a rule in arithmetic or algebra or in the calculus of *Principia Mathematica* – e.g. (x).fx – to say of any step in the series so generated, 'I meant this . . .' is not equivalent to picturing this step in the mind before taking it. The criterion for meaning something here is not the existence in the mind of the series but the mastery of a technique. It is this picture of meaning something as a mental activity that leads us to the idea that the formulation of a rule uniquely and unambiguously determines its application such that in the development of a series every step in the process already exists if not in reality then at least in the mind. What Wittgenstein seeks to show through a number of examples is that a rule is grounded in human agreement and practice and that what counts as conforming to a rule may be variously interpreted.

Where, then, does this compulsive notion of logical necessity come from? He falls back upon the analogy of picturing as illustrating the origins of the hardness of the logical must. For example, in our learning and practice with the word 'all' in various language-situations the word becomes 'surrounded with a whole lot of pictures (visual and others) of which one or another comes up when we hear and speak the word'. In our attempt to give an account of the 'meaning' of the word 'we first pull out *one* from this mass of pictures – and then reject it again as non-essential when we see that now this, now that picture presents itself, and sometimes none at all' (RFM 41). The Russellian 'all' disallows exceptions, i.e., 'all without exception', and one learns its meaning by learning that 'fa' follows from '(x).fx'. However, ordinary language also uses 'all' as a hyperbole, i.e. 'all with few exceptions' and both uses have their place in our language. It is the insistence on treating 'all without exception' as the correct use of 'all' that inclines us to say that 'fa' *must* follow from '(x).fx' and so to treat 'all' used as a hyperbole – or Wittgenstein's own example, 'all but one' – as improper. To say that 'fa' *does* rather than *must* follow from '(x).fx' is to see more clearly that logical relations are things deposited by human beings amongst the paradigms of our language-games and removes the illusion that we are tracing the steps determined by laws of thought or reality or some such thing.

Where we tend to go wrong is when a particular use of 'all' forces itself upon us such that we feel that 'something over and above the *use* of the word "all" must have changed if "fa" is no longer to follow from "(x).fx"; something attaching to the word itself' (RFM 42).

RFM explores a number of cases where logical necessity, compulsion and inescapability appear to be forced upon us by such things as mathematical proofs. In one example, he constructs various ways of proving equinumerousness by establishing a one-one correlation between the angles contained in a given geometrical figure and a series of vertical strokes. The object of these exercises is to dispel the persuasive and seductive picture of a proof as something which exhibits the essential properties of geometrical figures and instead see a proof as the deposition of a pattern or paradigm which may differ from one that we have accepted traditionally (RFM 48). A proof of equinumerousness between two figures

doesn't explore the essence of the two figures, but it does express what I am going to count as belonging to the essence of the figures from now on – I deposit what belongs to the essence among the paradigms of language. The mathematician creates *essence* (RFM 50).

The ultimate example of the type of misunderstanding which Wittgenstein is trying to clear up is provided by mathematical realists who project prescribed properties on to the world and treat them as though they are ingredients of things (RFM 63–4).

Once more the interlocutor objects; 'Can we do otherwise than accept the conclusion of a proof: does not the proof compel us?' Certainly in following a proof or inference we can always refuse to take the next step – but in that case have we not ceased following or inferring? Are we not being unreasonable if we accept the premises on which a proof is based and deny the conclusion? Wittgenstein wants to say that what appears to be compulsion is rather a matter of agreement; that is we agree to go *this* way and refuse any other path. It is easy to see that the axioms or premisses on which a proof is based are a matter of agreement but we are less inclined to concede that the steps leading to the conclusion are also a matter of agreement. Once we accept, adopt, invent or agree to the premisses then are we not compelled to follow through the implications of the premisses and accept the conclusion? Putting this another way, if we wish to deny the conclusion must we not do so by rejecting the premisses which is the whole point of the *reductio-ad-absurdum* type of argument? The interlocutor puts it this way: " 'But if you are right, how does it come about that all men (or at any rate all normal men) accept these patterns as proofs of these propositions?" It is true, that there is great – and interesting – agreement here' (RFM 50). As he puts it elsewhere, rather more positively, reading a proof and being convinced by it 'is a peculiar procedure: *I go through* the proof and then accept its result – I mean: this is simply what we *do*. This is use and custom among us, or a fact of our natural history'. If someone doesn't acknowledge a proof as a demonstration that *this* follows from *that* 'then he has parted company with us even before it comes to talk'. 'In a demonstration we *get agreement* with someone. If we do not, then our roads part before it comes to traffic by means of this language' (RFM 60–2).

In the *Philosophical Investigations* Wittgenstein refers to misleading philosophical analogues of our ordinary language games as pictures or images or representations of the grammar of our expressions. The use of the word 'object' provides a simple illustration of this tendency. When used of physical object the idea of spatial location may be said to be part of its grammar. When we talk of a mental object, however, we may be misled by the persistence of this grammatical picture and feel impelled to locate such objects in the mind or, even more inappropriately, in the brain. What we need to see, according to Wittgenstein, is that the grammar of 'physical object' and the grammar of 'mental object' are quite different and that this is best revealed by a comparison of their respective uses. Similarly, the grammatical picture of logical inference as a mechanical process in which logic is 'an all-pervading ethereal mechanism' is dissolved by construing the grammar of laws of inference as more like systems of measurement (RFM 82–4).

This also throws light on what seems to be Wittgenstein's advocacy of finitist mathematics and behaviourist psychology. 'Finitism and behaviourism are quite similar trends. Both say, but surely, all we have here is. . . . Both deny the existence of something, both with a view to escaping from a confusion' (RFM 142). His interest in finitism and behaviourism is in their therapeutic function in excorcising the ghostly entities conjured up by mathematicians and psychologists from the grammars of infinite sets and mental processes respectively. It does not represent a conviction that they are either the foundations of, or provide the justification for, mathematics and psychology. So far as mathematics is concerned 'the role of the proposition: "I must have miscalculated . . ." is really the key to an understanding of the "foundations of mathematics"' (RFM 221). This means, I take it, that mathematics is a practice, a technique, and a miscalculation represents some departure or other from the way in which we normally apply an agreed paradigm. He thinks that this way of looking at mathematics will deliver us from the temptation of 'giving a justification of our procedure where there is no such thing as a justification and we ought simply to have said: *That's how we do it*' (RFM 199).

Consider the grammatical differences between a finite series and an infinite series which, according to Wittgenstein, are frequently assimilated with misleading consequences. Imagine a series of 100 trees planted in a row and suppose we are asked, do four trees of the same species occur consecutively in the series? The grammar of a finite series includes the law of excluded middle, $p \vee -p$; either four trees of the same species occur consecutively in the series or they do not. If p is true then $-p$ is false and if $-p$ is true then p is false. Consider now another example which is one given by Wittgenstein. Does 7777 occur in the infinite expansion of π? Assimilation of the grammar of an infinite series with that of a finite series suggests that here too we have the law of excluded middle, $p \lor -p$; either we will come on 7777 in the series or we will not. But the two cases are different. Whilst there are conditions under which we could assert the truth of p, namely, we come across 7777 in the development of the series, there are no conditions under which we could assert the truth of $-p$. The absence of 7777 in the series developed to the nth place – however large n may be – would not entitle us to infer that 7777 does not occur in the infinite expansion of π. The inability to prove $-p$ does not imply the truth of p. Wittgenstein makes the point that the question is something that 'changes its status when it becomes decidable. For a connexion is made then, which formerly *was not there*' (RFM 266-7). The temptation to treat this question as though it were an application of the law of excluded middle arises from a grammatical picture which is perfectly appropriate for a finite series. That is to say, we have a definite picture of a finite series as something like a row of trees which we can survey. The retention of this picture with respect to an infinite series leads us to suppose that questions that may be asked significantly of a finite series have the same significance when asked of an infinite series. If the answer to the question about the occurrence of 7777 in the expansion of π is affirmative we imagine something like 3.145926536 . . . 7777 . . . which is a picture of a (more or less) completed series or row from its beginning to the occurrence of the pattern. This way of looking at infinite series is as though God saw the whole of it and we do not merely because we lack this omniscient vision (cf. PI 426). But suppose the answer to the question is negative? 'Then no such picture is of any use to me, and my supply of pictures gives out' (RFM 277). The application of $p \lor -p$ depends on there being significant pictures for both p and $-p$ and the total absence of anything that could be regarded as a suitable picture for $-p$ indicates that this question has only the surface grammar of the law of excluded middle (RFM 268).

The crux of Wittgenstein's argument is expressed by the following exchange with his interlocutor:

> To say of an unending series that it does *not* contain a particular pattern makes sense only under quite special conditions. That is to say: this proposition has been given a sense for certain cases.

Roughly, for those where it is in the *rule* for this series, not to contain the pattern. . . . Further, when I calculate the expansion further I am deriving new rules which the series obeys. 'Good – then we can say: "It must either reside in the rule for this series that the pattern occurs, or the opposite"'. But is it like that? – 'Well, doesn't the rule of expansion *determine* the series completely? And if it does so, if it allows of no ambiguity, then it must implicitly determine *all* questions about the structure of the series.' Here you are thinking of finite series. 'But surely all members of the series from the 1st up to the 1 000th, up to the 10^{10}-th and so on, are determined; so surely *all* the members are determined.' That is correct if it is supposed to mean that it is not the case that e.g. the so-and-so-many'th is *not* determined. But you can see that *that* gives you no information about whether a particular pattern is going to appear in the series (if it has not appeared so far). *And so we can see* that we are using a misleading *picture*.

If you want to know more about the series, you have, so to speak, to get into another dimension (as it were from the line into a surrounding plane). But then isn't the plane *there*, just like the line, and merely something to be *explored*, if one wants to know what the facts are? No, the mathematics of this further dimension has to be invented just as much as any mathematics (RFM 268–70).

In a rule for the expansion of an infinite series it seems as if the truth conditions for every step in the series, as well as the steps themselves, are already determined by the rule. To follow such a rule is to traverse an endless row of mathematical entities stretching into infinity beyond and independently of our application of the rule. A rule of inference determines a sequence of propositions and leads inescapably to a conclusion the truth of which is guaranteed by the truth of the premises and the validity of the rule of inference. Clustered around our concept of following a rule are all kinds of notions of mathematical objectivity, logical necessity, behavioural determinism, and the hardness and constraints of the logical must. Wittgenstein's analysis of the concept of following a rule has attracted more obloquy from his critics than any other aspect of his remarks on mathematics. The outright rejection of his remarks on following a rule because they are not consistent arises from a misunderstanding of what he is about. The various examples of following a rule that he considers do not comprise a uniform class of instances falling under a single concept. The rejection of uniformity is implicit in his rejection of the facile generality which he believed philosophers tended to invoke and which was the source of so many of their problems. Wittgenstein calls this tendency 'a grammatical obsession (which) can be described as taking some extremely simple form of grammar and so to speak conjugating all words according to its pattern' (Ambrose 110). Nowhere is this tendency more apparent than in treating the following of a rule as a uniform operation in all circumstances instead of seeing it as a family of instances with complex inter-relations. The later Wittgenstein's technique of philosophising and its importance is illustrated by some remarks on calculations and calculating which are relevant here.

> What I am doing is, not to show that calculations are wrong, but to subject the *interest* of calculations to a test. Test e.g. the justification for still using the word . . . here. Or really, I keep on urging such an investigation. I show that there is such an investigation and what there is to investigate there. Thus I must say, not: 'We must not express ourselves like this', or 'That is absurd', or 'That is uninteresting', but: 'Test the justification of this expression in this way'. You cannot survey the justification of an expression unless you survey its employment, which you cannot do by looking at some facet of its employment, say a picture attaching to it (RFM 142).

This succinctly expresses the nature of Wittgenstein's grammatical investigations of what he believed to be the extraordinarily complicated 'physiognomy of what we call "following a rule" in everyday life'. 'These things are finer spun than crude hands have any inkling of' (RFM 420, 422).

Of course Wittgenstein's remarks are not consistent; how could they be, given the grammatical differences, the changing circumstances, the varieties of interpretation, the conflicting pictures, images and models attached to following a rule? Saying that there are no determinate and consistent theses to which his remarks are addressed is not to place Wittgenstein beyond all criticism and disagreement. There is plenty of scope for that in assessing the force of the examples he chooses in order to test, and perhaps dissolve, particular pictures associated with the following a rule.

The simplest and most effective way of demonstrating the nature and range of Wittgenstein's enquiries concerning following a rule is to collect and tabulate many of the kinds of questions to which he addresses himself.

A. RULES AND THEIR JUSTIFICATION

Can we give a description which will justify the rules of grammar? Can we say why we must use *these* rules? (Lee 47; PI 217)

Can the use of language be compared to playing a game according to exact rules? (Ambrose 48)

Can we deduce the rules for the use of a word from its meaning? (Ambrose 50)

Can we say of a grammatical rule that it conforms to or contradicts a fact? (Ambrose 65)

Can we say of a rule that it is true or false or merely that it is practical or impractical? (Ambrose 70)

Is what we can say a priori only what we ourselves have laid down as rules for the use of a symbol? (Ambrose 86)

What is the relation between a rule and a proposition that conforms to an empirical fact? (Ambrose 161; RFM 327)

Is the expression of a rule for the development of a number series explained by the numerical values or are the values explained by the rule? Is the rule what is explained or what does the explaining? (RPP II 404–5)

Is following a rule indefinable or can it be defined in countless ways? (RFM 321)

Would we call something following a rule if it stood in isolation? (RFM 335, 349; PI 199, 202)

How does it come about that the question 'how can one follow a rule?' arises when I find no difficulty in following a rule? (RFM 341)

Could there be arithmetic without agreement on the part of calculators? (RFM 349)

'We take a number of steps, all legitimate – i.e. allowed by the rules – and suddenly a contradiction results.' Why does this wreck the whole game? (RFM 371)

Is calculation an experiment? (RFM 389)

Are not the rules of logical inference rules of *language-game*? (RFM 401)

Isn't a rule something arbitrary? (RFM 404; PI 497)

B. RULES AND MENTAL PROCESSES

Does using language according to grammatical rules mean that the rules of grammar run in our heads as we use language? (Lee 48)

There may be states of mind corresponding to every game such as chess but do these states presuppose or contain the rules? (Ambrose 49)

What is the distinction between states of mind and knowledge of the rules? (Ambrose 49)

Is the gap between a rule and its application a problem or a mental cramp? (Ambrose 90)

Does following a rule entail a new intuition or a new decision for each step? (Ambrose 133–4; RFM VI 44)

In following a rule of inference, is the conclusion thought when the premise is? (Ambrose 134)

Is seeing the regularity in a series a psychological fact? (RFM 327–8)

Could I give a general explanation of how a rule for the expansion of a series continues purely in the mind and so without any real language? (RFM 329)

Is the agreement of people in calculation an agreement in opinions or convictions? (RFM 332)

Is a recognition of uniformity presupposed in saying people are acting according to a rule? (RFM 348)

What is the role of teaching and learning in following a rule correctly? (RFM 392–3)

Does one learn to obey a rule by first learning the use of the word 'agreement' or the reverse? (RFM 405; PI 224)

Does understanding a rule reach beyond all the examples of following it? (RFM 417; PI 209)

Doesn't the technique (the *possibility*) of training someone else in following it belong to the following of a rule? (RFM 418)

May I not *believe* I am following a rule? Doesn't this case exist? (RFM 420; PI 202)

Is it correct for someone to say: 'When I gave you this rule, I meant you to . . . in this case'? Even if he did not think of this case at all as he gave the rule? (PI 692–3)

C. RULES AND INEXORABILITY

Are the steps taken in following a rule contained in it? (Ambrose 131)

Does giving a rule also give the infinite extension of its application? (Ambrose 179)

How does grasping a rule bind you in what you do further? (RFM 328)

Could it be said: 'In calculating, the rules strike you as inexorable; you feel that you can only do that and nothing else if you want to follow the rule'? (RFM 332)

If giving a rule an interpretation before following it *determines* what I have to do, what choice have I left. (RFM 332; PI §219)

Is it the case that once you have got hold of the rule, you have the route traced for you? (RFM 333)

How can I follow a rule when whatever I do can be interpreted as following it? (RFM 341)

Is there some *knowledge* which makes a rule followable only in *this* way? (RFM 341)

How can a rule guide us when various regularities correspond to it? (RFM 347)

Does 'If you follow a rule, this *must* come out', mean it must, because it always has or that it comes out is one of my *foundations*? (RFM 350)

'But at every step I know absolutely what I have to do; what the rule demands of me! Whence this certainty? But why do I ask that question? Is it not enough that this certainty exists? (RFM 350)

Isn't it possible to derive anything from anything according to some rule or other – nay, according to *any* rule with a suitable interpretation? (RFM 389; PI 198, 201)

Is not the sense of compulsion in following a rule a spell that enthralls us rather than the tracing of a ghostly line? (RFM 395)

'If you accept this rule you *must* do this.' Does this mean the rule conducts you like a gangway with rigid walls? Is it not the case that the rule could be interpreted in all sorts of ways? (RFM 406)

If a rule for the expansion of a series has been given us a calculation can tell us there is a '2' at the 5th place. Could God have known this without the calculation, purely from the rule of expansion? (RFM 408)

Are there not cases where whether someone does the same thing or keeps on doing something different does not determine whether he is following a rule? (RFM 416; PI 227)

Does following a rule mechanically, i.e. without thinking, entail comparing it with a mechanism? (RFM 422)

'Lets try what will come out now if I apply this rule.' Is the ensuing calculation an experiment? (RFM 424)

Why do I always speak of being compelled by a rule; why not of the fact that I can *choose* to follow it? (RFM 429)

In considering, 'How can one keep to a rule?', how useful is the picture of a handrail by means of which I let myself be guided further than the rail reaches? (RFM 430)

'If you really follow the rule in multiplying, you *must* all get the same result.' Is this hysterical university talk or the expression of an attitude towards the technique of calculation which comes out everywhere in our life? (RFM 430)

If the proof convinces us, then must we not also be convinced of the axioms? (RFM 345;

Whence comes the idea that the beginning of a series is a visible section of rails invisibly laid to infinity? (PI 218)

The philosophical fascination for Wittgenstein of the explanations that are offered of how and why we follow a rule is as prolific generators of a mythology surrounding our linguistic and mathematical activities. He does not deny that inexorability, logical necessity and compulsion are features of most of these explanations. It is not their impropriety and consequent abolition that is the object of his enquiries but their office. His central concern is, 'you say you must; but cannot say what compels you' (RFM 326). Wittgenstein's enquiries into following a rule are analogous to Hume's analysis of causality. That necessary connection between causally related events is a feature of our explication of the concept of causality Hume never denied, but what makes the connection *necessary*? Does necessity reside in objects, mysterious powers or minds? Wittgenstein's analysis of the sense of compulsion attaching to following a rule is as profound and important as Hume's examination of necessary connection and has been as grossly misunderstood. Wittgenstein's examination of the explanations we offer of following a rule and the examples of rule-following he considers are designed to reveal the complex network of largely mythological imagery with which we shroud such activities as calculating, expanding a series, inferring, playing games with fixed rules (like chess) and playing games without fixed rules (like beach-ball). Sometimes the picture drawn by mathematical realists seems appropriate and we are inclined to say the inexorability lies in the rule itself as an expression of mathematical objectivity. The series or the line is already there stretching before you and the rule determines the truth conditions enabling you to follow the steps of the series or to trace the line and thus give substance to the shadow. Recognition that a rule does not guarantee its interpretation might lead us to modify this picture and say that it is the rule together with an agreed interpretation that compels us to follow the steps that stretch out before us. For those who find quite unacceptable the notion of behavioural determinism implicit in this view of the inexorability of following a rule the picture drawn by intuitionist mathematicians seems more appropriate. Here the notion of compulsion plays no part and in developing a rule for the expansion of a series every step requires a new intuition. Those who find intuition an opaque notion may modify this picture and depict following a rule essentially as a mental process which accompanies and gives life to the activity of calculating. This too may dissolve when we recognise the different grammars of 'to mean a particular step in a series' and 'to think a particular step in a series'. Additionally, the postulation of another series in the mind running parallel with the series we actually develop on paper seems an unnecessary duplication. Perhaps we are inclined to go along with the formalists and identify the sense of compulsion with the regularity of the sequence of marks we make on paper when we write out a series, i.e. in following a rule we feel compelled to follow the pattern. Behavioural determinism is at its most persuasive when we say all rational human beings *must* follow rules of inference in this way and no other. This picture loses something of its persuasiveness as soon as one asks, 'have I no choice left?'

The crucial point in all these considerations that Wittgenstein seeks to establish is that 'the rule compels us' is a variable that changes with the different perspectives we adopt. Inexorability, logical necessity and compulsion are pictorial representations of our grammar, of our way of talking about and explaining following a rule. What are the practical consequences for actually following a rule of saying either that the rule determines the steps or the steps determine the rule? None! That should arouse our suspicions.

This illuminates another important strand of Wittgenstein's thought, namely, his insistence that description and explanation should be distinguished. The calculus that results from following a rule stands in no need of justification or explanation. Obeying a rule is a practice, a technique, that is learned and can be taught. All that is necessary is that the activity be described; it is our attempts at explanation that lead straight into the realms of grammatical mythology. The activities of calculating and following a rule no more require explanation than mathematics needs foundations. What the sense of inexorability, logical necessity and compulsion expresses is 'an attitude towards the technique of calculation which comes out everywhere in our life. The emphasis of the *must* corresponds only to the inexorableness of this attitude both to the technique of calculating and to a host of related techniques' (RFM 430). For Hume and Wittgenstein necessity does not lie in objects but in our attitudes.

7
Philosophical Investigations

LINGUISTIC ANALYSIS

One of the most misleading ideas suggested by logical analysis was that there was 'something like a final analysis of our forms of language, and so a single completely resolved form of every expression' (PI 91). As it was put in the *Tractatus*; 'a proposition has one and only one complete analysis' (3.25). This view led to two further mistakes; first, that the process of analysis was a search for greater exactness in our expressions, as though there were 'a state of complete exactness; and as if this were the real goal of our investigations'. Second, the supposition that 'the essence of language – its function, its structure' lay hidden 'beneath the surface . . . and which an analysis digs out' (PI 92). Both the goal and the method of philosophical investigation implicit in this view of language are decisively rejected. The proper role for philosophy is that of grammatical investigation directed to clearing away linguistic misconstructions and misunderstandings. 'Some of them can be removed by substituting one form of expression for another; this may be called an "analysis" of our forms of expression, for the process is sometimes like one of taking things apart' (PI 90). We might call this type of analysis, substitution analysis, to differentiate it from logical analysis. Whereas logical analysis was intended to dig for hidden forms and structures, substitution analysis surveys and rearranges what is already on the surface and open to view. Grammatical surveying replaces logical excavation as the method of philosophical investigation.

Precisely what linguistic activities comprise grammatical investigations?

The commonly used expression 'linguistic analysis' suggests a unity of method which is misleading. 'There is not a philosophical method, though there are indeed methods, like different therapies' (PI 133). To interpret Wittgenstein as saying that all philosophical problems are soluble by the application of a technique called 'linguistic analysis' is absurd. To suppose that this technique consists of the compilation of lists of word usages, as though the panacea for philosophical perplexity is lexicography, is to crown the absurdity. An examination of the *Investigations* shows that a grammatical investigation may consist of any of the following types of enquiry.

1. Constructing analogies between aspects of language and
    (a) games (in general) and chess (in particular) (3, 68–75; 31, 35)
    (b) pictures (59, 73, 96, 115, 194)
    (c) geometrical methods of projection (139, 141, 366)
    (d) tools, instruments and machines (14–15, 41–2; 16, 54, 57; 6, 156–7)
    (e) physical and mental processes (196, 303, 308, 363, 571)
    (f) physiognomy, atmosphere and corona (568, pp. 181, 210, 218; I. 117, 173, 213; p.181)
    (g) mathematics (124, 240, 463, p.226)
    (h) a private 'beetle' and a private diary (293, 258, 270)
    (i) conventions, customs and institutions (41, 355; 198–9, 206; 337, 380)
    (j) signposts (85, 87, 198)
    (k) actions and gestures (1, 7, 23, 36, 613; 433–4, 550, 590, 666, 673)
    (l) standards of measurement (50)
    (m) tables (53, 62, 73, 86, 162–3, 265)
    (n) illness and therapy (255; 133)
    (o) musical themes (22, 341, 523, 527)
2. The invention of
    (a) primitive language-games (2)
    (b) intermediate cases with respect to normal forms of representation (122)
    (c) language for particular purposes (492)
    (d) a language with two different words for negation (556)
3. Imagining the following cases
    (a) consulting a dictionary in the imagination (265)
    (b) the ascription of pain to dolls and stones (282, 284)
    (c) God giving a parrot understanding (346)
    (d) senseless combinations of words (I512)

  (e) a language having different psychological verbs (577)
  (f) a person or persons –
    – whose memory could not retain the meaning of 'pain' (271)
    – being in pain but concealing it (391)
    – who could only think aloud (331)
    – learning to do sums in his head without ever doing written or oral ones (385)
    – who are automata (420)
    – being shown a 'private' map of movements (653)
    – using 'abracadabra' as an expression of pain (665)
    – simulating pain (667)
    – being in pain while a piano is being tuned and saying 'it will stop soon' (666)
    – telephoning someone and illustrating what was said by pointing (67)
4. Attempting or undertaking the
  (a) logical analysis of sentences (60)
  (b) determination of what is common in games and language (66–7)
  (c) substitution of one form of expression for another (90)
  (d) restoration of metaphysical expressions to their everyday use (116)
  (e) uncovering of nonsense (119)
  (f) assembling of reminders for particular purposes (127)
  (g) revelation of what is hidden by its simplicity and familiarity (129)
  (h) doubting in real cases third-person ascriptions of pain (303)
  (i) consideration of the circumstances in which the use of a word is instituted (380)
  (j) justification of the use of words (382)
  (k) determination of criteria for our use of words (164, 182, 344)
  (l) investigation of the arbitrariness of signs (508)
  (m) conducting of language experiments (510)
  (n) comparisons of –
    – propositions and pictures (522)
    – knowing and saying (78)
    – negation and action (547)
    – beliefs and feelings (578)
    – two language-games for making predictions (630)
    – hopes and expectations (584–5)
    & etc.

The above list brings out the range and diversity of activities comprehended by Wittgenstein's notion of grammatical investigations and also how misleading it is to treat this notion as equivalent to a body of doctrine about language. One result of these enquiries is that 'we see that what we call "sentence" and "language" has not the formal unity that I imagined, but is the family of structures more or less related to one another' (PI 108). If this is the case, 'what becomes of logic now?' Logic had appeared to be 'sublime' with 'a peculiar depth'; a kind of 'super-order between super-concepts' expressing the essence of both thought and language and revealing the nature of all things (PI 89, 92, 97). Now, however, the unshakeable ideal of 'the strict and clear rules of the logical structure of propositions' hidden in the understanding is seen to derive it's sense of inescapability from the same source as if we looked at things through a pair of spectacles which it never occurs to us to remove (PI 102–3). In other words, we are inclined to hold this view of logic only because 'we predicate of the thing what lies in the method of representing it' (PI 104). This projection of logic on to reality and the understanding leads us to attribute a life to our symbolism – 'the nature of the *real* sign' – with the consequence that we mythologise thought, language and the world. Grammatical investigations are dedicated to demythologising these concepts. 'The *preconceived idea* of crystalline purity can only be removed by turning our whole examination round. . . . The philosophy of logic speaks of sentences and words in exactly the sense in which we speak of them in ordinary life' (PI 108). It is at this point that Wittgenstein reiterates and underlines two assertions made in the *Tractatus*, namely, that 'all the propositions of our everyday language, just as they stand, are in perfect logical order' and that 'our problems are not abstract, but perhaps the most concrete that there are' (5.5563 cf. PI 97–8). The degree of concreteness of these problems is indicated by the nature of the investigations Wittgenstein now proposes in order to solve them. Words like 'language', 'experience' and 'world' have a use as concrete and as humble as words like 'table', 'lamp' and 'door'. The same is true of the favourite mystery or ghostly-entity words of philosophy like 'knowledge', 'understanding' and 'meaning'. In spite of the aura of mysteriousness with which philosophy has invested these words they remain utility-words; practical, down to earth and simple instruments of our forms of life. If words that have been canonised in philosophy turn out to have everyday uses which are not problematical, we must not conclude that 'every sentence-like formation must have a use' and the cure for the tendency 'to count some quite useless thing as a proposition' is to consider its application (PI 520). The law of identity, that seemingly 'infallible paradigm' of identity – 'a thing is identical with itself', or 'p o p' – is dubbed the finest example of 'a useless proposition' (PI 215–16). As it stands such a proposition lacks grammar. On the other hand, an expression like 'war is war' does have a grammar and so 'is not an example of the law of identity' in spite of their outward similarity of form or surface-grammar (PI 221).

Grammatical investigations are not undertaken with a view to explaining and still less justifying ordinary language. 'Grammar does not tell us how language must be constructed in order to fulfil its purpose. . . . It only describes and in no way explains the use of signs.' Their aim is not the revelation of the nature, or essence or hidden logical structure of language, nor is it to justify any of our forms of representation; 'the aim of the grammar is nothing but that of the language' (PI 496–7). How, then, do philosophical problems arise? They arise because of the tendency of certain expressions to conjure up pictures which we assume to be integral parts of their grammar on all occasions of their use. He describes such pictures as 'a full-blown pictorial representation of our grammar. Not facts; but as it were illustrated turns of speech' (PI 295). Philsophical problems are engendered by carrying over a picture that is appropriate for particular uses of a word to other uses of it where the picture becomes misleading. Another tendency is that of expressing such pictures in the form of grammatical propositions and then interpreting them as empirical or experiential ones. This is the case with words like 'pain' and 'understanding' both of which Wittgenstein investigates with great thoroughness and subtlety. The generation of fictional entities is illustrated by the attempts to identify the logically private exemplar of 'pain' and the mysterious inner processes of 'understanding'. This is familiar ground; a grammatical fiction is a feature of certain sorts of expressions which we mistakenly interpret as a feature of reality. This is a more thorough-going delineation of the error which Wittgenstein detected in the 1929 paper on *Logical Form*, namely, that of projecting on to the world features that properly belong only to our method of representation. Grammatical investigations include in their purview the exploration of the concept of representation, the differences between our methods of representation and the exemplification of their multiplicity. In this respect, grammatical investigations set out to say what the *Tractatus* had declared to be unsayable. This is not to say that the doctrine that what shows cannot be said is completely abandoned. Rather is it the case that it is transformed to the thesis that what shows *need* not be said except to remove misunderstandings. Hence, with respect to grammatical investigations 'the concept of a perspicuous representation is of fundamental significance for us. It earmarks the form of account we give, the way we look at things' (PI 122). Hence, too, with respect to philosophy it 'may in no way interfere with the actual use of language; it can in the end only describe it. For it cannot give it any foundation either. It leaves everything as it is' (PI 124). Similarly:

philosophy simply puts everything before us, and neither explains nor deduces anything – since everything lies open to view there is nothing to explain. . . . If one tried to advance theses in philosophy, it would never be possible to debate them, because everyone would agree to them. The aspects of things that are most important for us are hidden because of their simplicity and familiarity (PI 126–9).

How our words and sentences represent simply *shows* in our mastery of the techniques of language. Philosophy cannot explain this because explanation is superfluous in the same way as a successful painter has no need to explain how a painted portrait represents a human face. To a most important question put by Wittgenstein's imaginary interlocutor, 'How do sentences manage to represent?', Wittgenstein replies: 'the answer might be: "Don't you know? You certainly see it, when you use them". For nothing is concealed' (PI 435).

The role of philosophy is not to provide foundations, explanations or justification for the functions of language; it is therapeutic in its efforts to remove linguistic malfunctions. These malfunctions lead to two kinds of philosophical errors:

1. The projection of grammatical pictures onto reality – the mistake of grammatical fictions; e.g., 'thought' and 'objects', 'pain' and 'private exemplars', 'understanding' and 'inner processes'.
2. The confusion of expressions whose different depth-grammars are obscured by similarities of surface-grammar – the mistake

of grammatical assimilation; e.g. propositional monism, physical and mental processes, 'I have an x' where x is a variable including among its values 'a gold tooth' and 'toothache'.

The conviction expressed in the *Tractatus* that much of philosophy was comprised of pseudo-propositions survived in the *Investigations* in a new form, namely, that it was comprised of sentences that were grammatical misconstructions. As in the *Tractatus* so in the *Investigations*, philosophical enquiry is essentially a matter of the elucidation of language both in its concern with the normal and the abnormal uses of our expressions. Philosophical propositions are nonsensical not because they fail to picture how things stand but because what they picture are either grammatical fictions or the result of mistaken grammatical assimilations. According to Wittgenstein, the end of philosophy is the end of philosophy.

Along with many other philosophers, Wittgenstein was acutely aware of the immensity of the intellectual labour involved in philosophy compared with the meagreness and seeming triviality of its results. Hume's remedy of carelessness, inattention and the pleasures of convivial company was a non-starter for Wittgenstein because of his solitary nature and he advocated the even more radical remedy of abolishing philosophy altogether. His first attempt to put an end to philosophy was to propound a final solution which although recognised in a sense as trivial seemed to him to justify its abandonment. Nevertheless, it is now clear that throughout the period of about ten years that he withdrew from philosophy the compulsive neurosis of philosophical enquiry was only dormant and not cured. Thereafter the proposed treatment was more radical still. If the problems of philosophy did not yield to a final solution then surely they could be abolished by a final dissolution by exhibiting the linguistic confusions in which they originated. However, the attempt to find peace from philosophical torment eluded Wittgenstein until life itself came to an end – and that too is significant.

Wittgenstein is insistent that it is *language* that is the source of philosophical pseudo-problems. Hence, his remarks about the craving for generality, the fascination exerted by certain of our forms of expression, the irresistable influence of the implications of our symbolism, and the misunderstanding, misinterpretation, bewilderment, seduction, bewitchment, enslavement, charm, illusions, spells, troubles, delusions, ghosts, false appearances and mistaken analogies produced by language. The question is, how do these tendencies arise in the first place? Presumably, they are not the linguistic counterpart of original sin since it is an affliction found principally, if not exclusively, among philosophers. To say that we are inclined to detach the meanings of words from particular uses like a physiognomy or picture which then collides with other uses of those words illustrates a kind of error but does not establish its origins. Even if we accept that it is only philosophers who err in this way, this application of the picture analogy leaves unexplained the prevalence and antiquity of these bad language-habits. We must not be fobbed off here by the assertion that demands for explanation have no final end and that we should simply note that this is what people do. This argument is acceptable in cases where we can indicate some bedrock of human activity, some form of life, in which human beings engage and agree. Wittgenstein's position, however, is that philosophy does not represent a genuine form of life, or, putting this another way, there is no such thing as a genuine philosophical language-game. If we choose to identify our philosophical tendencies or metaphysical yearnings with psychological cravings that expressed themselves in linguistic confusions then the exploration of these phenomena would be a matter for the psychology of philosophy and not a grammatical investigation.

It is at this point that the parallel between Wittgenstein and Kant, to which a number of writers have called attention, breaks down. Kant sets up an elaborate theory tracing the sources of philosophical perplexity back to the pretensions of the understanding, pure reason and the will. Wittgenstein declines the gambit of invoking mysterious inner mental states, processes or faculties; for him problem and remedy are both located at the level of language. 'Like everything metaphysical the harmony between thought and reality is to be found in the grammar of the language' (Z 55). The categories which Kant attributed to the understanding as necessary forms of experience of phenomena are for Wittgenstein part of the apparatus of grammar and our methods of representation are optional forms for our descriptions of phenomena. The transmutation of the Kantian attributes of the human psyche to the grammar of our language is one of Wittgenstein's greatest achievements. On the other hand, a consequence of this transmutation is that these problems lose their distinctive character of depth, persistence and universality which are themselves only grammatical illusions.

We must return again to the question, where does the tendency to generate grammatical fictions and the like originate? Wittgenstein's account of the grammatical origin of philosophical errors becomes credible only if we recognise that there are countless occasions in which we successfully find further employment for words whose meanings have been delineated in other usages. On all these occasions there is no collision between meaning and use, sense and employment, picture and application. In short, the detachment of meaning from use and the representation of meaning as a kind of picture which persists independently of that use is not itself a malfunction of language but part of its normal function. It is the picturability of meaning that enables us to select the right word for a particular use, to grasp in a flash a meaning derived from an extended use, to compare the meanings of words in terms of the compatibility of the pictures, to identify synonyms by the congruency of the pictures and to see negation as the reversal of a picture's sense. Again it must be emphasised that Wittgenstein's new sense of 'picture' is not restricted to paintings, drawings and visual images but embraces many concepts – including mathematical abstractions and the pseudo-concepts derived from grammar and methods of projection. To change the analogy, the comparison of words with instruments or tools lends itself to the interpretation that it is the meaning of a word which determines its use in the sense that we do not select a spanner to do the work of a chisel. What this means is that the generalisation 'the meaning of a word is its use in the language' (PI 43) would be better replaced by, 'meaning and use *interact*'. The idea that the meaning of a word is a kind of picture which can be detached from the use which gave it its structure, as it were, is perfectly harmless in most cases and part of the normal operations of language. It becomes troublesome when philosophers try to identify the location of the picture in the mind or the understanding and suppose that the associated picture must always be present whenever the word is used. What among ordinary men is a normal tendency becomes among philosophers a neurotic impulse.

The neurosis which was given expression in both Russell's *Principia Mathematica* and Wittgenstein's *Tractatus* was the comparison of language with a rule-bound calculus. The later Wittgenstein's therapy for this condition is to demonstrate that a rule-bound calculus is a bad paradigm for natural language.

To break the fascination of this paradigm Wittgenstein deploys two arguments. The first argument is designed to illustrate the fluctuating rules of our ordinary language. In the *Investigations* he remarks:

> In philosophy we often *compare* the use of words with games and calculi which have fixed rules, but cannot say that someone who is using language *must* be playing such a game. But if you say that our languages only *approximate* to such calculi you are standing on the very brink of misunderstanding. For then it may look as if what we were talking about were an *ideal* language. As if our logic were, so to speak, a logic for a vacuum. Whereas logic does not treat of language – or of thought – in the sense in which a natural science treats of a natural phenomenon, and the most that can be said is that we *construct* ideal languages. But here the word 'ideal' is liable to mislead, for it sounds as if these languages were better, more perfect, than our everyday language; and as if it took the logician to show people at last what a proper sentence looked like. All this, however, can only appear in the right light when one has attained greater clarity about the concepts of understanding, meaning, and thinking. For it will then also become clear what can lead us (and did lead me) to think that if anyone utters a sentence and *means* or understands it he is operating a calculus according to definite rules' (PI 81).

The early Wittgenstein's mistake lay in supposing that a calculus was needed to *underwrite* ordinary language: Russell's mistake lay in supposing that a calculus was needed to replace it.

It was Frege who advanced the thesis that unless the meanings of words had sharp boundaries they were unusable. Wittgenstein rejects this picture and says that the actual investigation of language suggests a different picture, namely, that the meanings of words are surrounded by a kind of penumbra rather than a sharp boundary and that this in no way renders them unusable.

> I said that the application of a word is not everywhere bounded by rules. But what does a game look like that is everywhere bounded by rules? Whose rules never let a doubt creep in, but

stop up all the cracks where it might? Can't we imagine a rule determining the application of a rule, and a doubt which *it* removes – and so on? But that is not to say that we are in doubt because it is possible for us to *imagine* a doubt (PI 84).

The aim of Wittgenstein's investigation is certainly the achievement of greater clarity but this is not to be construed as a programme of language reform. There are areas of language standing in need of improvement and greater precision, in the interests of science, for example, but the areas of confusion Wittgenstein wishes to remove are of a different kind which 'arise when language is like an engine idling, not when it is doing work' (PI 132). Indeed his declared objective is what he calls *'complete clarity'* which is not to be confused with complete exactness but simply means that the philosophical problems generated by this linguistic phenomenon should *'completely* disappear' (PI 133). Such problems do not derive from the inexactness or the fluctuation of our rules. 'It is not our aim to refine or complete the system of rules for the use of our words in unheard-of ways.' Rather is it the case that they derive from the picture of language as a calculus.

THE NEW PICTURE ANALOGY

We must examine in some detail a new sense of 'picture' which is increasingly invoked in the later philosophy.

Again and again in the later writings, Wittgenstein employs a picture analogy which clearly is not the same as the idea of the proposition as a picture elaborated in the *Tractatus*. Using the *Investigations* as the source of information the new picture analogy exhibits the following structure.

Pictures may be:

1. *Actual* – e.g. paintings, drawings, illustrations, models, samples, portraits, photographs and puzzle-pictures (73, 95, p.54n(b), 193–4, 280, 291, 295–7, 368, 422 (cf. II. p.178), 425–7, 515, 519, 522, 526, 548, 604–5; pp.178, 190, 193–229, 230).
2. *Mental* – e.g. visual images, sense impressions (experiential and imaginary), physiognomies, atmospheres, coronas and dreams (6, 37, 59, 113–15, 139–41, p.54n(a), 191, 218–22, 251, 293–5, 300–1, 305–8, 334–5, 352, 367, 368, 373–4, 397–8, 402,

449, 490, 534, 573, 607, 658, 663; pp. 175, 176, 181, 183, 184, 185, 193–229).

Using examples from either (or both) of these main types, Pictures may represent:

1. *Concepts and Models*
   (6, 37, 59, 73, 96, 139–41, 191, 218–22, 291, 293, 300–1, 305–8, 352, 367, 449, 490, 519, 526, 534, 604–5, 607, 658, 663; pp.175, 176, 178, 181, 183, 185, 190, 193–229).
2. *Grammar*
   p.54n(a), 193–4, 251, 295–7, 334–5, 348–9, 373–4, 398, 422–7, 548, 573; pp.178, 184, 193–229, 230).
3. *Methods of Projection*
   113–15, p.54n(b), 144, 280, 291, 368, 397, 402, 449, 515, 522; pp.193–229, 230).

The above schema is illustrative and suggestive rather than exclusive and exhaustive.

Apart from the discussion of 'seeing' and 'seeing as' in connection with the duck–rabbit picture, which has proved controversial, it is clear that one of the principal functions of the picture analogy is to illustrate ways in which language generates philosophical confusion.

Wittgenstein writes of a word having 'a field of force' and our feeling that it has 'a familiar physiognomy' (PI 568; pp.218–219). This notion of a physiognomy is a variant on the much-used analogy of grammatical pictures. It is precisely this tendency for words to acquire a particular physiognomy or to be associated with a grammatical picture that seems familiar to us that is philosophically troublesome. What in fact arises from a conflict between different grammars or systems or propositions now looks like a philosophical problem and we try to synthesise two different methods of representation. Wittgenstein's remedy for the haze that surrounds language as a result of 'this general notion of the meaning of a word' is quite other than the remedies offered in philosophical explanations as traditionally conceived.

It disperses the fog to study the phenomena of language in primitive kinds of application in which one can command a clear view of the aim and functioning of the words. A child uses such primitive forms of language when it learns to talk. Here the teaching of language is not explanation but training (PI 5)

What will exemplify primitive forms of language is not the logically simple but the childishly simple.

Wittgenstein considers another pair of words with which to explore the relationship of meaning and use, namely, picture and application. There are certain kinds of words for which it is credible to suggest that the meaning of a word is a visual image which comes before the mind whenever that word is used. The word 'cube' may conjure up a vivid mental picture of a cube whenever 'cube' is used. In such a case the problem is how do we understand the meaning of a word on the assumption that its meaning is its use? Understanding the meaning of a word is instantaneous 'and is surely something different from the 'use' which is extended in time' (PI 138).

If I know the meaning of the word 'cube' when it is uttered 'can the whole *use* of the word come before any mind when I *understand* it in this way?' Putting this another way, 'can what we grasp *in a flash* accord with a use, fit or fail to fit it?' This leads to the important question: 'What really comes before our mind when we *understand* a word? Isn't it something like a picture? Can't it *be* a picture?' Suppose that this is correct and that when someone hears or reads and understands the meaning of the word 'cube' his understanding the meaning consists in a picture that comes before his mind, like a drawing of a cube. In what sense could one say that a mental picture fitted or failed to fit a particular use of the word 'cube'?

> Perhaps you say: 'It's quite simple:- if that picture occurs to me and I point to a triangular prism for instance, and say it is a cube, then this use of the word doesn't fit the picture'. But doesn't it fit? I have purposely so chosen the example that it is quite easy to imagine a *method of projection* according to which the picture does fit after all. The picture of the cube did indeed *suggest* a certain use to us, but it was possible for me to use it differently (PI 139).

The view that understanding the meaning of a word consists of experiencing some kind of inner picture is exposed to the same objections that Wittgenstein himself had raised against his earlier idea that propositions were pictures which simply displayed their sense in their pictorial structure. Whether the picture is conceived as outer (a proposition) or inner (a visual image) both alternatives overlook the fact that by the adoption of a suitable method of projection anything can be a picture of anything. Even if a relationship of likeness or pictorial identity is established between a picture and an object, the picture can always be applied in a way that is a projection of an entirely different object. In understanding the meaning of a word, appealing to problematic pictures – either inner or outer – does not help us. Where it seems appropriate to invoke a picture associated with a word, what matters is not the picture but its application. In short, to understand the meaning of a word is to understand its use, its mode of projection, its grammar.

What makes the notion of an inner picture so persuasive is expressed thus by Wittgenstein:

> 'I believe the right word in this case is . . .' Doesn't this show that the meaning of a word is a something that comes before our mind, and which is, as it were, the exact picture we want to use here? . . . No: the fact that one speaks of the *appropriate word* does not *show* the existence of a something that etc. One is inclined, rather, to speak of this picture-like something just because one can find a word appropriate; because one often chooses between words as between similar but not identical pictures; because pictures are often used instead of words, or to illustrate words; and so on' (PI p.54n(a)).

The credibility of the inner picture as the meaning of a word is itself a projection of our use of pictures to explain or illustrate the meanings of certain words. A children's illustrated dictionary correlates words like 'apple', 'ball', and 'cabbage' with pictures and its seems a short step to suppose that there is a parallel correlation between words and mental pictures. Even if such psychical connections existed it is not the picture that fixes the meaning of the word with which it is associated. 'What is essential is to see that the same thing can come before our minds when we hear the word and the application still be different. Has it the *same* meaning both times? I think we shall say not' (PI 140).

Is it not possible to imagine an example where a picture, a method of projection and an application all come before the mind in connection with a particular word?

> Suppose I explain various methods of projection to someone so that he may go on to apply them; let us ask ourselves when we should say that *the* method that I intend comes before his mind.

Now clearly we accept two different kinds of criteria for this: on the one hand the picture (of whatever kind) that at some time or other comes before his mind; on the other, the application which – in the course of time he makes of what he imagines. (And can't it be clearly seen here that it is absolutely inessential for the picture to exist in his imagination rather than as a drawing or model in front of him; or again as something that he himself constructs as a model?) (PI 141).

In this example, too, the mental picture cancels out as irrelevant. It is not the case, as was said in the *Tractatus*, that 'a picture represents its subject correctly or incorrectly' (2.173). Of any representation alleged to be an incorrect picture we can devise a method of projection that will make it correct. The representational form of a picture is no longer to be thought of as *its* standpoint but *ours* and we may change our standpoint such that any representation becomes perspicuous. In that case, however, the problem arises if for every different application of a picture we can imagine a method of projection that makes the representation perspicuous how can picture and application collide in a way that generates philosophical perplexity? This collision comes about 'inasmuch as the picture makes us expect a different use, because people in general apply *this* picture like *this*. I want to say; we have here a *normal* case, and abnormal cases (ibid.)'.

He makes a similar point when he writes:

It is no more essential to the understanding of a proposition that one should imagine anything in connexion with it, than that one should make a sketch from it. Instead of 'imaginability' one can also say here: representability by a particular method of representation. And such a representation *may* indeed safely point a way to further use of a sentence. On the other hand a picture may obtrude itself upon us and be of no use at all (PI 396–397).

In this circumstance too, we can say that the normal case is the one where a method of representation suggests further uses for a sentence. For example, within the representational framework or standpoint adopted for the description of material things the sentence, 'this object has the following properties . . .', has any number of uses which are familiar and also may be used successfully of new discoveries in the realms of physical science. The abnormal case is where a picture of that method of representation obtrudes itself when we ought to recognise that there has been a change in standpoint. As, for instance, when one is tempted to describe the room in which one is sitting in the 'visual room' and then go to try and describe its properties.

The 'visual room' seemed like a discovery, but what its discoverer really found was a new way of speaking, a new comparison:

. . . you have a new conception and interpret it as seeing a new object. You interpret a grammatical movement made by yourself as a quasi-physical phenomenon which you are observing. (Think for example of the question: 'Are sense-data the material of which the universe is made?'). But there is an objection to my saying that you have made a 'grammatical' movement. What you have primarily discovered is a new way of looking at things. As if you had invented a new way of painting; or, again, a new metre, or a new kind of song (PI 400–1).

We may distinguish four strands in what Wittgenstein says about meaning and use.

1. That meaning and use, as it were, coincide; i.e. the meaning of a word or sentence simply is its use in particular situations.
2. That arising from the grammar of a particular use an expression acquires a meaning – like a physiognomy – that makes the expression appropriate in other uses.
3. That meaning and use *collide*; i.e. when an expression acquires a physiognomy of meaning from the grammar of a particular use that conflicts with the meaning of the expression used in the context of a different grammar.
4. That a picture of a method of representation used in connection with an expression obtrudes itself and obscures the meaning that the expression has when used in connection with a different method of representation.

The first and second cases are part of the normal physiology of language. The third and fourth cases belong to the abnormal pathology of language and are the philosophically interesting ones. Like any good diagnostician Wittgenstein approaches pathology via physiology and it is this that lends weight to his post-mortem reports on various philosophical theories of language.

What emerges clearly from all this is that the relation between meaning and use is not one of identity but a complicated, perhaps even a very elastic one. The meanings of our expressions are elucidated by their use in ordinary language, in invented language-games and through the complex analogies of grammar, methods of projection and pictures. These analogies are not necessarily mutually consistent since they do not comprise a body of ideas that could be called a theory of language but are designed to illustrate various facets of our expressions which are different in scope and function. To treat 'the meaning of a word is its use' as even an approximation to an identity statment is to repeat in the interpretation of the *Investigations* the mistake of interpreting representation in the *Tractatus* as pictorial likeness. 'Propositions are pictures' and 'meaning is use' have both been too narrowly and simply conceived – as have the links between them. Most of the examples Wittgenstein considers in the *Investigations* are abnormal cases in which the detachment of expressions from their normal applications, grammar and the like, and, particularly their incorporation in philosophical propositions, generate all manner of pseudo-problems. The result is that we fail to see how these problems arise and consequently how easily they may be resolved. Hence, Wittgenstein's expressed aim in philosophy is 'to show the fly the way out of the fly-bottle' (PI 309). The philosopher is not the savant who elucidates what the common man does unwittingly when he uses language – rather the reverse: 'When we do philosophy we are like savages, primitive people, who hear the expressions of civilised men, put a false interpretation on them, and then draw the queerest conclusions from it' (PI 194). This sharpens the point of his remark that ordinary language is all right as it stands. He is not concerned with the elucidation or the analysis or the replacement or the syntactical, grammatical and notational revision of ordinary language which functions normally in its countless different ways, precisely because such operations are unnecessary. The sense in which ordinary language is all right is that it adequately performs the multiplicity of tasks for which it was adopted by its users who are civilised human beings. It is the would-be elucidator, analyst and revisionist – the philosopher –

who is the muddled and muddling barbarian. His final retort to Russell's criticisms of the abominable syntax of ordinary language is that the most misleading paradigms of language are those derived from the artificial tautological constructions and atypical generalisations of *Principia Mathematica*. Thus Wittgenstein's concern is less with the use of language by ordinary men than with its misuse by philosophers.

The task of philosophy is not to create a new ideal language, but to clarify the use of our language, the existing language. Its aim is to remove particular misunderstandings; not to produce a real understanding for the first time (PG 72b, 115).

It is not those who are well but those who are sick, who need treatment and Wittgenstein's linguistic homoeopathy is a species of that most primitive of all remedies – the hair of the dog that bit you.

PHILOSOPHY AS GRAMMATICAL FICTION

We have already noticed Wittgenstein's tendency to treat the ontology of the *Tractatus* as the projection on to the world of a particular view of language. His view of reality as comprising configurations of objects is a shadow cast by the grammar of propositional pictures whose arrangement of names displayed how things stand. In this sense, objects are not entities but grammatical fictions. Plato's primary elements, Russell's individuals and Wittgenstein's objects are all features of the grammar of a particular method of representation of the world and not of the world per se; change the method of representation and they disappear. In philosophy, what appears to be an ontological commitment is only the mythologising of our grammar.

The development of what is known broadly as British Empiricism has produced a variety of phenomenalist accounts of the nature and structure of language and the world. Inevitably, there are differences between these accounts concerning the logical status of mathematical propositions, the relation of universals to experience, the solution of the problem of solipsism and so on. Nevertheless, there are a number of common features concerning language which include two theses which occupied Wittgenstein's attention in the *Investigations*. The first is that what descriptive propositions describe are sense-data, i.e. the sensory impressions that comprise the items of immediate experience. Thus our knowledge is essentially knowledge of the contents of our minds such that the world is a construction out of sense-data. The second thesis arises out of the first in that, given that propositions describe sense-data, then the criteria for understanding the meaning of a word are to be located in a variety of mental events, acts, states and processes. Most of the examples given to illustrate this phenomenalist account of language trade upon sense-data of a visual kind, usually colour words, to render credible the idea that understanding a word consists in possessing a corresponding private image or inner picture. For example, we understand the meaning of the word 'red' because we can conjure up in our minds a visual image of a red colour patch. Wittgenstein examines at some length the kinds of things that phenomenalists have said about language and failure to realise which stalking horse he is using is to miss the point of some of his most important remarks in the *Investigations*. It seems likely that his extended examination of the idea that the meaning of 'pain' is an inner sensation which constitutes a private exemplar of pain is undertaken, at least in part, because in this example sense-data analysis is robbed of the initial plausibility of the idea that what a word means is a visual image which the word conjures up in the mind when it is used.

The viability of an account of language, knowledge and the world in terms of sense-data depends upon finding a satisfactory solution to three inter-related problems. First, there is the ontological problem of the adequacy of ephemeral sense-data as the material out of which we construct an external world existing permanently and independently of our perception of it. Second, there is the epistemological problem that if knowledge is confined to objects of personal and immediate experience that we have sensed and we cannot experience another's sensations, their reports of them can only be a matter of belief and not knowledge for us. Third, there is the linguistic problem of how words that mean or refer to logically private sensations come to have a public use in common language.

Wittgenstein's comments range over all these problems with particular reference to Russell's views. We have mentioned earlier the fact that Russell held that a logically perfect language would be 'very largely private to one speaker. That is to say all the names that it would use would be private to that speaker and could not enter into the language of another speaker'.[1] It is clear from this that Russell did not think that any one at present possessed a private language. A logically perfect language would be largely private and belonged to the future. Nevertheless, he thought that the objects designated by logically proper names are private in as much as the frame of reference from which all descriptive language derived its significance is logically private experience. This is shown by the fact that Russell gives as examples of the fundamentals of language the 'egocentric particulars' 'I', 'this', 'here' and 'now' – with 'this' as the most fundamental of all.[2] These four words are words of ordinary language in common use but the objects denoted by them on each occasion of their use are private to the speaker. The emphasis here is on a private *object* rather than a private *language* and the basic model of Russell's phenomenalist account of language is that of logically private exemplars connected with the proper names of common language by means of ostensive definitions.

Thus an ostensive definition points, as it were, in two directions; outwardly and inwardly. The outward direction is to a common perceptual object and the inward direction is to the logically private sense-datum which each perceiver of the object has and which may be qualitatively different for all perceivers except, possibly, for certain structural similarities. The bestowing of a name accompanying an ostensive gesture enables us to talk about the common object in spite of the privacy of each person's perception of it. This might be called the double reference theory of names and in most phenomenalist accounts is not explicitly formulated with the result that there is an oscillation between inner and outer objects that is confusing and problematical. Wittgenstein calls attention to the misleading nature of talking about colour and colour-impressions 'as if we detached the colour-*impression* from the object, like a membrane'. The uncertainty of the ontological status of the sense-datum, which seems to oscillate between that of a mental image and that of a surface of a visual object 'ought to arouse our suspicions' (PI 276). The difficulty here is that the sense-datum appears to be a kind of quasi-object interposed between material things and our perception of them and, instead of explaining perception, introduces a puzzling new entity for further explanation. There are two ways in which this oscillation between inner and outer may be abolished. One is the solipsist version of phenomenalism which simply cancels out the outer object altogether. Common objects, other people and reports of their perceptions all comprise a family of sense-data qualitatively indistinguishable within the realm of logically private inner objects. For the solipsist the inner object is the only logical type of object that there is, and the only ground of dispute between two solipsists would concern which of them is the figment of the other's imagination.

The other way of avoiding the awkwardness of an oscillation between inner and outer objects is Wittgenstein's proposal that we cancel out the inner object. In a specific repudiation of Russell's views he observes:

'I' is not the name of a person, nor 'here' of a place, and 'this' is not a name. But they are connected with names. Names are explained by means of them. It is also true that it is characteristic of physics not to use these words (PI 410).

He continues with an examination of the idea that one can ostensively define a sensation – which is the paradigm case of the inner object. Specifically, he invites consideration of a number of questions including, 'are these books *my* books?', and, 'is this sensation *my* sensation?'. He asks:

Which sensation does one mean by '*this*' one? That is: how is one using the demonstrative pronoun here? Certainly otherwise than in, say, the first example (are these books *my* books). Here confusion occurs because one imagines that by directing one's attention to a sensation one is pointing to it (PI 411).

The plausibility of an ostensive definition of an inner object is a grammatical sleight of hand deriving from the assimilation of two different cases, namely, that directing one's attention to an inner sensation – 'this' sensation – is the same as pointing to an object – 'this' book. The phenomena of directing one's attention and pointing to an object are not comparable and this fact is obscured by the similarity in surface grammar between the two questions. Once this grammatical assimilation is detected and the different depth grammars of the two cases is revealed then the credibility of an ostensive definition as an inward pointing to a private exemplar is called in question. The interlocutor objects at this point: 'But when I imagine something or even actually *see* objects, I have *got* something which my neighbour has not.' Wittgenstein responds:

I understand you. You want to look about you and say: 'At any rate only I have got THIS'. What are these words for? They serve no purpose. Can one not add: 'There is here no question of a 'seeing' – and therefore none of a 'having' – nor of a subject, nor therefore of "I" either'? Might I not ask: In what sense have you *got* what you are talking about and saying that only you have got it? Do you possess it? You do not even *see* it. Must you not really say that no one has got it? And this too is clear: if as a matter of logic you exclude other people's having something it loses its sense to say that you have it (PI 398).

Expressions like 'only I have *this* sensation' and 'another person cannot experience *my* sense data' presupposes the grammar of ownership appropriate in ordinary statements of possession but which have no application with respect to the inner object.

How, then, are language and sensations related? What is the grammar of those statements that purport to describe sensations, inner experiences and sense data? As we have seen, most phenomenalist answers to this question concerning the relation of sensation and language trade upon the model of *inner* object and *outer* designation. Wittgenstein's examination of this model reveals that it is defective as an illustration of the grammar of our actual expressions of sensation and the like. How this model is set up is exhibited by a consideration of the word 'pain'. It seems indisputable that 'pain' describes an experience of which only the user is personally aware. However, Wittgenstein points out, if it is the case that it is only from my own experience that 'I know what the word "pain" means – must I not say the same of other people too? And how do I generalise the *one* case so irresponsibly?' (PI 293). What would appear to confirm this initial supposition is if 'someone tells me that *he* knows what pain is only from his own case'. This sets up the model of 'inner' and 'outer'; the word 'pain', although in common use as part of the language, refers to a private exemplar which each person has and which no one else can experience or observe directly. Against the persuasiveness of this model Wittgenstein deploys his celebrated beetle-in-the-box argument. If we suppose that each person had a box containing his own private 'beetle' and no one else could look into another's box, then everyone could say 'he knows what a beetle is only by looking at *his* beetle'. On this supposition, everyone could have something different in his box, or the contents could be constantly changing;

> But suppose the word 'beetle' had a use in these people's language? – If so it would not be used as the name of a thing. The thing in the box has no place in the language-game at all; not even as a *something*: for the box might even be empty. No, one can 'divide through' by the thing in the box; it cancels out, whatever it is. That is to say: if we construe the grammar of the expression of sensation on the model of 'object and designation' the object drops out of consideration as irrelevant (PI 293).

The point is that the picture of a *private* beetle makes no contribution to the grammar of 'beetle'. The model of a something about which nothing can be said, except that it is a *something*, might as well be replaced by nothing. One might object to this and say that what is in the box is a something which cannot be experienced, viewed or described by someone else, but this is not at all the same as saying that nothing can be said about it. Nothing can be said about it by *others* but the possessor of the box can say something about it and can not only designate but describe it. Changing from the 'beetle' analogy back to the example of pain, one could say this is why doctors may ask a patient to describe his pain and not simply designate its location and this is precisely what the patient who is in pain, and only he, can do. The words, 'I have a pain here' accompanied by an appropriate ostensive gesture locates the region of the pain and the words 'it burns, stabs or throbs' describes its type and provides additional detail. This makes it appear as if one had a private picture or image of 'pain' which one can scrutinise more closely if required – as though one can peer into one's box and describe the private 'beetle' in more detail. This is a persuasive account of 'pain' but consider what it is we do when we describe a picture more closely. Supposing someone is shown a picture of Rembrandt's 'Night Watch' and he is asked to describe it. He might begin by saying, 'It is an oil painting of a 17th Century Dutch Militia Company.' Asked to describe it more closely he might say, 'it is typical of Rembrandt's style in that the background is dark but the figures in the foreground appear to glow with a strange illumination'. Pressed to describe it more closely still he might say, 'the Captain of the Company is dressed characteristically as follows . . .'. This is what is meant by describing a picture more closely in an actual case. Is this possible with the private inner picture? If we attempt such an exercise we are quickly reduced to giving up the idea of a picture and saying instead that there must be *something* before us. To this Wittgenstein retorts that it is as if we were to say of someone, 'He *has* something. But I don't know whether it is money, or debts, or an empty till' (PI 294). Thus when we assess the value of the private exemplar it turns out to be bankrupt.

A further problem with regard to the model of inner object and outer designation concerns the criteria for correctness of our descriptions of the inner object. Wittgenstein highlights this problem with a typically ingenious example:

> I describe a room to someone, and then get him to paint an *impressionistic* picture from this description to show that he has understood it. Now he paints the chairs which I describe as green, dark red; where I said 'yellow', he paints blue. That is the impression which he got of that room. And now I say: 'Quite right. That's what it's like' (PI 368).

The point here, I take it, is that if descriptions of things are really descriptions of our private inner impressions or pictures of things then whatever we say will be right and we are bereft of criteria for *correct* descriptions. If it is the case that a phenomenalist description can never be wrong it is only because we have chosen a method of representation that makes being right tautologous and that means that the distinction 'correct' and 'incorrect' can have no significant application. The indubitability of our sensations or sense-data is a feature of our chosen method of representation and its expression in words is a grammatical proposition, not an experiential one.

He returns to the temptation to invoke an inner picture in his discussion of the duck-rabbit picture-puzzle in relation to 'seeing' and 'seeing as' where he says:

> And above all do *not* say 'After all my visual impression isn't the *drawing*: it is *this* —— which I can't show to anyone'. Of course it is not the drawing, but neither is it anything of the same category which I carry within myself. The concept of the

'inner picture' is misleading, for this concept uses the *'outer* picture' as a model (PI 196).

The concept of the 'inner picture' proves to be equally problematical with respect to its outer designation, i.e. its description in words. The idea of a private ostensive definition is defective because 'I could not apply any rules to a *private* transition from what is seen to words. Here the rules really would hang in the air; for the institution of their use is lacking' (PI 380). Additionally, if the use of a word is in need of justification 'it must also be one for someone else', and to say 'whatever seems right is right' provides neither an institution nor a justification of its use nor a rule for its correct use. If asked to justify the application of the word 'red' to a particular colour patch is it an answer to say, 'I know it is red because I see it as *this*' – pointing inwardly to my private exemplar? But this *what?* – This something? How could that justify the application of the common word 'red'? Wittgenstein observes, on the other hand, 'It would be an answer to say: "I have learnt English"' (PI 381). Similarly, 'you learned the concept "pain" when you learned language' (PI 384). For Wittgenstein to learn a concept is to learn the use of the concept-word in the language; its content, station and boundaries (whether sharp or blurred) are functions of its grammar. Is he asserting, then, that concepts are *only* words and nothing more? No, but whatever else we may want to say that they are, as psychological phenomena or as conditions of the intelligibility of experience their elucidation is a matter for grammatical investigation.

Wittgenstein again emphasises the fluctuation between inner and outer implicit in phenomenalist analyses of colour words whose meanings seem to oscillate between the private 'visual impression' and the 'colour known to everyone' (PI 277). Sentences of the kind, 'I know how the colour green looks to *me*' or 'only I know that I am in pain' are not *senseless*; but what is their use? What is important to see is that such constructions do not elucidate the grammar of 'green' or 'pain' in normal use. His response to the phenomenalist attempts to 'define the concept of a material object in terms of "what is really seen"' is to point out that 'what we have rather to do is to *accept* the everyday language-game, and to note *false* accounts of the matter *as* false. The primitive language-game which children are taught needs no justification; attempts at justification need to be rejected' (PI p.200).

Wittgenstein recognises that the attempt to describe things exclusively in terms of their appearances to the speaker – 'this is how x looks to me' – is primarily the adoption of a new method of representation. It represents a new standpoint, a new way of looking at things, like the invention of a new style of painting, or a new standard of measurement, or even a new song (PI 401). The curious habits of staring ahead, looking about one and repeating a name to oneself over and over again are activities characteristic of doing philosophy. Hence the following caricature of Moore:

> I am sitting with a philosopher in the garden; he says again and again 'I know that that's a tree', pointing to a tree that is near us. Someone else arrives and hears this, and I tell him: 'This fellow isn't insane. We are only doing philosophy' (OC 467).

When we engage in these activities the adoption of a new method of representation – 'the world is a construction out of sense data' – or that 'a name *means* its bearer' or the conviction, 'I *know* that this is a hand', seem peculiarly appropriate. From this position it is only a small step to a sense of discovery, as though these new ways of speaking were the revelation of new facts about the world. In the case of the sense data method of representation the change in standpoint demands new criteria for the applications of words like 'real', 'material object', 'world', 'knowledge' and 'belief' which differ from those we employ in ordinary language. Wittgenstein does not object to the adoption of new methods of representation but only to the confusion which results from the oscillation between old and new criteria for the applications of these words. Instead of recognising this oscillation as the source of our confusion we compound it by saying that our old way of speaking in ordinary language

> does not describe the facts as they really are. . . . For *this* is what disputes between Idealists, Solipsists and Realists look like. The one party attack the normal form of expression as if they were attacking a statement; the others defend it, as if they were stating facts recognised by every reasonable human being (PI 402).

What appear to be experiential conflicts are merely collisions between grammars. There would be no objection, for example, to a phenomenalist proposal which reserved 'the word "pain" solely for what I had hitherto called "my pain" and others "L.W's pain"'. No factual consequences would follow from the adoption of such a representation; the world would be unchanged, 'other people would still be pitied, treated by doctors and so on' (PI 403). Confusion reaches its zenith when we insist that the new representation of pain is the correct analysis of the word 'pain' as it is used in ordinary language; that 'pain' *really means* 'my pain' and that all talk about other people's pain is based upon a logically insecure inference from my own case.

Wittgenstein asks:

Is a sum in the head less real than a sum on paper? – Perhaps one is inclined to say some such thing; but one can get oneself to think the opposite as well by telling oneself: paper, ink, etc. are only logical constructions out of our sense-data' (PI 366).

This is an illuminating comment on the grammar of the word 'real'. The history of philosophy is littered with proposals to reserve the word 'real' for a variety of uses that are then treated as representations of reality or disclosures of the nature of the world. To say that 'the *real* world is x' where for x we substitute the Parmenidean plenum, Platonic forms, Democritean atoms, Lockean ideas, Humean impressions, Russellian sense-data or Wittgensteinian objects, only fixes the grammar of 'real' – and, perhaps more importantly, the grammar of 'unreal' – with respect to a particular method of representation.

Against this however it must be remarked that not all phenomenalist analyses commit the error of reading a grammatical proposal as an experiential one. A. J. Ayer, for example, in his treatment of material objects in terms of sense data explicitly recognises that 'we are not disputing about the validity of two conflicting sets of hypotheses, but about the choice of two different languages'. Thus, 'a proposition which is expressed by a sentence referring to a material thing can equally well be expressed by an entirely different set of sentences which refer to sense data; and this is what those who assert that material things are "logical constructions" out of sense data must be understood to claim'.[3] The central problem of this version of phenomenalism, which is both more moderate and more sophisticated than many alternative accounts, is the establishment of a credible relation between the material object language in common use and the private sensory language which Ayer holds it is possible, in principle, to construct.[4] Clearly, Wittgenstein's investigation of the grammar of phenomenalism is not complete until he has examined the possibility of a private language.

What all this brings out once again is the grammatical nature of Wittgenstein's investigations. He is not refuting phenomenalism; he is examining its grammar. He is not denying it as though it were an empirical thesis about our perception of the world. Nor is he placing such new ways of speaking on the Index, as though he is seeking an injunction against all but our ordinary modes of speech. However, from the fact that these new ways of speaking collide with our old ones we should not conclude that our ordinary expressions are defective and not performing their office. Repeatedly he contrasts what such new methods of representation incline us to say about our everyday expressions with the way that these expressions actually and successfully discharge their functions. His concern is not to reject phenomenalism in favour of some other theory of perception and knowledge but to reveal the confusing consequences that follow the attempt to superimpose its grammar on the grammar of our ordinary language for expressing sensations. Furthermore, such a superimposition sends us searching for mental entities, doubting the ascription of 'pain' to others, endeavouring to formulate a private language and all the time we overlook how our ordinary forms of expression work and that they are in perfectly good order as they stand. What Wittgenstein says to the phenomenalist is not that you must not speak in this way, but that you must command a clear view of what it is to speak in this way. It is also the case that he wishes to draw attention to interior confusions in some of the proposed new ways of speaking. Particularly is this so with the defective model of inner and outer pictures, and inner object and outer designation on which phenomenalism trades so heavily. Nevertheless, Wittgenstein's primary question about phenomenalism is not concerned with its *truth* but its *point*.

THE GRAMMAR OF 'PAIN' AND 'UNDERSTANDING'

To the assertion that the meaning of a word is some kind of mental picture, state, process, sensation or feeling which may be associated with the word Wittgenstein replies,

The meaning of a word is not the experience one has in hearing or saying it, and the sense of a sentence is not a complex of such experiences. . . . The sentence is composed of the words, and that is enough (PI p.181).

But what of the idea of meaning as a picture or physiognomy or atmosphere which seems to be a feature of certain familiar words, like 'a "corona" of lightly indicated uses' that float before the mind? Surely, these are characteristic experiences associated with the meanings of words which cannot be ignored in any account of meaning? 'If the possible uses of a word do float before us in half-shades as we say or hear it – this simply goes for *us*. But we communicate with other people without knowing if they have this experience too' (PI 181). That there are characteristic experiences which accompany the use of certain words is undeniable but *they* cannot be the criteria for the use of the word in communication with others. The logically private experience cannot be the criterion for the use of the publicly communicable expression. The word 'infinite' when used by a mathematician or a metaphysician may be accompanied by a sensation of mind-reeling but this is not part of the meaning of the word.

Nevertheless, there are words, such as 'pain' and 'understanding', where we seem compelled to elucidate meaning in terms of inner mental sensations and processes. In order to break the persuasiveness of this picture of meaning Wittgenstein undertakes a meticulous and protracted grammatical investigation of both of these words. Taking the case of 'pain' first, if we give a phenomenalist account of its grammar it seems that the criterion for the correct application of a sensation-word like 'pain' is the occurrence of the sensation itself. If we accept this opening gambit in the game it then seems that there is a striking difference between first person and third person ascriptions of 'pain'. In the case of 'I am in pain' the criterion for the correctness of this expression is the occurrence of a sensation of which I am directly aware and which is inaccessible to others. No such criterion is available in the case of 'he is in pain', for, however convincing his display of pain-behaviour may be, this may or may not be accompanied by the appropriate sensation. The obvious line of defence here is to say that 'pain' always describes a sensation of which in my own case I am directly aware. In the case of another person I infer from his behaviour that he is having the same sort of sensation that I have had. The epistemological consequence of this is that whereas I can never be mistaken about the truth-value of 'I am in pain' I can never be certain of the truth-value of 'he is in pain'. In short, I can *know* that *I* am in pain but I can only *believe* that *he* is in pain.

Against this picture of the privacy of sensations Wittgenstein observes that 'if we are using the word "to know" as it is normally used (and how else are we to use it?) then other people very often know when I am in pain. Yes, but all the same not with the certainty with which I know it myself'. 'It can't be said of me at all (except perhaps as a joke) that I *know* I am in pain. What is it supposed to mean – except perhaps that I *am* in pain' (PI 246). An instance where it would be perfectly appropriate for someone to say 'I *know* I am in pain' would be as a denial of a charge of malingering. Ayer has pointed out that the claim to knowledge in such cases may be superfluous but this does not mean that it is inapplicable or unjustified.[5] 'I *know* I am in pain' is not just a joke or a form of emphasis – 'I *am* in pain' – it is a claim to direct awareness. In fact, Wittgenstein recognises this when, in the passage quoted above, he concludes, 'The truth is: it makes sense to say about other people that they doubt whether I am in pain; but not to say it about myself'. The difference between Ayer and Wittgenstein here is illuminating. Ayer wishes to treat 'I *know* I am in pain' as an experiential proposition and the paradigm case for all propositions about knowledge and pain. The criterion for the correct application for these words in such propositions is the occurrence of the appropriate sensation. Wittgenstein, on the other hand wishes to treat 'I *know* I am in pain' as a grammatical proposition which expresses a fragment of the grammar of 'knowledge' and 'pain', namely, that it makes sense to say about others that they doubt whether I am in pain but not to say it about myself. Although it is possible to devise an experiential use for 'I *know* I am in pain' it is misleading to adopt such a use as the paradigm case for the applications of 'know' and 'pain'. Above all he wishes to deny that the only criterion for the correct use of 'know' and 'pain' is the occurrence of a sensation. For then it looks as if I must *reserve* the use of 'know' for *my* pain and speak of 'belief' in the case of *his* pain. But the boundaries between 'know' and 'believe' are not coincident with those between 'my pain' and 'his pain'. A consideration of the way we actually operate with these words reveals forms of life in which we find it impossible to doubt another's pain.

I can be as *certain* of someone else's sensations as of any fact. . . .
'But, if you are *certain*, isn't it that you are shutting your eyes in
face of doubt?' – They are shut. Am I less certain that this man is
in pain than that twice two is four? – Does this show the former
to be mathematical certainty? – 'Mathematical certainty' is not a
psychological concept. The kind of certainty is the kind of
language-game (PI p.224).

The point that must be emphasised, and about which there has
been a great deal of misunderstanding of Wittgenstein, is that he
is not denying the occurrence of pain-sensations nor their importance in the grammar of our expressions of pain. But the occurrence of a sensation is not the *only* criterion that we accept without
doubt for many uses of 'pain', including its ascription to others.
Our language-game is such that we accept pain-behaviour as a
criterion for the assertion, 'he is in pain'. Not only that, but the
norm for most of these cases is not doubt, or at best an uncertain
belief about the truth of 'he is in pain', but *knowledge* and
certainty. Furthermore, we do not arrive at this certainty via the
route of an inference, i.e. that from his pain-behaviour I infer that
he is having the sensation that I have had and therefore he is in
pain. The private exemplar is simply irrelevant and plays no part
in determining the truth-value of 'he is in pain'. The criteria that
we adopt for this determination depend only upon physical
characteristics – including behaviour and symptoms – and the
circumstances in which the expression is used. In short we can
legitimately claim to know that 'he is in pain' in the circumstances
of a serious road accident, although we may be in doubt in the
circumstances of an army sick parade on the eve of an attack. The
question of *justification* of knowledge and doubt in these cases
does not arise except to say this is how the language-game is
played. Hence Wittgenstein's comment; 'I would like to reserve
the expression "I know" for the cases in which it is used in normal
linguistic exchange' (OC 260; cf. 230, 249). One can indeed say 'I
know . . . only from my *own* case', but this proposition is not an
experiential one; it is a grammatical one. The picture that we get
'when we look into ourselves as we do philosophy' and say 'I
know what pain is only from my own case' is an example of a
'pictorial representation of our grammar' (PI 295). Thus,

one can make the decision to say 'I believe he is in pain' instead
of 'he is in pain'. But that is all. What looks like an explanation

here, or like a statement about a mental process, is in truth an exchange of one expression for another, which, while we are doing philosophy, seems the more appropriate one (PI 303).

To say that the criterion for the correct application of 'pain' must always be a sensation of a certain sort treats 'pain' as though it always functions as a name of a sensation. How, then, do words refer to sensations?

> We talk about sensations every day and give them names. But how is the connection between the name and the thing named set up? This question is the same as: how does a human being learn the meaning of the names of sensations? – of the word 'pain' for example. (PI 244)

In answer to this question he advances what he calls one possibility, which is worth quoting in full:

> Words are connected with the primitive, the natural, expressions of the sensation and used in their place. A child has hurt himself and he cries; and then adults talk to him and teach him exclamations and, later, sentences. They teach the child new pain-behaviour. 'So you are saying that the word 'pain' really means crying?' – on the contrary: the verbal expression of pain replaces crying and does not describe it. For how can I go so far as to try and use language to get between pain and its expression? (PI 244–5).

According to this possibility 'I am in pain' is not a *description* but an *expression* of pain; it is a sophisticated act of pain-behaviour which I have learned from others. If we adopt this possibility then the grammar of 'I know I am in pain' is as vacuous as 'I know I am crying' and its seemingly privileged and paradigm status simply disappears.

Does this mean that Wittgenstein was a behaviourist and that the programme of the *Investigations* is designed to replace statements about sensations by equivalent statements which refer only to behaviour? Certainly, he has been so interpreted. The interlocutor asks;

> 'But doesn't what you say come to this: that there is no pain, for example, without *pain-behaviour*?' – It comes to this: only of a living human being and what resembles (behaves like) a living

human being can one say: it has sensations; it sees; is blind; hears; is deaf; is conscious or unconscious (PI 281).

The interlocutor persists:

'Are you not really a behaviourist in disguise? Aren't you at bottom really saying that everything except human behaviour is a fiction?' – If I do speak of a fiction, then it is of a *grammatical* fiction (PI 307).

Wittgenstein is not advocating any behaviourist thesis. He does not deny that there really are sensations and that there is the greatest possible difference between 'pain-behaviour accompanied by pain and pain-behaviour without any pain'; indeed – 'what greater difference could there be?' His intention is not to deny sensations, but the grammatical interpretation of our sensation-words that treats them all uniformly as descriptions of inner objects. It is not the sensation itself but the picture of it as an inner object or private exemplar that is a grammatical fiction. The sensation itself

is not a *something*, but not a *nothing* either! The conclusion was only that a nothing would serve just as well as a something about which nothing could be said. We have only rejected the grammar which tries to force itself on us here (PI 304).

The defective model of object and designation does not arise from a psychological mistake but a linguistic one, namely; 'that language always functions in one way, always serves the same purpose: to convey thoughts – which may be about houses, pains, good and evil, or anything else you please' (PI 304). He offers a grammatical answer to the question. 'How does the philosophical problem about mental processes and states and about behaviourism arise?' What we fail to recognise is that in putting the question in that form we have already taken the decisive step. Talking of 'processes' and 'states' commits us to a particular method of representation,

for we have a definite concept of what it means to learn to know a process better. . . . And now the analogy which was to make us understand our thoughts falls to pieces. So we have to deny the yet uncomprehended process in the yet unexplored medium. And now it looks as if we had denied mental processes. And naturally we don't want to deny them (PI 308).

To deny mental processes would entail saying that the phenomenon of dreaming was nothing but the dream narrative and Wittgenstein explicitly repudiates this. On the other hand, 'why should dreaming be more mysterious than the table?' He emphasises that 'the verbs "believe", "hope", "wish", "intend" and so on, exhibit all the grammatical forms that are also possessed by "eat", "talk", "cut"' (RPP I 371, 378, 494). To sensationalists and behaviourists alike Wittgenstein says, 'Not to explain, but to *accept* the psychological phenomenon – that is what is difficult' (RPP I 509).

His investigation of the grammar of 'pain' is a special case illustrative of a general interpretation of language which he consistently repudiates, namely, 'if you want to understand a sentence, you have to imagine the psychical significance, the states of mind involved' (PI 652). It is this view of language which Wittgenstein examines and discards, not the reality of sensations or other mental events. With respect to what might be called mental phenomena he says,

> *Certainly* all these things happen in you. And now all I ask is to understand the expression we use. The picture is there. And I am not disputing its validity in any particular case. Only I also want to understand the application of the picture. The picture is there; and I do not dispute its *correctness*. But *what* is its application? Think of the picture of blindness as a darkness in the soul or in the head of the blind man (PI 423–4).

Once again he concedes that in numberless cases when we look for a picture and find one 'the application as it were comes about of itself'; i.e. the meaning fixes the use of the expression. But in the case of this picture of a mental mechanism which 'forces itself upon us at every turn' we are not helped out of the difficulty which begins at the point we ask 'what is its application?'. 'A picture is conjured up which seems to fix the sense *unambiguously*. The actual use, compared with that suggested by the picture, seems like something muddied' (PI 425–6).

The concept of mind is prone to grammatical illusions, that is to say the grammar of our mental expressions is prolific in its generation of pictures of the private exemplar, the inner state, the hidden process, the mysterious mechanism, pain-sensations as images of 'pain', objects of thought, contents of consciousness, mental previews of orders, intentions, expectations, wishes and hopes and the like. As pictures these are harmless enough and there are many occasions where picture and application present no problems. In other cases, however, the application of a picture gets in the way of our understanding how an expression is actually used. For example:

'While I was speaking to him I did not know what was going on in his head'. In saying this, one is not thinking of brain-processes, but of thought-processes. The picture should be taken seriously. We should really like to see into his head. And yet we only mean what elsewhere we should mean by saying: we should like to know what he is thinking. I want to say: we have this vivid picture – and that use, apparently contradicting the picture, which expresses the psychical (PI 427).

This picture of the mental process going on in the head is what inclines us to suppose that the real meaning of the verbal expressions of thought must be a kind of description of this inner process. Here picture and application collide. In such cases, what is to be done with the picture 'must be explored if we want to understand the sense of what we are saying. But, the picture seems to spare us this work: it already points to a particular use. This is how it takes us in' (PI p.184).

We can again see that Wittgenstein's grammatical investigations are much more than a consideration of the uses of words. Also included is the exploration of the pictorial representation of grammatical pictures and a comparison with their actual applications with special reference to those philosophically interesting examples where picture and application collide. The most prolific source of conceptual confusion is grammatical misunderstanding and for this psychology with its reliance on experimental method is of no help; for here 'problem and method pass one another by'

(PI p. 232). Thus, a mental process is not a picture of a brain process but of a feature of grammar.

The word 'understanding' presents more problems than is the case with 'pain' and is even more prolific in its generation of grammatical fictions. Consider the following cases: To understand

(a) the meaning of a word is to have an appropriate mental image of it;
(b) an order is to see in advance the execution of the order in the mind's eye.
(c) the development of an infinite series is like seeing a visible section of a track which continues indefinitely;
(d) something in a general sense is a state of mind;
(e) sentences in a language is a mental process;
(f) the meaning of an expression in a flash must be an act of recognition of a picture rather than an instantaneous parade of different usages.
(g) a word when it is being used is a mental process lying behind it's use.
(h) how to go on with the expansion of a series is a feeling like a glad start;
(i) a sentence when reading it differs from reading it without understanding in terms of the different mental phenomena that accompany the two cases;
(j) the meaning of a colour-word, 'blue' for example, is to have an image of blue in the mind as a kind of sample.
(k) when spoken of another, i.e. 'He understands', is a hypothesis but 'I understand' is not.
(l) intentions, wishes, hopes and expectations is to think of their fulfilment in advance,
    & etc.

The above list includes the kind of psychical grammar which we are tempted to attribute to 'understanding' and its cognates. Wittgenstein takes this picture of the grammar of 'understanding' seriously and in a series of brilliantly conceived examples illustrates the actual uses of the word and, more importantly, the collision that occurs frequently between this picture and its applications. The purpose of this examination is to reveal the extent to which the criteria for correctness for the use of 'understanding' are located in the grammar of the language-game and not in feelings, sensations, states or processes in the mind. Putting this the other way round, whatever the mental accompaniments of 'understanding' may be, our descriptions of them tend to be projections of our grammar. That there are such mental accompaniments Wittgenstein has no wish to deny but they do not have the office with regard to the use of 'understanding' to which we are inclined to appoint them.

The kind of picture which he rejects is that expressed in a remark already quoted, namely, that 'to understand a sentence you have to imagine the psychical significance, the states of mind involved' (PI 652). According to this, understanding a sentence is a process of inferring, imagining or somehow divining the state of mind of the user of the sentence. To say 'he understands', therefore, is a hypothesis that he has the appropriate state of mind, but 'I understand' is not because I am directly aware of my state of mind. This picture is at its most compulsive with sentences that declare the user's intention or meaning, for then it looks as if what is intended or meant must already exist in the mind of the user and that someone else who understands such sentences does so as a result of reproducing for himself the user's state of mind. In other cases, for example the expansion of a series according to a rule, we are inclined to separate understanding the series from its application and say that 'the understanding itself is a state which is the *source* of the correct use' (PI 146). Against this picture Wittgenstein says:

> Meaning is as little an experience as intending. But what distinguishes them from experience? – They have no experience content. For the contents (images for instance) which accompany and illustrate them are not the meaning or intending. The intention *with which* one acts does not 'accompany' the action any more than the thought 'accompanies' speech. Thought and intention are neither 'articulated' nor 'non-articulated'; to be compared neither with a single note which sounds during the acting or speaking, nor with a tune. . . . The *interest* of the experiences one has while speaking and of the intention is not the same. (The experiences might perhaps inform a psychologist about the 'unconscious' intention.) . . . The language-game 'I mean (or meant) *this*' (subsequent explanation of a word) is quite different from this one: 'I thought of . . . as I said it'. The latter is akin to 'It reminded me of . . .' (PI p.217).

Wittgenstein's point is that the criteria which we accept for the application of 'understanding' are much more extensive than we are inclined to think. The model of the inner something (state, process, act, object, etc.) as *the* criterion for the use of 'understanding' proves to be as defective here as was the case with the model of the private exemplar as the criterion for the use of 'pain'. He considers at some length an example of 'Now I understand' which is closely related to 'Now I can do it' or 'Now I know how to go on'. In this example A writes down a series of numbers watched by B who tries to discover some principle which will enable him to continue the series. If B is successful, he exclaims; 'Now I can go on!' (PI 151). In this example, understanding is something that makes its appearance in a moment – rather like grasping the meaning of a word in a flash. More specifically, this is a use where we would say that understanding made its appearance at the moment that B said, 'Now I can go on'. Now, just what is it that makes its appearance here? The various possibilities that suggest themselves here include the following:

1. B discovers an algebraic formula which enables him to continue the development of the series.
2. B discovers a regularity in the differences between successive steps in the series which enables him to continue it.
3. B recognises the series as one with which he is familiar and continues it from memory.
4. B makes no remark about the series but with what might be called the expression 'that's easy' simply continues it.

Clearly, one could imagine other equally appropriate responses but Wittgenstein's point is; 'are the processes which I have described here *understanding*?'. For now it seems:

'He understands' must have more in it than: the formula occurs to him. And equally, more than any of those more or less characteristic *accompaniments* or manifestations of understanding. We are trying to get hold of the mental process of understanding which seems to be hidden behind those coarser and therefore more readily visible accompaniments. But we do not succeed; or, rather, it does not get as far as a real attempt. For even supposing I had found something that happened in all those cases of understanding – why should *it* be the understanding? And how can the process of understanding have been hidden, when I said 'Now I understand' *because* I understood?! And if I say it is hidden – then how do I know what I have to look for? I am in a muddle (PI 152–3).

As the model of the inner object collapses when we try to scrutinise the object, so too the picture of understanding as an inner process dissolves when we try to trace the process. The therapy that Wittgenstein prescribes for the compulsion to identify the meaning of a word with something inner is to examine several different examples of the use of the word and see whether or not the model serves the office of a common denominator. What justifies saying 'I can go on' is not something that lies *behind* any of our expressions but the particular circumstances in which we say it.

Try not to think of understanding as a 'mental process' at all. For *that* is the expression which confuses you. But ask yourself: in what sort of case, in what kind of circumstances, do we say, 'Now I know how to go on', when, that is, the formula *has* occurred to me? – In the sense in which there are processes (including mental processes) which are characteristic of understanding, understanding is not a mental process. (A pain's growing more or less; the hearing of a tune or a sentence: these are mental processes.) (PI 154).

The picture of understanding as a mental state which is logically and temporally prior to the process of actually going on is a grammatical fiction arising from the adoption of a method of projection which takes as paradigm 'I *know* when I understand because of my direct awareness of my mental processes; you can only *infer* my understanding from my behaviour.' The crucial point is that even the most convincing examples of the private applications of 'understanding' by ourselves to ourselves are governed by outer criteria, otherwise there would be no difference between understanding and thinking one understood when one did not. Unless one can differentiate between understanding and thinking one understood, the word 'understanding' could have *any* application and hence no significant role in the language. This differentiation is not provided by any set of sensations, mental accompaniments, feelings like a glad start or the dawning of an aspect since these may all be present when we think we understand but do not. In the example of the development of a series, the occurrence of the formula $a_n = n^2 + n - 1$ for the continuation of 1, 5, 11, 19, 29 . . . cannot be called the moment of understanding because what could equally well have occurred to us is the formula $a_n = n^2 + n + 1$ which is the rule for a different series. We only know that we understand, or can go on, when we can continue the series correctly according to the rule, i.e. we proceed 41, 55, 71, 89 . . . and this criterion of understanding is the same for myself as for others. What is true, and Wittgenstein recognises this, is that often we treat the sensation or feelings that may accompany understanding as signals of understanding (cf. PI 179–80). The question then becomes, do we accept these signals of whatever sort as criteria for the application of 'understanding'? Once again the answer is that it depends upon the particular circumstances; in some cases we would and in others we would not. The words 'Now I know how to go on' or 'Now I understand' are used in particular circumstances and are surrounded by behaviour of a certain kind and also some characteristic experiences. The phenomenalist locates the criteria for 'understanding' only in these experiences and the behaviourist locates them only in behaviour. Wittgenstein insists upon the variety of our criteria and it would be surprising if the uses of 'understanding' did not trade upon the acceptance of both sorts of criteria.

Wittgenstein's own statement of his objectives with respect to his examination of understanding is illuminating.

Some people say that understanding a sentence consists in the impression made by every word. (Compare William James, who said that special feelings attach to 'if . . . , then . . .', 'but', 'and'). This sounds like a simple statement but is really extremely complicated. I could of course say there are sensations attached to 'if . . . , then . . .', etc. There are the sounds of the words, and all sorts of bodily sensations connected with gesture and intonation. Where we are liable to go wrong is in supposing that sensations connected with words are somehow 'in the mind'. The phrase 'in the mind' has caused more confusion than almost any other in philosophy. Sensations need not always be present when the words are uttered. It is not wrong to say there are bodily sensations accompanying a word so long as you do not say these sensations must be there whenever you say the words or understand the sentence in which it occurs. . . . The trouble with words such as 'understanding' comes through thinking of a few cases and trying to carry over their analogy to all other cases. For example, conscious mental acts do play a great role in understanding, but we should not try to make every case of understanding look like these cases. For there are cases where no conscious experience mediates between understanding an order, say, and carrying it out. Nor should we construe what we cannot do in mathematics after the case of human frailty. Troubles we get into in philosophy come through constantly trying to construe everything in accordance with one paradigm or model. Philosophy we might say arises out of certain prejudices. The words 'must' and 'cannot' are typical words exhibiting these prejudices. They are prejudices in favor of certain grammatical forms (Ambrose 114–15).

8

Grammar and the World

It is inevitable in tracing the historical development of Wittgenstein's thought that it should be classified by his interpreters and critics into the early, middle and later periods. However, it is a serious misunderstanding of the wholeness of his philosophy to suppose that there is little connection between them. From some of the literature on Wittgenstein it might be supposed that the *Tractatus* and the *Philosophical Investigations* were written by different authors. It is certainly the case, as we have seen, that logical atomism and the picture-theory of meaning are explicitly repudiated in the later philosophy but important strands of the *Tractatus* persist and are developed in the middle and later periods. With respect to the picture-theory itself, important elements of the concept of representation raised by the theory survive its overall rejection. Professor Anscombe has recorded an interesting remark of Wittgenstein's about the *Tractatus* made many years after its publication, to the effect that it was not a bag of junk but like a clock that did not tell the correct time. As he wrote in the preface of the *Investigations*:

It suddenly seemed to me that I should publish those old thoughts and the new ones together: that the latter could be seen in the right light only by contrast with and against the background of my old way of thinking (PI VIII).

This background is one of unity as well as diversity as the following tabular arrangement of some of the main features of Wittgenstein's thought illustrates.

There is an interesting example of role-reversal between the philosopher and the plain man in the early and the later writings. According to the *Tractatus* the plain man used language 'without having any idea of how each word has meaning or what its

Features of Wittgenstein's thought

The early period	*Common elements*	*The later period*
	That language and reality have a common logical form	
means that language mirrors the world.		is a grammatical mistake.
Propositions picture facts.		By a suitable choice of method of projection anything can be a picture of anything.
	The general form of the proposition	
displays how things stand in reality.		is the product of a craving for generality.
The point at which language hooks on to the world is the name-object relation.		The world does not divide into facts; facts do not divide into objects and there is no such thing as *the* name-object relation.
	The way in which reality is projected into	
propositions is through their logical structure.		sentences is through representational conventions.
	Agreement or disagreement with reality	
is what is displayed by a proposition.		cannot be read off by inspection of a proposition.
	Elementary propositions	
are logically independent of one another.		are not logically independent of one another.

Features of Wittgenstein's thought (contd)

The early period	Common elements	The later period
Sentences are truth-functions of elementary propositions.		A truth-functional calculus is a bad paradigm for most of language.
	Names have meanings only in propositions.	
	The Theory of Logical Types	
attempts to say what shows in the symbolism.		is a hierarchical arrangement of grammar.
	Logical connectives are not representatives.	
		Logical constants are not constant.
	What is laid against reality like a yardstick is	
a proposition.		a system of propositions.
	The meaning of a proposition is revealed in its	
being a logical picture of actual or possible states of affairs.		use, mode of projection, application and grammar.
	Signs that have no use have no meaning.	
	A proof is a	
tautology.		paradigm.
	Mathematics is a	
method of logic using equations for the purpose of sign-substitution.		body of activities for various purposes rooted in practice and agreement.

Features of Wittgenstein's thought (contd)

The early period	Common elements	The later period
	The boundary between sense and nonsense is	
picturability.		use.
	To use and understand language is to	
operate a calculus.		be master of a technique.
	The rules of logical inference are	
the scaffolding of language.		the rules of the language-game.
	The hardness of the logical must	
reflects the common logical form of reality and language.		reflects an attitude towards inference paradigms.
	Categories of thought are	
conceptual frame works		grammatical paradigms
	which prescribe forms for our descriptions.	
	What a proposition displays in its form of representation	
cannot be said; i.e. cannot be a subject of further representation.		can be said; i.e. it can be made explicit by specifying its mode of projection.
Logical analysis will reveal the hidden logical structure of language.		Grammatical investigation will reveal the variety of functions of language.

Features of Wittgenstein's thought (contd)

The early period	Common elements	The later period
	A proposition can have	
One and only one analysis.		many different uses.
Language does not comprise a hierarchy of logical types.		Grammar is a theory of logical types.
	Ordinary language is fundamentally in sound logical order provided	
we penetrate the disguised forms of the facts represented.		we relate it to its appropriate forms of life.
	Thought-processes are elucidated by the study of	
sign-language		grammar
	in which psychology is irrelevant.	
	Psychological propositions of the form 'A believes p' do not represent a relation between the	
proposition 'p'		picture of 'p'
	and an object 'A'.	
	Language does not picture how things stand in the mind.	
		The psychological verbs, 'to understand', 'to intend', 'to mean' & etc. do not picture mental objects, states or processes.

Features of Wittgenstein's thought (contd)

The early period	Common elements	The later period
		Private experience is not the proto-phenomenon of language.
		The elucidation of sensation-words is a grammatical not a psychological investigation.
	Philosophy does not aim at the construction of an ideal language.	
elucidatory	Philosophy is purely	descriptive
	and must not come between language and reality.	
	The stated problems of metaphysics are not genuine propositions because	
they fail to picture anything.		they arise from grammatical misunderstandings.
set of propositions.	Philosophy does not comprise a genuine	language-game.
	The fundamental confusions of philosophy arise from a misunderstanding of language.	
The plain man		The philosopher
	does not understand the workings of language.	

Features of Wittgenstein's thought (contd)

The early period	Common elements	The later period
	Philosophy is a critique of language.	
	Philosphical problems are not solved but	
abolished.		dissolved.
	The end of philosophy is the end of philosophy.	
	The notion of perspicuous representation remains of fundamental importance.	
		Any fact whose obtaining is a presupposition of a proposition's making sense is to be counted as belonging to language.
		The words of public language need public criteria of correctness.
		A private language lacks the criteria required for it to be language.
	Reality	
is mirrored in language.		is a grammatical construction.

meaning is' (4.002) and as a consequence needs the elucidations of the philosopher. According to the *Investigations* it is the philosopher who labours under misconceptions about meaning and who needs the plain man to show him how language works. That physicians may need to heal themselves is a commonplace;

that they need to be healed by their former patients is revolutionary.

WELTANSCHAUUNG

It would not be inaccurate to describe the central theme from which Wittgenstein's philosophy stems as a concern with the question, how does language represent the world? In particular, what makes a representation a perspicuous one? The consideration of these questions lead to the exploration of a variety of important issues of langauge and ontology including the epistemological status of mathematics. The objective of this book is to trace the development of Wittgenstein's answers to these questions from the representational unity of propositional pictures through the recognition of the multiplicity of our methods of representation to the investigation of the grammatical diversity of our language-games. The paradox between Wittgenstein's desire to put an end to philosophy and its perpetuation in his own writings arises from the fact that on the one hand how sentences represent is already perfectly clear in the way we use them and on the other hand there is a need to explicate and explore the notion of perspicuous representation. If one had to sum up in a single sentence the point of Wittgenstein's philosophy it could be expressed as an investigation of the grammar of representation. Reality as mirrored in language was an obsessive concern throughout his life.

One of the most important links of continuity in Wittgenstein's thought concerns the directness of the connection between language and reality or the way language hooks on to the world. According to the *Tractatus* the directness of this connection is assured by the name-object relation in which the concatenation of names in a proposition pictures the configuration of objects in the situation depicted. Such a proposition was laid up directly against reality analogously with the application of a scale of measurement to an object. The directness of this connection enabled Wittgenstein to disallow the interpolation of thought processes or metalanguages between language and the world. This in turn explains why he assigned such a negative role to thought and philosophy. The logical structure of thought reveals itself in the logical structure of its expression in a proposition so that although reality, thought and proposition stand in line, thought is a passive or neutral term in the series. The dominant idea of thought in the *Tractatus* is that the 'self', 'soul', 'mind' and the 'I that thinks' are ontological fictions. On the other hand, a subordinate idea of thought in the *Tractatus*, which gives it a more active role, is connected with Wittgenstein's analogy of nets as conceptual frameworks or optional forms for our descriptions of the world. As has been remarked, according to this account, thought is both structured and structuring with respect to the connection between language and the world.

In the later philosophy both the structured and structuring roles of thought are located in the grammar of language and the categories of thought, understanding and reason are grammatical categories. In a sense, reality is a grammatical construction. The dominant idea of thought in the *Investigations* is that the 'self', 'soul', 'mind', the 'I that thinks', along with mental states and processes, are grammatical fictions. Just as the idea of substance as a subject which can never be a predicate of anything else is an illusion generated by the subject–predicate form of expression so the grammatical form of some of our descriptions of reality incline us to give a substantive status to thoughts and the like. Confusion is compounded when an expression such as 'A thinks p' inclines us to look beyond and behind 'p' to a mysterious mental process accompanying 'p' which gives it life and significance. This is a distortion of the image of reality in language.

According to the *Tractatus*, in spite of the semantic route to ontology, reality per se has a definite structure. The requirement of a definite world is the satisfaction of the need to give language definiteness of sense. Nevertheless, when Wittgenstein likens scientific laws, as forms for our descriptions of reality, to nets applied to a surface covered with dots, it is important to realise that the dots represent the given or raw data of reality. The raw elemental data of reality remains invariable and what varies are the optional forms or categorial frameworks that we use to render the data intelligible. Thus the laws of mechanics impose a unified form on phenomena which makes the world intelligible but does not explain it because in an important sense the laws are about the net and not the world. This analogy is an early hint of the conceptual relativism later worked out in detail in Wittgenstein's remarks on grammar and the world. But what now becomes of the idea of the fixed and determinate structure of the world? A world that no longer divides into facts, where objects as primary elements are abolished and that does not share a common logical form with language, which no longer reduces to a single propositional type, cannot remain the same world. Given the semantic route to ontology of the *Tractatus*, the shift from the elucidation of language-structure to the investigation of language-functions must have profound ontological implications. In the *Tractatus* it is reality that gives language its determinate logical structure but in the later philosophy Wittgenstein denies that it is reality that shapes grammar. This becomes clearest and most explicit in his examination of the grammar of colour words and the grammar of mathematics. The principal reason for this is that in the later philosophy language is not a mirror of a fixed and determinate reality but reflects our forms of life and, as such, is intention orientated. Its representational standpoints or *Weltanschauung,* its methods of projection, its applications and grammars are reflections of our life-styles, uses, needs and purposes. We shape language in accordance with a variety of different aims and activities such that the grammar of a language-game has a structure and a point determined by those aims and activities, that is, the form of life of which the language-game forms a part. For example, arithmetic derives its structure and point from the activity of counting. Even in the case of our use of colour words where reality or the laws of physics seem to fix the concepts for us a question such as 'are there three or four primary colours?' is a grammatical rather than an empirical one (RC III 26). Much of the analysis of colour concepts has nothing to do with physics, physiology or psychology but on the other hand some 'sentences are often used on the borderline between logic and the empirical, so that their meaning changes back and forth and they count now as expressions of norms, now as expressions of experience' (RC II 16; III 180, 188, 206; I 32, III 19). As a result of this oscillation between logic and the empirical we generate various species of grammatical fictions such that, for example, 'the primary phenomenon is a preconceived idea that takes possession of us' (RC III 230). A further consequence of this view leads to a complication of the idea that grammar reflects our forms of life – as though the two were separate and distinct. As Wittgenstein puts it: 'Would it be correct to say our concepts reflect our life? They stand in the middle of it. The rule-governed nature of our languages permeates our life' (RC III 302–3).

The investigation of the grammar of 'to know' reveals Wittgenstein's mind at its best in his subtle illustrations and his penetrating observations on proof, certainty, doubt, illusion, belief, surmise, evidence and other related concepts. To follow up all these lines of enquiry would take us too far afield but some of his remarks with respect to Moore's claims are important and relevant for our purposes here:

> What is the proof that I *know* something? Most certainly not my saying I know it. And so when writers enumerate all the things they *know*, that proves nothing whatever. So the possibility of knowledge about physical objects cannot be proved by the protestations of those who believe that they have such knowledge. For what reply does one make to someone who says 'I believe it merely strikes you as if you knew it'? (OC 487–9).

The grammar of 'to know' is very complex and extends over a large family of instances variously related but amongst them is not found Moore's 'metaphysical emphasis' on 'I know' (OC 482). What Moore is seeking is already part of our normal language-games: 'Every language-game is based on words "and objects" being recognised again. We learn with the same inexorability that this is a chair as that $2 \times 2 = 4$' (OC 455). The possibility of knowledge of physical objects is a prerequisite of ordinary language; it is part of its grammar. The final solution to the problem of 'how language hooks on to the world' can only be found by an elucidation of the grammar of 'world' and 'language'.

It is in grammar that our problems arise and it is in grammar that they will be abolished.

Wittgenstein's final answer to his own great question: 'How does language hook on to the world?', at last becomes explicit. Propositions about reality do not reach out to the world; their grammar includes it.

THE METAPHYSICS OF SENSE

It seems to me that an important weakness of the *Tractatus* has its counterpart in the *Philosophical Investigations* and the later philosophy generally. In the *Tractatus*, as Wittgenstein himself came to recognise, the demand for the crystalline purity of logic and the notion of a common logical form linking together the world and language were not the result of enquiry but a requirement of the view he held then of language structure. This is what was meant by saying that Wittgenstein took a semantic route to ontology. Some, at least, of what Wittgenstein says in the later philosophy about the world and grammar is open to the same objection. The point is made clearer by Wittgenstein's own remarks:

> If I want to tell someone what colour some material is to be I send him a sample, and obviously that sample belongs to language; and equally the memory or image of a colour that I conjure by a word belongs to language. The memory and the reality must be in *one* space. I could also say: the image and the reality are in *one* space . . . I will count any fact whose obtaining is a presupposition of a proposition's making sense as belonging to language (PR 38a, b . . . 45a).

This decision to categorise as language what others would count as non-linguistic facts of reality is the key to understanding many of Wittgenstein's remarks on grammar and the world. It places in perspective and lessens the shock-value of such remarks as: 'How do I know that this colour is red? It would be an answer to say; "I have learnt English"' (PI 381). In the *Tractatus* and the *Investigations* although the boundaries of language are differently drawn, both are prescriptions resulting from two different views of language function. In the earlier work features of language are attributed to the world and in the later work features of the world are attributed to language. The principal difference between Wittgenstein and Moore hinges on a boundary dispute with respect to the demarcation between grammar and the world. Propositions which Moore took to be straightforward empirical descriptions Wittgenstein insists are grammatical prescriptions or forms for descriptions. In terms of the analogy of conceptual nets they are about the net and not about that to which the net applies.

The recognition of the elasticity of the notion of a picture in the *Tractatus* lead to the realisation that a picturing relation where anything can be a picture of anything is of little value in elucidating the sense of language. Coupled with this recognition of elasticity is Wittgenstein's rejection of generality as exemplified in his own attempts to find the general form of propositions, the

Russellian 'all', the assimilation of the grammars of finite and infinite series and the universalising of particular paradigms. This rejection of generality is crucial for Wittgenstein's method of analysing concepts by the meticulous examination of particular instances and their differentiation in ways that dispel the persuasiveness of the generality invoked by philosophers. The skilful deployment of these methods and the sharpness of the questions raised must not be allowed to obscure the fact that the later philosophy itself trades upon a new variety of generality whose elasticity is as problematical as the earlier concept of representation proved to be. This relates to Wittgenstein's concept of grammar. Throughout the middle and later periods of Wittgenstein's philosophical development the tendency to broaden this category is noticeable so that grammar comes to include the following:

1. The rules governing sentence construction.
2. The rules differentiating sentence types.
3. The logical characteristics of language-games.
4. The activities and forms of life of which language-games are part.
5. Any fact whose obtaining is a prerequisite for a proposition's sense.
6. Colour samples which give sense to colour words.
7. Mental images enabling us to paint pictures or recount dreams from memory.
8. Representational conventions.
9. Methods of projection.
10. Universal law-like forms for descriptions.
11. Actual applications and uses of sentences.
12. Ways in which propositions may be verified.
13. Construction of paradigms.
14. Systems of sentences to which propositions belong.
15. The source of:
    (a) ontological fictions, like primary elements or objects;
    (b) psychological fictions like mental processes and objects of thought;
    (c) philosophical puzzlement.
16. Those investigations which constitute the only proper methods of philosophy.
17. Weltanschauung or world pictures or categorial frameworks.

It is partly because Wittgenstein has prescribed the inclusion in language of facts which determine the sense of a proposition and partly because of the expanding boundaries of the concept of grammar that it becomes impossible to demarcate sharply between the world and language. As has been noted, for Wittgenstein there is no uniform logic of colour words which reflects the structure of reality because he has chosen to incorporate the facts about colour patches into the grammar of language-games about colour. The convolutions that the maintenance of this viewpoint entails are clearly manifest in the *Remarks on Colour*. Take, for example, this passage:

> What is there in favour of saying that green is a primary colour and not a mixture of blue and yellow? Is it correct to answer: 'You can only know it directly, by looking at the colours'? But how do I know that I mean the same by the words 'primary colours' as someone else who is also inclined to call green a primary colour? No, here there are language-games that decide these questions (RC III 158).

One of the reasons for incorporating colour samples into the language-games using colour words was due to the conviction that 'an ostensive definition can be variously interpreted in *every* case' (PI 28). The success with which children learn through ostensive definition to correlate names and objects does not demand the postulation of a primitive proto-language to show what station in grammar a name occupies. The protophenomenon simply is the ostensive definition itself; it is not the grammar. One might echo Wittgenstein's own words in another connection and say that ostensive definition is a form of life which under normal circumstances enables us to connect words and non-linguistic entities. The treatment of colour samples as part of grammar is unnecessary and, in many ways, misleading.

According to Wittgenstein it is not only ostensive definitions that may be variously interpreted in every case but also methods of projection, correlations and rules. This is consistent with his rejection of generality but, it might be argued, seems to be at variance with the common agreement comprising the normal practice of projecting, correlating and following a rule.

These considerations call in question the role of grammar in Wittgenstein's later philosophy. To deny the incorporation of colour samples into language is to undermine the view that reality does not shape grammar. To resist the assimilation of mental events like memory-images with language is to construe such events not as parts of grammar but as the proto-phenomena of grammar and puts phenomenalism back on the agenda. To re-assert the external (vertical) relation of world and thought with respect to language instead of Wittgenstein's proposed internal (horizontal) relation would be to rehabilitate ostensive definition as a vehicle of ontology. To maintain a logical distinction between words and actions would be to drive a wedge into their assimilation in the concept of the language-game.

Adopting any or all of these proposals does not arise from a desire to put the clock back but from a disquiet about the generality of Wittgenstein's concept of grammar and the suspicion of circularity about his argument. So broad a category of grammar is not the result of his philosophical investigations but a requirement for them. Grammar in the later Wittgenstein is another chapter in the metaphysics of sense.

A thinker as acute as Wittgenstein could hardly have been unaware of the possibility of this kind of objection. Hence his insistence that the object of his investigations is only to *describe* and not to *explain* language. According to him the temptation to which philosophers are prone is to offer explanations of language-functions that only mythologise grammar and impede a clear view of language actually at work.

Mere description is so difficult because one believes that one needs to fill out the facts in order to understand them. It is as if one saw a screen with scattered colour-patches, and said: the way they are here, they are unintelligible; they only make sense when one completes them into a shape – Whereas I want to say: Here is the whole. (If you complete it you falsify it.) (RPP I 257).

Wittgenstein cannot have it both ways. If our Weltanschauungen are embedded in the grammar of our language-games then the possibility of neutral theory-free description is ruled out. In Wittgenstein's investigations of language what purports to be description turns out to be explanation; i.e. the facts filled out by the concept of grammar. The incorporation into language of activities associated with language-games, colour samples, mental events and the analogies of methods of projection, games, tools and the later picture-theory of meaning all pertain to the apparatus of explanation rather than description of language. Wittgenstein's special and elaborate vocabulary of grammar transcends the facts just as much as any other philosophy of language which he claimed only falsified language. The assertion that (his) philosophy only demolishes houses of cards and in no way interferes with language but leaves everything as it is, is at best tendentious and at worst nonsense (PI 118, 124). The replacement of the analogies of propositional picture and logical calculus by the grammatical analogies of the later philosophy is the replacement of one house of cards by another. Grammar as conceived by Wittgenstein does not give us the facts but another interpretation of the facts. Although so much that he discusses is illuminated by his incandescent intelligence Wittgenstein once again falls victim to his own generality and the life-long impulse to put an end to philosophy. Nevertheless, for those who understand philosophy, the erection of not one but two such impressive houses of cards is a considerable achievement and a not wholly inappropriate monument to Wittgenstein's genius.

Having denied that reality determines grammar and admitted that the demarcation between them is not always clear, Wittgenstein does not wish to embrace an opposite extreme and say that grammar is purely arbitrary. Although in the later philosophy it is recognised that, given appropriate representational conventions, any linguistic complex can represent any state of affairs and that such notions as 'agreement with reality' and 'fitting the facts' are slippery and not easy to characterise sharply they are not totally vacuous. To say that 'a reality corresponds to $2 + 2 = 4$' may be understood as a claim that 'a reality corresponds to a scale of measurement' and that in turn may be taken to mean that 'it is a useful scale'. Similarly, to say that reality requires that if '$(x)fx$' is true then necessarily 'fa' must be true simply reflects a fixed point of human agreement with respect to our practise of logical inference. It is the paradigms of our descriptive forms that reveal what we count as belonging to reality and in this sense it is true to say that reality is a grammatical construction. In Plato's Weltanschauung ordinary material objects are counted as being less real than the abstract universals and values of the world of Forms. According to Berkeley's Weltanschauung the concept of an external material world is a grammatical illusion of common parlance and all real existence is mind-dependent. In modern physics the old Newtonian Weltanschauung of discrete particles moving determinately in universal space and time is replaced by that of particle/wave/energy moving indeterminately in four-dimensional space-time. The Weltanschauung embedded in our ordinary language owes much to Newtonian mechanics and presupposes a world of material entities which persist independently of our perceptions and are causally related to them and comprise a body of common perceptual objects having public criteria for their individuation and description. To the question, 'how do you know that there is an external world of material objects which may be individuated, recognised, named, remembered and described by human beings? Wittgenstein might reply; 'I have learned language'. For these are fixed points of the grammar of our ordinary discourse about the world and many questions about these points that have the outward form of empirical questions are grammatical in nature.

From this it is clear that without going to the extreme of claiming that reality is *only* a grammatical construction – the world will not cease to exist if we were to stop talking about it – what we count as being real is a function of the grammar of our language about it. This interconnection of reality and grammar is clearly illustrated in Wittgenstein's remarks on the nature of religious belief.[1] When someone says, 'I believe in the Last Judgement and the resurrection of the dead', Wittgenstein finds it impossible to say either that he believes the same or the opposite. What seems to be a matter of a simple application of the law of excluded middle, either p or not-p is true, fails to represent the problem appropriately. The assertion of p or the assertion of not-p both depend on there being agreement on an appropriate picture of p. It might seem that this requirement could be met by representing 'the Last Judgement' by a picture of God presiding over a great assize and representing 'the resurrection of the dead' by a picture of the recombination of constituent parts of the human body. But if we represent the meaning of this claim by invoking such pictures we find that our usual interpretation of pictures is of no help here. Ordinary pictures may be compared with what they are pictures *of*, as is the case, for example, with photographs, landscape drawings and painted portraits. With what do we compare our pictures of God and bodies being resurrected? With respect to this particular claim the concept of a picture turns out to be useless and gets us no further. Wittgenstein's point is that he finds himself unable to assert p and also unable to assert not-p because with respect to this claim he is unable to attach any significance to p. The significance of p for Wittgenstein is not an empirical issue but a grammatical one. For him the Weltanschauung of religious belief was not a concomitant of his form of life. The difference between believer and unbeliever is not that the former advances assertions which the latter denies. That is, it is not like two believers disputing whether the future life is entered by resurrection from the dead or the survival of death. The world of the believer and the world of the unbeliever are not the same – a view that will come as no surprise to those theologians who say: belief cannot *argue* with unbelief; it can only preach to it.

What Wittgenstein is saying here is a special version of Hume's devastating criticism of metaphysics and theology, namely, that the claims made by them are not false but meaningless. A counter-objection to Hume and Wittgenstein is that both have rigged their definitions of meaning such that the exclusion of metaphysics and theology is not a discovery following from theory-neutral definitions but a built-in requirement of them. At the stage in his development in which these lectures were given, Wittgenstein still tended to think of a picture as being intelligible only if it is a picture of something such that it was possible to compare the picture with the something of which it was a picture. It is tempting to think of the world and our images of it as separable in a way that makes verification of our pictures a matter of comparison with reality. This is not the case with our conceptual pictures of the electron, electromagnetic waves or fields of force, let alone God. Christian apologists might well argue against Wittgenstein here that God's revelation is not in a word that was *about* God but in a word that *was* God. This is a matter which may be left to theologians to pursue but the point that is important here is that Wittgenstein's more mature reflections on grammar move still further away from the idea of the separation and verification by comparison of reality and our conceptual pictures. Reality and our images of it are inseparably linked in grammar. An anticipation of this is found in Wittgenstein's remarks on Luther's claim that theology is the grammar of the word 'God' (Ambrose 32). Wittgenstein's route to ontology is still a semantic one except that in the earlier philosophy the relation between the world and language was an external one in which reality and propositional pictures were linked together by a common logical form. In the later philosophy this external relation is replaced by an internal relation in which the world and language are linked together in grammar.

The oscillation from one Weltanschauung to another leads to problems of colliding grammars. For example, the concept of a person in the grammatical context of ordinary language depends upon bodily criteria for its identification and application. Those theologians who say that God is a person or that God is a unity of three persons are not invoking bodily criteria in making such a claim. The question is, what place, if any, does the concept of a person have in the grammar of talk about God? Various answers to this question may be possible but what we cannot accept as an answer is the logical sleight of hand that passes off the criteria for the use of bodily person and immaterial person as the same. A related problem emerges in philosophical attempts to devise a consistent and self-contained grammar of phenomenalism. The difficulty here is to individuate sense-data without doing so in terms of the names and supporting grammar of our ordinary words for material objects. The oscillation from one grammar to another inclines us to think of sense-data both as mental impressions and as membranes arising from the surface of perceptual objects. Hence the grammatical collision between the logical privacy of sense-data and the public criteria of the identification of material objects.

Wittgenstein returned to the sense in which Weltanschauung is a grammatical construction in material written during the last eighteen months of his life. These remarks have been published posthumously in the volume *'On Certainty'*. This work contains Wittgenstein's last reflections on epistemology and the relation between reality and language. Some of his remarks are concerned with an investigation of G. E. Moore's celebrated claim to know for certain the truth of a number of empirical propositions such as, 'Here is one hand and here is another', and, 'I have never been far from the earth's surface.'

Wittgenstein concedes that the propositions Moore claims to *know* are 'all of such a kind that it is difficult to imagine *why* anyone should believe the contrary' (OC 93). However, the reason for this is not because we have determined their truth by some process of verification or other experiential procedure. They do not belong to that system of propositions that have been tested empirically but rather belong to the rules of empirical testing or to our methods of representation. As such they are deposited among the paradigms of language and what they picture is our world-view or standpoint which is not something accepted because we have satisfied ourselves empirically of its correctness but because it is part of the inherited background against which we distinguish between true and false (OC 94). 'The propositions describing this world-picture might be part of a kind of mythology. And their role is like that of rules of a game; and the game can be learned purely practically, without learning any explicit rules' (OC 95). Moore's propositions belong to the grammar of the language-game in which we represent the world as comprised of material objects. This is not to say that the grammar is fixed for us by the structure of reality since this role can be filled by mythology and 'the mythology may change back into a state of flux, the river-bed of thoughts may shift'. In that case it is true to say that 'the same proposition may get treated at one time as something to test by experience, at another as a rule of testing' (OC 97–8). The sense of certainty attaching to Moore's propositions is a classic illustration of a grammatical fiction generated by taking as a representation of the world what properly belongs to our method of representation of the world. As a consequence of this Moore thought that these propositions *established* what in fact their grammar *presupposed*.

If we change our standpoint or method of representation to that of the phenomenalist picture of the world then propositions about my hands lose their privileged status and are indistinguishable from any other propositions descriptive of sense-data; they no longer constitute a paradigm for such a language-game. Part of Moore's confusion springs from a life-long tendency to oscillate between material-object and sense-data methods of projection without regard to the different grammars of the two systems.

The picture of the earth as a fixed and immovable disc suspended in space was for centuries a method of representation in the light of which all observations of the movements of heavenly bodies were interpreted. When it was found that these movements did not fit the picture, the appearances were saved by the introduction of epicyclic motion. The multiplication and consequent complications of epicyclic orbits, among other things, finally led to the adequacy of the picture being called in question. It was replaced by the picture of the earth as a free-floating ball in space moving elliptically round the sun. Wittgenstein remarks: 'The picture of the earth as a ball is a *good* picture, it proves itself everywhere, it is also a simple picture – in short, we work with it without doubting it' (OC 146–7). Moore has overlooked the fact that the propositions he enumerates as certain and indubitable have 'a peculiar logical role in the system of our empirical propositions'. Furthermore

> Moore does not *know* what he asserts he knows, but it stands fast for him, as also for me; regarding it as absolutely solid is part of our *method* of doubt and enquiry. I do not explicitly learn the propositions that stand fast for me. I can *discover* them subsequently like the axis around which a body rotates. This axis is not fixed in the sense that anything holds it fast, but the movement around it determines its immobility (OC 136, 151–2).

Again Wittgenstein remarks:

> I have a world-picture. Is it true or false? Above all it is the substratum of all my enquiry and asserting. The propositions describing it are not all equally subject to testing. . . . It is clear that our empirical propositions do not all have the same status since one can lay down such a proposition and turn it from an empirical proposition into a norm of description (OC 162, 167).

To employ an empirical proposition as a norm of description is to convert it to a grammatical proposition, for example 'every event has a cause'.

Moore, in claiming to *know* the truth of various propositions as a matter of certainty, is attempting to map out the foundations of empirical knowledge that are proof against all scepticism and so demonstrating the possibility of knowledge in general and knowledge of an external world in particular. Wittgenstein's doubts concerning these claims are not those of the sceptic bent on demolishing all pretensions to knowledge – he would assert that we can claim to know all kinds of things and that there is not necessarily a doubt wherever we can imagine a doubt. His doubt of Moore's propositions do not concern their truth-value but their office. In particular he rejects the assumptions that our empirical propositions 'form a homogeneous mass' and that the idea of 'agreement with reality' has a clear application (OC 213, 215). Moore has missed the vital distinction which Wittgenstein laboured to demarcate between representations and methods of representation, descriptions and forms of descriptions, language-games and their rules, propositions and their grammar. Moreover, the kind of agreement which appears to fix our world-pictures has little to do with reality but is agreement between human beings.

> But what men consider reasonable or unreasonable alters. At certain periods men find reasonable what at other periods they found unreasonable. And vice versa. But is there no objective character here? *Very* intelligent and well-educated people believe in the story of creation in the Bible, while others hold it as proven false, and the grounds of the latter are well known to the former (OC 336).

Thus Wittgenstein concludes;

> To say of man, in Moore's sense, that he *knows* something; that what he says is therefore unconditionally the truth, seems wrong to me – It is the truth only inasmuch as it is an unmoving foundation of his language-games (OC 403).

Wittegenstein also illustrates his aim with respect to Moore's claim to *know*, by distinguishing between 'I know that that's a . . .', as it might be used in ordinary life, and the same utterance when a philosopher makes it' (OC. 406). It is not that we cannot imagine a use for 'I know that this is a hand' or 'I know that this is a tree' but their employment in philosophy is disengaged from any such usages. It is only in their disembodied state that such expressions appear to generate a picture of knowledge and certainty on which Moore trades. This is why when the philosopher and the ordinary man say 'I know that . . .' Wittgenstein feels impelled to say to the former but not the latter, 'You don't *know* anything!' (OC 407).

Notes

CHAPTER 1: THE STRUCTURE OF THE WORLD

1. G. H. von Wright and G. E. M. Anscombe (eds). *Notebooks: 1914–1916*, 2nd edn (Blackwell, 1979) p.130.
2. E. Stenius, *Wittgenstein's Tractatus: a Critical Exposition*. p.31.
3. G. E. M. Anscombe (ed.), op. cit., p.132; cf. P. Engelmann, *Letters from Ludwig Wittgenstein* (Blackwell, 1968) p.31.
4. 'Some Remarks on Logical Form', *P.A.S. Supp.*, vol. IX (1929) 168–71.
5. E. Stenius, op. cit., pp.32–4.
6. M. Black, *A Companion to Wittgenstein's Tractatus*. pp.43–4.
7. G. E. M. Anscombe, *Introduction to Wittgenstein's Tractatus*, p.30.
8. G. Frege, *The Foundations of Arithmetic*, trans. J. L. Austin (Blackwell, 1959) p.x.
9. 'Concept and Object' in *Philosophical Writings of Gottlob Frege*, trans. P. Geach and M. Black, 2nd edn (Blackwell, 1980) p.43.
10. G. E. M. Anscombe and P. T. Geach, *Three Philosophers* (Blackwell, 1963) p.161.
11. Ibid., p.162.
12. 'On Sense and Reference' in *Philosophical Writings of Gottlob Frege*, trans. P. Geach and M. Black, 2nd edn (Blackwell, 1970) p.58.
13. von Wright and Anscombe (eds), op. cit., p.15a.
14. Ibid., p.37j.
15. Ibid., p.67g
16. Ibid., p.69c.
17. J. Griffin, *Wittgenstein's Logical Atomism* (Oxford University Press, 1964) p.71.
18. Ibid., p.5.
19. von Wright and Anscombe (eds), op. cit., pp.61a, b.
20. Ibid., p.64g.
21. Ibid., p.62i.
22. Ibid., p.63d.
23. Ibid., p.64b.
24. Ibid., p.60c.
25. Ibid., p.62g.
26. Ibid., p.20e.
27. Ibid., p.65g,i.
28. Cf. G. E. M. Anscombe, 'Retraction', *Analysis*, XXVI (1965).
29. von Wright and Anscombe (eds), op. cit., p.61b.

30. D. Lee, W. Wittgenstein's Lectures: Cambridge 1930–1932 (Blackwell, 1980) p.120.

CHAPTER 2:   THE STRUCTURE OF LANGUAGE

1. von Wright and Anscombe (eds), *Notebooks: 1914–1916*, 2nd edn (Blackwell, 1979) p.60f
2. Ibid., p.60h.
3. Ibid., p.61g.
4. Ibid., p.61i.
5. Ibid., p.62b.
6. Ibid., p.67i.
7. Ibid., p.69i,j.
8. Ibid., p.71g.
9. Ibid., p.70d-e.
10. B. Russell, *Logic and Knowledge: the Philosophy of Logical Atomism*, ed. R. C. Marsh (Allen & Unwin, 1966) p.179.
11. von Wright and Anscombe (eds), op. cit., App. III, p.132.
12. B. Russell, *Introduction to the Tractatus*, pp.ix–x.
13. *The Philosophy of Bertrand Russell: Reply to Criticisms*, ed. P. A. Schilpp, pp.690, 694.
14. von Wright and Anscombe (eds), op. cit., p.70b.
15. A. N. Whitehead and B. Russell, *Principia Mathematica* (Cambridge University Press, 1967) p.37.
16. Ibid., p.53.
17. Ibid., p.55.
18. *Logic and Knowledge: Mathematical Logic as Based on the Theory of Types*, ed. R. C. Marsh (Allen & Unwin, 1956) p.76.
19. von Wright and Anscombe (eds), op. cit., App. III, p.123.
20. Ibid., pp.28e,f.
21. Ibid., p.30d.
22. M. Black, *A Companion to Wittgenstein's Tractatus*, p.156.
23. Ibid., p.9.

CHAPTER 3:   THE PICTURE-THEORY OF MEANING

1. von Wright and Anscombe (eds), *Notebooks: 1914–1916* (Blackwell, 1979) App. III, p.130.
2. Ibid., p.130.
3. Cf. G. H. von Wright, 'Biographical Sketch in N. Malcolm in *Ludwig Wittgenstein: a Memoir*, (Oxford University Press, 1958) pp.7–8.
4. Black, *A Companion to Wittgenstein's Tractatus*, p.14.
5. E. Stenius, *Wittgenstein's Tractatus: a Critical Exposition*, p.108.
6. Ibid., pp.91–3.
7. Ibid., pp.148–9.

8. Ibid., p.96; cf. also E. Stenius, 'Wittgenstein's Picture-Theory: a Reply to Mr H. R. G. Schwyzer', *Inquiry*, vol. 6 (1963).
9. Black, op. cit., p.175.
10. Anscombe, *An Introduction to the Tractatus*, p.82n.
11. Cf. P. Gardiner, *Schopenhauer* (Penguin, 1963) pp.275ff.

CHAPTER 4: LANGUAGE AND THE PROJECTION OF REALITY

1. *Proceedings of the Aristotelian Society*, vol. IX (1929).
2. *Tractatus*, p.163.
3. Ibid., pp.163–4.
4. Stenius, *Wittgenstein's Tractatus: a Critical Exposition*, p.42.
5. Ibid., p.213.
6. Ibid., pp.164–5.
7. Ibid., p.166.
8. Ibid., p.163.
9. Ibid., p.169.
10. Ibid., p.169.
11. Cf. *PG* 62a p.102; 98c p.146.
12 Cf. P. F. Strawson, *Introduction to Logical Theory* (Methuen, 1971) ch. 3: II: 'Truth-Functional Constants and Ordinary Words', pp.78–101.
13. F. Waisman's Notes *PR* p.317; cf. 846-c p.112; 152e-i p.178.
14. D. Lee, *Wittgenstein's Lectures: Cambridge* 1930–1932 (Blackwell, 1980).
15. Ibid., p.25.
16. Ibid., p.25–6.
17. Ibid., p.28.
18. Ibid., p.29.
19. Ibid., pp.42–3.
20. A. Ambrose, *Wittgenstein's Lectures: Cambridge* 1932–1935 (Blackwell, 1979) p.55.
21. Lee, op. cit., pp.38–9.
22. Ibid., p.85.
23. Ambrose, op. cit., p.52.
24. Cf. Ibid., p.96.

CHAPTER 5: FROM PICTURES TO GRAMMAR

1. G. Ryle, 'Systematically Misleading Expressions', *P.A.S.*, XXXII (1932) pp. 139–70.
2. B. Russell, *Human Knowledge: Its Scope and Limits* (Allen & Unwin, 1948) p.107.
3. B. Russell, *My Philosophical Development* (Allen & Unwin, 1959) p.239.

4. Ibid., p.240.
5. Ibid., pp.244–5.
6. N. Malcolm, *Dreaming* (Routledge & Kegan Paul, 0000) p.90.
7. *Remarks on the Philosophy of Psychology*, vol. II, eds G. H. von Wright and H. Nyman (Blackwell, 1980) p.39, §203.
8. B. Russell, *Philosophy of Logical Atomism: Logic and Knowledge*, p.243.
9. Ibid., pp.195–8.
10. N. Malcolm, *Ludwig Wittgenstein: a Memoir* (Oxford University Press, 1958) p.65.
11. G. Frege, *Frege Against the Formalists: Philosophical Writings of Gottlob Frege*, eds P. Geach and M. Black (Blackwell, 1970) pp.182ff.

CHAPTER 6: THE GRAMMAR OF MATHEMATICS

1. G. Frege, *The Foundations of Arithmetic*, trans. J. L. Austin (Blackwell, 1950) p.99.
2. Ibid., p.80.
3. G. Frege, *Frege Against the Formalists: Philosophical Writings of Gottlob Frege*, eds P. Geach and M. Black (Blackwell, 1970) p.187.
4. G. H. Hardy, 'Mathematical Proof', Mind, vol. XXXVIII (1929) p.4.
5. Cajori F. Newton, *Principia*, note 6, p.632.
6. G. Frege, 'On Euclidean Geometry', *Gottlob Frege, Posthumous Writings*, eds Hermes, Kambartel and Kaulbach (Blackwell, 1979) p.169.

CHAPTER 7: PHILOSOPHICAL INVESTIGATIONS

1. B. Russell, *The Philosophy of Logical Atomism, Logic and Knowledge*, p.198.
2. B. Russell, *Human Knowledge: Its Scope and Limits* (Allen & Unwin, 1948) p.107.
3. A. J. Ayer, *Foundations of Empirical Knowledge* (Macmillan, 1961) pp.18, 233; cf. Lee 80–1, 110.
4. Ibid., p.238.
5. A. J. Ayer, 'Privacy', *The Concept of a Person*, p.59.

CHAPTER 8: GRAMMAR AND THE WORLD

1. Cyril Barrett (ed.), *Lectures and Conversations on Aesthetics, Psychology and Religious Belief* (C. Blackwell, 1970).

Index